Number Four
Eastern European Studies

Stjepan G. Meštrović, Series Editor
Series Editorial Board
Norman Cigar
Thomas Cushman
Bronislaw Misztal
James Sadkovich
Keith Tester

The Conceit of Innocence

The CONCEIT of Innocence

Losing the Conscience of the West in the War against Bosnia

EDITED BY STJEPAN G. MEŠTROVIĆ

Contributors: *Akbar S. Ahmed, Brad K. Blitz, Keith Doubt, Georgie Anne Geyer, Marshall Freeman Harris, Richard Johnson, Slaven Letica, Chandler Rosenberger, Stephen W. Walker, Albert Wohlstetter*

Texas A&M University Press
College Station

Copyright © 1997 by Stjepan G. Meštrović
Manufactured in the United States of America
All rights reserved
First edition
04 03 02 01 00 99 98 97 5 4 3 2 1

The paper used in this book meets the minimum requirements
of the American National Standard for Permanence
of Paper for Printed Library Materials, Z39.48-1984.
Binding materials have been chosen for durability.
⊗

Library of Congress Cataloging-in-Publication Data

The conceit of innocence : losing the conscience of the West in the
　　war against Bosnia / edited by Stjepan G. Meštrović ; contributors,
　　Akbar S. Ahmed . . . [et al.]. — 1st ed.
　　　　p.　cm. — (Eastern European series ; no. 4)
　　Includes bibliographical references and index.
　　ISBN 0-89096-770-9 (alk. paper)
　　1. Yugoslav War, 1991–　2. Ethnopsychology.　I. Meštrović,
Stjepan Gabriel.　II. Ahmed, Akbar S.　III. Series: Eastern European
series (College Station, Tex.) ; no. 4.
DR1313.C66　1997
949.703—dc21　　　　　　　　　　　　　　　　　　97-17417
　　　　　　　　　　　　　　　　　　　　　　　　　　CIP

To the memory of Albert Wohlstetter

CONTENTS

    Preface   xi
    Introduction   3
    STJEPAN G. MEŠTROVIĆ

1. Ethnic Cleansing: A Metaphor for Our Time   35
   AKBAR S. AHMED

2. The Pinstripe Approach to Genocide   65
   RICHARD JOHNSON

3. How the Conscience of the West Was Lost   74
   GEORGIE ANNE GEYER

4. "We Had to Jump Over the Moral Bridge": Bosnia and the Pathetic Hegemony of Face-work   120
   KEITH DOUBT

5. Labeling Theory and the Wars in Croatia and Bosnia-Herzegovina   142
   SLAVEN LETICA

6. Idle Curiosity and the Production
of Useless Knowledge:
Academic Responses to Genocide 158
BRAD K. BLITZ

7. Serbia and Russia: U.S. Appeasement
and the Resurrection of Fascism 181
RICHARD JOHNSON

8. Boris Yeltsin as Abraham Lincoln 200
ALBERT WOHLSTETTER

9. A Tale of Two Serbias 208
CHANDLER ROSENBERGER

10. Genocide: We Are Responsible 230
STEPHEN W. WALKER

11. Clinton's "European" Bosnia Policies 238
MARSHALL FREEMAN HARRIS

Contributors 253
Index 255

PREFACE

I have many colleagues and friends to thank for their direct or indirect contribution to this volume, although none should be blamed for any possible objections by the reader to how their insights were assimilated by this editor. David Riesman impressed upon me the importance of the concept of innocence for understanding American social character at the time of the publication of *The Lonely Crowd*. Through our correspondence, he expressed strong support for how I would apply his ideas to a new topic, genocide against Bosnia. It was Keith Tester who proposed the title, *The Conceit of Innocence,* when I discussed with him how I would make use of Riesman's ideas in this book, namely, extrapolating the concept of innocence to the 1990s vis-à-vis American attitudes toward Bosnia. C. G. Schoenfeld, Norman Cigar, Robert Marquand, and Chris Rojek made invaluable criticisms of earlier drafts of chapter 1. Philip J. Cohen put me in touch with or introduced me to many of the contributing authors. I would also like to offer my sincere thanks to my undergraduate and graduate students for their feedback during classes to the ideas that were finally formulated in this book.

A number of conferences hosted and organized by Thomas Cushman, Marshall Harris, Stephen W. Walker, and Keith Doubt also helped to crystallize my ideas and, of course, exposed me to many of the contributing authors.

The present volume is intended to be read as a self-contained work that makes a unique argument. Nevertheless, I should state that it constitutes a logical development of my previous publications in social theory as well as on Bosnia. Regarding the former, it is a sequel to *Postemotional Society* (London: Sage, 1997) and regarding the latter, it is a sequel to *This Time We Knew*, coedited with Thomas Cushman (New York: New York University Press, 1996). Given that my concept of postemotionalism is an extension of David Riesman's concept of other-directedness, the present volume should be read as a discussion of how this new state of social character in the West impacts traditional and inner-directed notions of law and morality in foreign policy. And the present volume is intended to promote discussion, not to present anything like a final statement on how postemotionalism impacts foreign policy.

All of the essays in this volume are printed for the first time except for those by Akbar S. Ahmed, Georgie Anne Geyer, and Stephen W. Walker. We are grateful to *Race and Ethnic Relations* for permission to reprint Ahmed's chapter, to Universal Syndicate for permission to print portions of Geyer's opinion pieces, and to *Tikkun* for permission to print Walker's chapter.

The Conceit of Innocence

Introduction
STJEPAN G. MEŠTROVIĆ

How does one begin to comprehend the now historical fact that Serb-sponsored genocide against Bosnian Muslims and Croats — an event that was widely covered by the information media — went on for five years without decisive Western military action to stop it and with the imposition of a weapons embargo on Belgrade's victims?[1] This question becomes more problematic, and interesting, when one considers that the West took *indecisive* military action against Serbs (the so-called "pinprick" North Atlantic Treaty Organization [NATO] air strikes) that failed to stop the slaughter in Srebrenica and other UN-declared "safe areas." In addition, "the Clinton administration followed the 'letter of the law'" in enforcing the weapons embargo, yet "the president secretly gave a green light to Iranian arms shipments to Bosnia."[2] Other, similar contradictions abound: How can Westerners, steeped in a tradition derived from the Enlightenment, make sense of the West's responses to this documented genocide, namely: the sending of humanitarian aid in the midst of war, the imposition of a peace accord in 1995 that stripped NATO forces of any police powers that are necessary to maintain peace, and the absolute refusal (as of this writing) to seek out and apprehend indicted war criminals?

Can these contradictions be explained by modernist theories, or are the postmodernists right that the West has entered a new era in which moral and political events no longer make sense? Or is there an alternative to both explanations? Against the modernists, Thomas Cushman and I argue in *This Time We Knew*[3] that knowledge of genocide in Bosnia and Rwanda, both of which received massive coverage by the information media, did not lead to moral action. Similarly, modernists who envisioned a post–Cold War world of increased tolerance, democracy, and human empowerment were simply off the mark: As argued by Akbar S. Ahmed in this volume, "ethnic cleansing" in Bosnia — and in many places outside of Bosnia, from Kashmir to Rwanda — has become a metaphor for our times. Also against the modernists, and against the "grand narratives" of the Enlightenment, postmodernists such as Jean Baudrillard envision a world of rootless, circulating fictions in which chaos and meaninglessness reign.[4] But I have argued in *Genocide After Emotion*[5] that this view is also erroneous, because the many fictions surrounding genocide in Bosnia, from the "safe havens" that were never safe and were hell for their inhabitants to the many "peace plans" that never led to lasting peace and actually supported war plans by the Belgrade regime, did and still do betray a certain order and meaning. That meaning is the gnawing realization that specific Western countries resort to *feigning* heart, resolve, and commitment to principles derived from the Enlightenment even though postmodernism has eroded the capacity for genuine empathy, boldness, and faith in these principles. The complexity of the present situation stems from the fact that in the present fin de siècle, the West is set on a course of faking, imitating, and synthetically recreating an inner-directed[6] mode of relating that seems to have vanished. The West seems to be engaged in a parody of power that Georgie Anne Geyer calls the "will to impotence."

Thus, had the West's commitment to its Enlightenment-based tradition been sincere, it would have honored the sovereignties of the new countries it recognized (Croatia and Bosnia-Herzegovina), lifted the illegal and immoral weapons embargo imposed on Serbia's victims, taken all steps necessary to prevent genocide (as mandated by the UN Charter), and apprehended indicted international war criminals. The West failed on each of these counts. Instead, the West pretended to be acting in accordance with its Enlightenment tradition by passing a flurry of resolutions through the United Nations that condemned genocide, backing a peace plan that destroyed the sovereignties of Bosnia-Herzegovina and Croatia, turning a blind eye to Iranian arms shipments to Serbia's victims, and engaging in a highly publicized concern for the victims of Belgrade-sponsored genocide after they had died by poring over the many mass graves. All of this activity amounted to a false peace enshrined in the Dayton Peace Accords, a fake humanitarianism, and a fake commitment to the rule of law.

As an alternative to both modernist and postmodernist explanations, I have argued in *Postemotional Society*[7] that the West has entered a new phase of development—one that succeeded the phase that David Riesman called other-directedness—in which dead emotions are taken out of context and manipulated by governments, media, and individuals. Postemotionalism is a wide-ranging new phenomenon that goes well beyond Bosnia, but in the Bosnian case, it centered on rationalizing savage acts committed by Serbs on the basis of their fear of the Muslims dating back to 1389 (the Battle of Kosovo)—more than a century before Columbus set foot on America—and of the Croats, dating back to World War II (the Ustashe). In this new, postemotional scenario, the West found that it could not punish Serbs who committed savage acts of genocide *in the present* based on empathy for Serbs as victims *in the past*. Other postemotional phenomena include America's long-standing collective neurosis known as the Vietnam syndrome, Britain's penchant for supporting the strongest party in any regional conflict (regardless of which party's cause is just), the West's suspicion of German motives regarding the former Yugoslavia based on German history in the First and Second World Wars, and Russia's anti-Western attitudes. All of these postemotional syndromes focus emotional energy on the past rather than the present. The significance of this observation is that modern, Western countries seem to act under the power of socially constructed memories *despite* widespread homage paid to rationality and principles derived from the Enlightenment. In this volume, I extend and deepen this argument by focusing on the postemotional manipulation of *innocence*. The many and seemingly diverse essays in the present volume all illustrate some aspect of the argument that Western appeasement of and even collaboration with Belgrade-sponsored genocide in the current Balkan War was made possible by the creation and manipulation of synthetic, hence post-emotional, innocence.

The Revival of the Age of Aquarius Versus the Ronald Reagan Era

What is collective innocence, sociologically speaking? As suggested by David Riesman,[8] post–World War II American innocence included a general mood of optimism, a sort of temporal hubris in which the United States was perceived to be an invincible power, a provincial self-righteousness, and an overconfident faith in the American dream. To be sure, the current popularity of postmodernism has made all of these tenets of collective innocence seem foolish, because postmodernists champion ethical and moral relativism, ambivalence, and ambiguity.[9] Nevertheless, at least in the 1950s, the American dream presupposed the moral superiority of American values (made clear in the victory over the Fascists), and a confidence in what David Riesman called inner-directed standards that were assumed to be stable enough to be passed on as a precious commodity to future generations. The American dream was not yet mean-spirited, nor was it stingy (recall the Marshall Plan). Innocence is not exactly the same as naïveté. Rather, innocence involves a collective and easy confidence in tackling large problems on the basis of limited evidence, an American can-do attitude. Americans in the 1950s thought that social problems were accessible to understanding and even, in some measure, to resolution. Even academics and journalists in the 1950s were innocent: many had not yet learned the methodological rules pertaining to their disciplines or professions in a formal way and, by today's sophisticated standards, were amateurs. A knowledge of basics sufficed, and with this limited knowledge, most professionals thought they could cure America's, even the world's, ills. In many ways, these American traits from a bygone era exhibited a boldness, courage, and "happy confidence" that are the hallmarks of what sociologists call "integrated" societies.[10]

But things are much different in the United States and the rest of the West in the postinnocent 1990s. If Americans learned to hate and fear the Soviet Union during the Cold War—on the basis of a collective faith in American moral superiority in relation to the evils of communism—many of them now hate and fear their own government (consider the Oklahoma City bombing, the rise of militias, the Unabomber's manifesto, and many related incidents in America's Far West). Optimism has given way to widespread pessimism concerning the future. The decrease of voter turnout in elections, a palpable decrease in general trust, and an increase in cynicism all serve to mark the end of American innocence. Americans are much more cosmopolitan and knowledgeable about the world today than they were in the 1950s, yet all this knowledge only makes them feel helpless in tackling what seem to be insurmountable social problems domestically as well as internationally. They have become what David Riesman prophesied in *The Lonely Crowd*, "inside-dopesters" who want to *know* what is going on in the world as a compensation for their deep-seated yet hidden suspicion that they cannot really *do* anything to alter the course of world events.[11] In contradistinction to Anthony Giddens's writings on empowerment,[12] Americans feel increasingly powerless and blasé as they become more knowledgeable. The American dream in the 1990s is mean-spirited toward immigrants, the have-nots, and the disadvantaged. It has also become stingy: Americans questioned why the United States should spend any money to reconstruct war-shattered Bosnia when that money could be used to reconstruct tattered American cities. And let us note that most of the money earmarked for Bosnia went to pay for the salaries and comfort of U.S. troops, not to the Bosnian victims of genocide.[13] There is little confidence in tackling large problems. The more common reactions include exasperation and "compassion fatigue," evidenced by the refrain, "America is not the world's policeman." This cautious attitude—in stark contradistinction to American boldness of bygone days—resulted in the paradox enshrined in the Dayton Peace Accords, such that American and other Western Implementation Force (IFOR) troops consistently refused to apprehend indicted international war criminals and refused other police action that might have led to genuine peace and catharsis. Social problems are no longer seen as accessible to understanding or resolution. Rather, highly socialized academics, journalists, opinion-makers, diplomats, and government officials tend to promote a stance that includes ambivalence, ambiguity, and a sense of helplessness concerning world events. The era of innocence is over.

Thinkers ranging from Alexis de Tocqueville to David Riesman,

Jean Baudrillard, and others are right to hold that America is, despite these negative developments, nevertheless still the cultural center of the world. Japan and Germany have powerful economies; Britain and France may be right to point to a richer cultural history; Russia may have a point in demanding to be taken seriously on its own cultural terms; the Islamic world may be an important focus of cultural resistance to the West — but, as noted by Arnold Toynbee in *America and the World Revolution*,[14] all these and other cultures still try to imitate what the United States once represented as a moral force in the world. To be sure, the United States is no longer Alexis de Toqueville's[15] beacon set upon a hill that beams the light of democracy to the rest of the world. Contemporary Americans no longer want that responsibility, commitment, or seriousness. Yet, perhaps more important, America is still the *artificial,* Disneyesque beacon of light that beams to the rest of the world a fake optimism, a contrived hubris, and an imitation of the old-fashioned can-do attitude. In short, the Europeans still exhibit a "won't-do" attitude, but increasingly Americans exhibit a "can't-do" attitude.

Moreover, the contemporary attempts to fake innocence are widely divergent from the political left to the political right. The members of the political left involved in American policymaking regarding Bosnia include former Secretary of State Warren Christopher, former Secretary of State Cyrus Vance, and former president Jimmy Carter. As a response to the perceived immorality of the Vietnam War, these three men sought and still seek to avoid the use of military force at almost any cost. During the Iranian hostage crisis, Christopher and Vance resisted any attempts by the U.S. military to rescue the hostages held in Iran, and Jimmy Carter consented only after extensive public pressure. One might have thought that they would have been relegated to the dustbin of history, yet all three were chosen by President Bill Clinton to engage in critical action relative to genocide in Bosnia. Vance appeased the Serbs and with Lord David Owen represented the West during the most brutal phase of Serb-sponsored genocide against Croats and Muslims. Christopher's "pin-stripe" approach to genocide is exposed brilliantly in this volume by Richard Johnson. And President Clinton asked Jimmy Carter to represent the United States in further negotiations with the Bosnian Serb leader and indicted international war criminal, Radovan Karadžić. Carter presented Karadžić with flowers at their first meeting. These three Americans transferred their postemotional reaction from the Vietnam era (that U.S. military action in Vietnam was immoral) to Bosnia, as if all military action is always immoral. In addition to Vance, Christopher, and Carter, a host of liberals took a similar postemotional stance on Serb-sponsored genocide in 1990 by advocating negotiation rather than military action as a response to genocide.

The ghost of Vietnam is the single most important factor that haunts U.S. foreign policy in general in the 1990s and with regard to Serb-sponsored genocide in particular. After the humiliating defeat and moral confusion that resulted from the Vietnam War, liberals seek to avoid the use of military force even with regard to obvious dictators such as Saddam Hussein. One should recall that Jimmy Carter wrote letters in an effort to subvert George Bush's leadership in the Gulf War. This is the essence of the liberal attempt to recapture American innocence: Restore American goodness by refusing to kill enemies for the sake of any cause, just or unjust, and opt for the 1960s ethic of love and peace as a way to deal with dictators. American "military" action in Somalia and Haiti should be regarded as refractions of the Vietnam syndrome.

But the political right is also haunted by the ghost of Vietnam, albeit in a different way. The conservatives seek to orchestrate short, winnable wars that make use of overwhelming U.S. military superiority and that minimize U.S. casualties in order to restore American prestige in the post-Vietnam era. This is what Ronald Reagan attempted in a series of short military actions against Libya and Grenada, and what George Bush attempted in the Gulf War. These and other military actions were "successful" in relation to their limited goals and the resultant, albeit brief, euphoria among the American public, but failed in terms of long-term goals such as establishing a post–Cold War "new world order." For example, as of this writing, Saddam Hussein is still in power, and the American public is left wondering what the Gulf War was really all about. Conservatives generally favor the use of Tomahawk missiles or other strong military responses to events such as Fidel Castro's shooting down of U.S. civilian aircraft in the spring of 1996, but are unable to articulate a set of inner-directed moral and political goals for the future.

The conservative attempt to recapture American innocence centers on restoring or preserving American prestige through the use of limited yet overwhelming military strikes. Yet the conservatives, like the liberals, suffer from an other-directed inability to commit themselves to specific, long-term values.

The overall result for American foreign policy, in general and with regard to Serb-sponsored genocide in particular, is that America *follows* European (particularly British and French) policies and no longer leads what used to be called the free world. In this volume, Marshall Freeman Harris exposes the irony of President Clinton's "European" policy regarding Bosnia. In their chapters, both Keith Doubt and Georgie Anne Geyer expose and analyze the pitiful aspects of the American inability to take a moral stand against genocide in the 1990s if such a stand involves inner-directed resolve. Geyer seems to imply that a generalized will to impotence has emerged in the West. For example, even NATO — which is a *military* alliance — has now been transformed into an organization for peace: "NATO is a regional grouping of those who consider themselves to be part of the world of its values and it wants to cooperate with others for the sake of world peace."[16]

Thus, most Westerners in general and Americans in particular went along with a lukewarm sort of optimism that the Dayton Peace Accords would work, even though many previous truces involving the Belgrade regime were broken by that regime. The hidden insincerity of that optimism is betrayed by the startling lack of joy among any participants in these accords, save for the Serbs, who immediately expressed delight that they had attained most of their territorial goals under the ethnic partition of Bosnia-Herzegovina and that United Nations sanctions imposed against them would be lifted.[17] Contrast this lack of joy with the palpable joy expressed on the streets of Western capitals and the front pages of Western newspapers following the defeat of the Nazis. Similarly, President Clinton's imitation of Western resolve expressed by previous U.S. presidents, that America must lead the Western world in moral causes, fell flat. Most Americans expressed uneasiness at the fact that U.S. soldiers might die in Bosnia for reasons they did not fully comprehend — *because the president of the United States failed to explain the moral reasons for acting.* The seeming overconfidence of the Americans, that they could achieve what the Europeans tried and failed to achieve, namely, lasting peace in Bosnia, was also not genuine. From the start, the American side resisted police actions in Bosnia, which meant that the policing would be done by local militias, many of whom had participated in the genocide that is the subject of the present discussion. The artificial American can-do attitude quickly dissolved, and the real question on most Americans' minds emerged: Would President Clinton keep his pledge to bring the U.S. troops back to America by November of 1996? He did not.

The postemotional president of the United States, Bill Clinton, tries to come across as John F. Kennedy but cannot recapture Kennedy's genuine, daring, and risky resolve against the Soviet Union. The postemotional first lady, Hillary Clinton, similarly tries to recapture the charisma of Eleanor Roosevelt but can never match her inner-directed resolve. Hillary Clinton became the first first lady since Eleanor Roosevelt to visit U.S. troops on front lines when she traveled to Bosnia on March 25, 1996: "The First Lady told a couple of thousand of the 19,300 Americans serving in Bosnia that they were here to advance United States interests and values. She said they were part of 'the kind of peacekeeping mission every American should be proud of and support.' . . . Mrs. Clinton repeated that the United States had a genuine interest in keeping Europe stable."[18] But "Mrs. Clinton's message that American interests and moral values are at stake in Bosnia is not universally accepted among the people she came to thank."[19] The *New York Times* elaborated: "'I joined the Army to defend my country,' said Sgt. Michael Tucker. 'There's no one threatening America here, and we don't have a fight here.' . . . 'When she leaves, she'll go back to her family, maybe have a drink, and relax. We can't do any of that.' . . . 'For what?' asked Specialist Ingersoll. 'So that we can run over a mine, or slide off the road and get killed? And there's no one going to tell me that when we finally do get home the fighting won't start up again.'"[20]

Specialist Ingersoll's assessment is in line with the U.S. government's own conclusion: "The Pentagon has offered its grimmest assessment of the prospects for peace in Bosnia to date, warning that without an enormous international aid program to rebuild its economy and political institutions, the country will probably fragment after the withdrawal of NATO peacekeeping troops."[21] Clinton "announced that the United States was donating $25 million to repair 2,500 homes damaged in the war,"[22] a paltry sum when compared with the more than $5 billion[23] that is needed to rebuild Bosnia-Herzegovina.[24] Later in this analysis, we shall suggest reasons other than Western stinginess for why the Dayton Peace Accords will probably fail. As of this writing, an assessment published in the *New York Times* holds: "The future is a shaky one, compared with the vision painted in the Dayton accords—that of a peaceful Bosnia with ethnically integrated cities, awash in international donations to rebuild what war had torn down, a country equipped to conduct the free elections vital to its survival."[25]

But the Clinton administration portrayed the import of U.S. involvement in grandiose and nostalgic terms. For example, U.S. Secretary of Defense William Perry, in a speech at Harvard University on May 13, 1996, connected the U.S. peace plan in Bosnia with the Marshall Plan:

> The immediate payoff for our joint training with the Partnership For Peace nations and our efforts to build a cooperative relationship with Russia has come, ironically, in Bosnia. Up until late last year, to say that "the future history of Europe is being written in Bosnia," would have been a profoundly pessimistic statement. Today, however, this statement qualifies as guarded optimism; not only because there is satisfactory compliance with the Dayton peace agreement, but because of the way IFOR has been put together and because of the way it is performing. IFOR is not a peacekeeping exercise—it is the real thing . . . a Russian brigade is operating as part of an American division in IFOR. . . . NATO itself has a renewed sense of purpose and sense of its own ability to put together a force for a post–Cold War military mission. This is all positive history, and it shows why I believe that *Bosnia is turning out to be the crucible for the creation of Marshall's Europe*. (emphasis added)

In general, postemotional society tries desperately to synthetically re-create the innocence of the era that followed immediately after World War II. President Clinton, who began his presidency on the uninspiring note that the United States is just one nation among many, tried to recreate the sense that America is special in his address to the nation concerning U.S. involvement in Bosnia. His speech seemed to touch all of the hallmarks of American civil religion:[26] that America is a nation blessed by God that must lead the rest of the world in moral causes such as peace and democracy. Yet he did not convince most Americans or Congress. President Clinton used a pale imitation of American civil religion that failed to inspire Americans, because he left out commitment to a just cause and the use of military force to achieve such a cause. The Dayton Peace Accords were dressed up as being in the service of peace but in fact were an effort to impose ethnic partition on Bosnia-Herzegovina, reward Serbian aggression, and shove the issue of justice aside.[27]

The 1950s and 1960s serve as a focal point for postemotional recycling in politics as well as popular culture. As mentioned previously, President Clinton tries to come across as his idol, John F. Kennedy, even though he clearly lacks Kennedy's boldness. Popular culture tries to recreate the innocence of the past through nostalgia. Consider, for example, the "Camelot Auction" in which Mrs. Kennedy's fake pearls, which cost about $45, sold for $211,500.[28] The unusually high prices paid by auction goers suggest, to this author, a postemotional obsession on the part of many with the innocence of JFK's era. Democracy and capitalism are still touted as American gifts to the world — and especially to the former Soviet Union — but there is a sense that these have become empty slogans. If America tried to democratize and capitalize the former Soviet Union, it was a halfhearted and stingy effort at best, and it failed in any case.

Innocent faith in values enshrined as good by one's culture is essential for healthy societal functioning. America in particular has always possessed a childlike belief that good triumphs over evil, that "bad guys" do not go unpunished. Yet it is precisely this aspect of innocence that has been most damaged in the 1990s. This is because Bosnia is not just one instance of genocide among many: its uniqueness stems from the fact that it was followed closely, often day by day, by Americans (and others) on television. This time (as opposed to World War II genocide or other instances of genocide since then, such as Cambodia), nearly everyone in the United States knew about this most evil of crimes, in "real" time, often on live television, yet felt impotent to stop it. The innocent American can-do attitude of bygone days was shattered. Europeans took the typically European attitude toward Bosnia (namely, it is an instance of tribalism characteristic of the Balkans), and various European countries took positions along the cleavages of traditional alliances and the widespread, racist feeling that genocide is what the subcivilized, not-yet-European people in the Balkans do. France, Britain, and Russia essentially became secret collaborators with Serbia. But Americans agonized over Bosnia, yet could not act for various reasons: The ghost of Vietnam haunted them; they were suspicious of their post-emotional president, Bill Clinton, whose foreign policy is driven by domestic politics; and they were bombarded with so much emotion-laden information that they felt confused and complained of compassion fatigue. The most important point is that the television coverage of Bosnia forced Americans to take on the role of passive voyeurs. Because such a stance is out of character for Americans, President Clinton had at least to pretend to "do something" about Bosnia in order to "look" presidential. Yet he did not do something that would have ended the suffering once and for all and would have been perceived as a bold and just solution, namely militarily defeating Belgrade and its proxies; lifting the illegal weapons embargo on Belgrade's victims; and pursuing indicted international war criminals, most of whom are Serb.

It is very important to note that President Clinton called for the Dayton peace talks at precisely the time when the Croat-Bosnian Federation was poised to take Banja Luka, a Bosnian city that was ethnically cleansed by Serbs, and to defeat the Bosnian Serbs militarily and decisively. A bold victory against a Serbian regime that orchestrated mass rapes, brutal killings, mass deportations, and other genocidal policies was denied the victims by the United States. Some analysts have attempted to rationalize away the import of the timing of Dayton by suggesting that the Croat-Bosnian Federation never worked very well and that in due time the Croats and Bosnian Muslims would have turned on each other. Even if that prophecy comes true *after* Dayton, no amount of rationalization can undo the historically recorded fact that the Croatian and Bosnian armies scored a series of decisive military victories against their tormentors despite an illegal weapons embargo in force against them, and despite efforts by the French and the British to bolster the Serbian regime.

An Interactive Parody of Innocence

A discussion of the sort being proposed here would be incomplete without taking into account other key players in what has come to be known as the current Balkan War. Georgie Anne Geyer's chapter, which is a compilation of opinion pieces that she has written on this war over the course of several years, serves as an excellent launching point for such a discussion. She links her portrait of Yakushi Akashi as a kind of pacifist who eschewed the use of military force to back up UN resolutions to a generalized Japanese cultural belief in pacifism at all costs as a response to World War II. In this way, Akashi's pacifism dovetails into the general hostility exhibited toward militarism exhibited by Jimmy Carter, Cyrus Vance, Warren Christopher, and the Clinton administration.

Akashi's refusal to use military force even in the face of genocide is also in tandem with UN secretary-general Boutros Boutros-Ghali's strange interpretation of the UN Charter as prohibiting the use of military force. This is also documented in Geyer's intimate interviews with Boutros-Ghali, reproduced in this volume. It is one interpretation among many, and contrasts sharply with former NATO secretary general Manfred Woerner's belief that the lessons of World War II were quite different: Military force should be used to preserve post-Nuremberg principles. Geyer quotes Woerner as having said to her, "I am head of the most powerful military organization in world history — and I can do nothing."

In his contribution to the present volume, Marshall Freeman Harris exposes a similar tendency by America's post–World War II European allies toward appeasement. In a strange interplay of fake innocence imitating fake innocence, the Europeans justify appeasement in the face of genocide as the lesson of World War II, and the Americans, under President Clinton, seek to imitate the Europeans in order to preserve the NATO alliance. The end result is that the entire post–World War II structure of military and political alliances is exposed as being devoted to impotence masquerading as power.

The Serbs, too, have engaged in the conceit of innocence. In his contribution to the present volume, Chandler Rosenberger exposes the deceit in the nationalist myth surrounding the Serbian "Alamo," the Battle of Kosovo in 1389. According to this mythology, the valiant Serbs lost to the Turks and have been struggling for freedom ever since, against Nazis, Communists, Muslims, Croats, and others throughout the world who fail to understand their innocent cause. In fact, as Rosenberger demonstrates, the Serbs collaborated with the Ottomans leading up to the Battle of Kosovo and, in their history since then, have collaborated with various enemies when it suited their purposes of establishing an ethnically pure Greater Serbia. Philip J. Cohen's *Serbia's Secret War* further documents a tradition of anti-Semitism and Nazi collaboration, all disguised by Serb propagandists with the false claim that Serbia has been a consistent ally of the United States and Europe against the Nazis.

Similarly, Brad Blitz exposes the strange sympathy expressed by many Western intellectuals for Serb rationalizations for crimes committed in the wars against Croatia and Bosnia-Herzegovina. The picture that emerges from these and other analyses is one of an *affinity* between many Westerners steeped in an Enlightenment tradition and Serbs who claim that they are oppressed by that same tradition.

But perhaps the most important discussion of how various mythologies interact is the one by Richard Johnson on the similarities between Serbia and Russia. His chapter may be summarized as follows: Russia dominated the Soviet Empire much like Serbia dominated the Yugoslav Empire. When these two Empires began to disintegrate because of the collapse of Communism and the drive for emancipation exhibited by many nations that no longer wanted to be a part of them, Serbia and Russia sought to restore some of their empires through the use of brute military force. Few analysts other than Johnson have noted that during the years that Serbia terrorized its former internal colonies, Russia terrorized many of the newly formed nations that used to be part of the Soviet Empire. The rhetoric of restoring Russian glory and power did not seem to concern the Clinton administration. On the contrary, the administration took the position that Russia had the right to a sort of "Monroe Doctrine" to impose its will on the territories of the former Soviet Union. In another postemotional twist on this same theme, President Clinton went so far as to compare Boris Yeltsin to Abraham Lincoln, the great liberator! Albert Wohlstetter exposes the ironies of this comparison in his contribution to the present volume.

The importance of these analyses is that they point to a post–Cold War scenario that was not anticipated by most analysts: Serbia's war against Croatia and Bosnia-Herzegovina served as a harbinger for Russia's brutality against Chechnya as well as other nations that used to constitute the Soviet Union. Instead of leading to democracy and free markets in formerly communist nations (though this occurred to some extent in some Eastern European nations), the end of the Cold War could lead to new authoritarian regimes that will again threaten the West. Yet this unwelcome scenario seems to have been aided by faulty, other-directed, postemotional policies set into motion by Western governments, the United Nations, and many Western organizations.

It is beyond the scope of this chapter to analyze further the many interactions among the several myths that this volume exposes. For example, it is curious how the West has generally accepted the Serbian myths of innocence as a way of promoting the West's strange interpretation of the lessons of World War II. Serbia was *not* the West's consistent ally against the Nazis, and to the extent that it was an ally, its behavior resembles that of the French and the Italians, who became allies only when it became clear that Fascism would not triumph. But the conclusion that appeasement is the lesson of history to be drawn from victory over the Fascists in World War II needs to be contrasted sharply with Riesman's portrait of post–World War II American innocence. The Americans of previous generations did *not* draw the European conclusion, nor the one now promulgated by Akashi and Boutros-Ghali.

Imitating Innocence

As stated previously, innocence is not the same as naïveté. Rather, innocence implies a sort of boldness and courage based on limited information. One can hardly surpass Émile Durkheim's phrase, "happy confidence," as a way to capture the innocence of children, healthy adults, and healthy societies. In contrast to such confidence, regarding Bosnia, Americans simply went along with a "peace plan" that they never really believed in. Specifically, the West sent humanitarian aid to the Bosnian and Croat victims of genocide instead of stopping the genocide. This pathetic gesture was hailed repeatedly by governments and the media as a sign of Western resolve and generosity. Similarly, the West expressed indignation at the president of Croatia, Franjo Tudjman, for proposing the ethnic partition of Bosnia-Herzegovina, and then proposed a nearly identical plan for ethnic partition under the rationalization that it was the only way to achieve peace in the former Yugoslavia. France and Britain proposed ethnic partition as a solution to Belgrade-sponsored genocide, followed by President Clinton's version of a similar partition plan. President Clinton could thereby take credit for being a peacemaker. But in these as well as many other aspects of dealing with genocide in Bosnia, the West acted timidly on the basis of vast amounts of information all the while it pretended to act boldly on the basis of limited information. Hence, the conceit of innocence. In his contribution to this volume, Stephen Walker exposes the West's hypocrisy concerning what it knew and the responsibility for that knowledge concerning genocide in Bosnia.

For example, even though the Western media went along with the Serbian propaganda line that the Serbs wanted to preserve Yugoslavia and protect their minorities in the former Yugoslav republics, the real motives of the Belgrade dictatorship were known. Thus, according to the *New York Times,*

> It has become clear that Mr. Milošević's real interest in preserving Yugoslavia was slight. When Slovenia seceded on June 26, 1991, it was allowed to go with scarcely a fight: there was no Serbian minority there. The real aim, as a senior presidential aide, Borislav Jović, recently explained, was to use wars in Croatia and Bosnia to take the Serbian-occupied areas and so forge a Greater Serbia. In extensive interviews with the BBC for a documentary on the destruction of Yugoslavia, Mr. Jović . . . said that in April 1991, more than two months before war broke out in Croatia: "We decided to change tactics. We would deploy troops in Serb areas of Croatia, the Croats would provoke war, and we would then take those territories. We knew that when Bosnia was recognized, we'd be seen as aggressors because our army was there," Mr. Jović said. "So Milošević and I talked it over, and we realized we'd have to pull a fast one. We transferred all the Bosnian Serbs in our Yugoslav Army to

their forces and promised to pay all their costs." Thus was an extremely well-armed Bosnian Serb force created.[29]

Similarly, in July of 1995, the UN-protected "safe area" of Srebrenica was handed over to Serbs by Dutch UN peacekeeping forces. The initial rationalization offered by the Dutch peacekeepers was that they "didn't know" that the Serbs committed genocide in Srebrenica by killing more than six thousand men and boys in the town: The Dutch defense minister "criticized senior Dutch officers for saying soon after the Srebrenica operation that they had seen no evidence of genocide and that the Bosnian Serbs' conduct had been militarily correct."[30] By November, 1995, evidence that was known to the West from the start was finally released to suggest that Serbs had committed genocide against Bosnian Muslim civilians under the watchful eyes of Dutch UN peacekeepers who were given direct orders to protect them: "The Dutch commander, Colonel Karremans, and his sector commander, Col. Charlie Brantz, read that the battalion was ordered to 'take all reasonable measures to protect refugees and civilians in your care.'"[31] The evidence included U.S. spy satellite photographs and a completed report based upon a Dutch government inquiry, which blamed the UN and NATO for the massacre.[32] It was revealed that "General Bernard Janvier, the United Nations commander for Bosnia, vetoed the air strikes that Dutch peacekeepers in Srebrenica requested to defend the town."[33] Yet between July and November of 1995, the UN claimed that it did not know what had happened to the six thousand men and boys that were taken away by the Serbs. Nevertheless, under a headline, "Serbian Villages Know of Killings," the *New York Times* reported,

> The fact that thousands were killed is plain fact in the Serbian villages surrounding Srebrenica on the west bank of the Drina River. People interviewed in those villages this week said it was well known that Muslims were held captive in schools along the 13-mile stretch from Zvornik to Šepak before they were killed. Bratislav Grubačić, editor in chief of the VIP Daily News Report in Belgrade, said he was in Bratunac and Potočari in mid-July. "It is common knowledge in eastern Bosnia about what happened," he said Friday. His reporters said there were as many as 10 mass graves in

the area, each containing several hundred bodies. . . . A priest near Šepak confirmed that the schools had been used to imprison the Muslims and that the prisoners had been shot. He expressed no remorse at the killings, but regretted the style in which they were conducted. "I would kill a Turk, but I wouldn't torture them," the priest said.[34]

John Shattuck, the assistant secretary of state for human rights, said that CIA spy satellite photographs of mass graves in Srebrenica were evidence of "direct acts of genocide."[35]

Regarding the role of the Germans in Nazism, Thomas Mann wrote on September 25, 1949: "They desire neither to hear nor to know anything about the atrocities of the Nazi regime, which they declare to be propaganda, lies and exaggerations. They exhibit an ostentatious indifference toward court cases dealing with such atrocities. They are equally indifferent to the havoc which Hitler's war wrought in other countries."[36] The attitude of many Serbs toward atrocities committed by the Belgrade regime and its proxies is hauntingly similar:

> Many Bosnian Serbs refuse to concede that war crimes were committed in their name, no matter what the evidence. Rather, they say, investigations of war crimes allegedly committed by Serbians are only an effort to vilify them as a people. Perhaps more than anywhere else in Bosnia, the people here are living surrounded by the evidence of atrocities. It is not even buried; it does not come just from witness statements. The people here do not refute the obvious. They counter it much more effectively than that: They simply do not see it. Below the hill with the human remains is a warehouse where hundreds of men from Srebrenica were allegedly executed. Bullet holes and blood stains mar the walls. Local Bosnian Serb workers have made no obvious attempt to clean the stains or patch the holes during the last nine months. It is as if they have not noticed what is there. Or, perhaps, since they have convinced themselves that nothing happened here, they see nothing to cover up. In this village, people say they have not heard the reports, which have reached much of the world, that right here, and in villages nearby, thousands of men from Srebrenica were murdered by Bosnian Serb soldiers. "We don't know anything

about it," said Mira Stjepanović, 41, sweetly and, to all appearances, sincerely. "We didn't know. We don't know anything."[37]

On the surface, there seems to be little difference between German and Serb denials of horrible crimes committed in their names. But the important difference is that this time, in the 1990s, much of the world knew what had happened as it was happening, whereas a skeptical world had to wait for the end of World War II for the evidence of Nazi atrocities. This time, there can be no doubt that the contemporary Serbs who engage in denial are feigning innocence.

Nor is this process of obfuscation limited locally. Contradictions as to what Western officials really knew and what they claimed publicly abounded in the same issue or even the same page of leading newspapers. For example, when President Clinton addressed the American people in a televised speech on November 27, 1995, he claimed that all three "warring parties" accepted the terms of the U.S. brokered peace agreement signed in Dayton, Ohio. In reality, the Bosnian Serbs vowed to defy the agreement. "In contravention of their cease-fire obligations, the Bosnian Serbs have been delaying and harassing convoys," UN spokesman Chris Vernon said.[38] On the same page of the *New York Times,* one learned that America's allies did not agree with the terms of the peace agreement,[39] that Serbs in Sarajevo threatened to leave the city rather than live in a multiethnic Bosnia because "the world doesn't know the bad things that the Muslims did to the Serbs,"[40] and that a UN report was issued in which "Secretary General Boutros Boutros-Ghali said Bosnian Serbs had been engaged in a 'consistent pattern of summary executions, rape, mass expulsions, arbitrary detentions, forced labor and large-scale disappearances.'"[41]

Indeed, the Serbs who lived in those suburbs of Sarajevo that were eventually handed over to Bosnian government control under the terms of the Dayton Peace Accords did leave, but not before many of them vandalized, set ablaze, or otherwise destroyed those same neighborhoods.[42] Fleeing Serbs even looted Muslim cemeteries in Sarajevo.[43] Yet these clear examples of malice were characterized by American military officers, diplomats, and media as acts motivated by fear, the same fear of Croatian Ustashe and Bosnian "Turks" (Muslims) that is typically used to rationalize the origins of the current Balkan War. For example, Stephen Kinzer wrote in the *New York Times,* "In yet another of the heart-rending refugee flights that punctuated the Bosnian war and that now mar the peace, thousands of terrified Serbs trekked over snowy mountains today, away from their homes near Sarajevo."[44] The photograph caption that accompanied this front-page story read, "Bosnian Serb refugees, fearing Muslim reprisals for the long siege of Sarajevo, slogged along a snow-covered mountain road to Pale yesterday."

But in another article on the same subject, Kinzer made it clear that the fear of these Serbs was not spontaneous. It was instigated by Serb officials: "In violation of the spirit if not the letter of the Dayton peace agreement, Bosnian Serb leaders are urgently pressing all Serbs living near Sarajevo to abandon their communities before the Muslim-dominated Bosnian Government assumes control in the coming weeks. . . . 'This is all part of a campaign of manipulation to get people out, to create a psychosis,' said Kris Janowski, a spokesman for the United Nations High Commissioner for Refugees."[45] Nevertheless, despite documentation that the Serb exodus was orchestrated by the Serb leadership, and accompanied by malicious destruction—"They even took the windows and roof tiles, leaving only bare walls"—this exodus earned expressions of Western sympathy: "'It's sad to see those people leave their homes in such a fashion,' said U.S. Army Captain Nick Charles of Washington."[46] Western journalists were all too eager to rationalize Serb criminality on the basis of fear and Western standards of human rights: "It is inconceivable to them [Serbs] that after more than three years of war, forces of the Muslim-led Government will respect their rights."[47]

A headline in the March 18, 1996, *New York Times* captures the West's response to the destruction of Sarajevo by Serbs that followed the Dayton Peace Accords: "NATO Forces Watch as Sarajevo Burns" (A4). In line with the frame of reference that all sides are equally guilty, "Secretary of State Warren Christopher criticized Muslims and Serbs in the Sarajevo suburbs tonight for violence intended to push Serbian residents to flee areas handed over to the Bosnian Government. But he said those abuses 'are not a threat at this moment to the overall peace process.'"[48] If all sides are equally to blame, then the West can feign innocence, because it allegedly cannot tell the "good guys" apart from the "bad guys."

Even when Western forces in Bosnia could make out clearly who the culprits were, they refused to take on police functions. Consider the following news report as an illustration of this misplaced innocence:

> Smoke spiraled from the last Serb-held area of Sarajevo Sunday night as gangs of Serb toughs set buildings ablaze, raped old women and ransacked apartments in a final spasm of violence before this desolate stretch of battered high-rises returns to Muslim control. . . . Italian soldiers arrested up to 10 Serb men involved in breaking and entering and possible arson. Hands raised above their heads, the men were marched to a nearby Serb police station. Within an hour, however, *they were set free. NATO officers said they had to rely on "local authorities" to deal with thugs. The Serb police are widely cited as being responsible for much of the trouble.* . . . Over the last few weeks, NATO spokesmen have issued statements telling the Serbs that they "have the right to burn their own houses; and that the international force "is not a police force and will not undertake police duties." Such a position has been interpreted by Serb gangs to mean a green light to terrorize the local population. (emphasis added)[49]

Similarly, "The U.S. ambassador to the United Nations, Madeleine Albright, was stoned here Thursday by militant Serbs shouting, 'Sieg Heil, Fascists,' and 'Get out of Yugoslavia.' Local Serb police watched without intervening as rocks shattered a large glass pane on a UN van, raining glass on Albright's senior aides."[50]

Several ironies in the West's response to these events need to be accentuated. IFOR supplied trucks and otherwise assisted the Serbs who chose to evacuate Sarajevo, but IFOR not only failed to assist Bosnian refugees who sought to return to their homes, it actively blocked their return: "NATO troops blocked several hundred Muslim refugees from visiting their former homes and cemeteries in Serb-held sections of Bosnia on Sunday, saying that they feared an eruption of violence . . . Though refugees are guaranteed the right to return under the terms of the Dayton, Ohio, peace accord, NATO spokesmen said Sunday that it was up to the local authorities in those areas to secure safe passage, not NATO ... 'Freedom of movement is enshrined in the Dayton accord, but it is a broad issue,' said Lt. Col. Max Mariner from Sarajevo."[51] The typical, neo-Orwellian rationalizations for NATO impotence followed this violation of the Dayton peace accord: "NATO officers insist they have no responsibility under the Dayton agreement to guarantee that refugees can go home ... NATO officers said that Bosnian Serb officials were told last week that it was up to them to insure that Muslim refugees would be allowed at least to visit their homes for a day."[52] Mobs of Serbs attacked Bosnian refugees who attempted to return to their homes, despite the presence of NATO troops and Serbian police. The explanation offered by NATO for *not* protecting the refugees was that "responding to attacks like those today was a task for Bosnia's police, not NATO peacekeepers."[53] Another rationalization given by NATO was that "both sides bear a heavy responsibility for what happened."[54]

Anyone who engages in a serious analysis of the West's involvement in this war must confront this question: What did the West expect would happen in Bosnia following the Dayton Peace Accords when the West relinquished police functions to the same local police forces that engaged in horrible crimes prior to the accords? Given that Serb police units were often involved in genocide, how could the West have expected these units to maintain law and order? The West's actions constitute a feigned innocence, because brutality committed by Serb police and militias had been documented extensively. But again, the West rationalized this illogical faith in local police forces by blaming all sides equally: "International police officers are not expected to bring law and order to Bosnia, where violence and vandalism from all sides are making life treacherous for civilians, many of whom are resettling after being displaced during the war. Local people are 'better attuned' to the policing culture of their country, said Shashi Tharoor, an assistant to the head of the United Nations peacekeeping department.... An annex to the Dayton peace agreement makes the limited role of the police monitors clear. But the international police are expected to see that local police forces are keeping the peace."[55]

In general, the West tried to paint a "happy face" on post-

Dayton developments. For example, Stephen Kinzer strolled through Sarajevo and concluded: "People are walking, people are smiling, people are buying and selling. It's as if they've just woken up from a terrible nightmare."[56] When Serbs detained Muslim men in Sarajevo who were supposed to have had free passage under the terms of the Dayton Peace Accords, and when Serb snipers fired on Bosnian civilians following the supposed implementation of these same accords, Western officials dismissed these acts as mere "glitches" in the peace process.[57] Gangs of Serbs engaged in night beatings of Muslim as well as Serb civilians as NATO forces looked on.[58] IFOR troops located but did not destroy or remove Serbian heavy weapons that violated the Dayton Accords: "Officials said that the order to begin demolishing the weapons had been recalled because of the talks in Rome this weekend on preserving the peace agreement."[59] In general, despite signs of Serb defiance of the peace agreement that were evident from the moment it was signed, the West pretended that all sides agreed to it voluntarily and in good faith.

The Refusal to Arrest War Criminals

As of this writing, fifty-seven war criminals have been indicted by the International Tribunal in the Hague. Forty-six are Serbs, eight are Croats, and three are Muslims. Not a single one has been arrested by IFOR. IFOR was able to locate but refused to arrest a number of indicted war criminals, including the leader of the Bosnian Serbs, Radovan Karadžić, and his military commander, General Ratko Mladić. Said one newspaper journalist, "It strains credulity that a suspect as well known as Dr. Karadžić has apparently passed through IFOR checkpoints without being arrested."[60] General Mladić went skiing on the same hills of Sarajevo from which he orchestrated the killing of civilians. Journalists found him and beamed back to Western newspapers a picture of the general smiling—but IFOR troops were not there to arrest him.[61] Western officials tried to feign innocence but ended up engaging in Orwellian double-speak:

> Officials of [IFOR] peacekeeping force suggested that the approximately 60,000 troops deployed in Bosnia would not seek to detain

> any of the 52 people indicted for war crimes so far, including the Bosnian Serb commander, General Ratko Mladić, and the Bosnian Serb political leader, Radovan Karadžić. The peace agreement, *when it was drawn up in Ohio last fall, called on the soldiers stationed here to detain war criminals if they encountered them.* "IFOR troops have the authority, but not the obligation, to detain indicted war criminals," said an IFOR spokesman, Lieut. Colonel Mark Rayner. "Our primary mission remains the overriding one of seeing that war does not resume and providing military security. We are not engaged in identifying them [war criminals], searching for them or tracking them down." (emphasis added)[62]

When the Bosnian government arrested two suspected Serbian war criminals on its own—an act permitted under the terms of the Dayton Accords—Western governments criticized Bosnia for jeopardizing the peace process,[63] and the Serbs temporarily stopped complying with the terms of the peace agreement.[64] The Bosnian government was forced by the West to promise that it would not arrest indicted war criminals in the future. IFOR refused to guard sites of mass graves despite evidence that Serbs had removed bodies of victims and other evidence of atrocities.[65]

There are several dimensions to the West's refusal to arrest indicted war criminals in this war that beg for analysis. The first has to do with interpreting the fact that most of the indicted war criminals are Serb. This fact is commensurate with other findings that Serbs have committed the overwhelming majority of the atrocities and the genocide in the current war.[66] But some Western intellectuals have interpreted this fact as meaning that the International Tribunal has not been fair to Serbs and needs to indict more Croats and Muslims.[67] In general, the West has a postemotional need to maintain the frame "all sides are equally guilty" in order to support its feigned innocence. It is true that all sides in the current war have committed atrocities, but this is not different from other wars. In World War II, all sides committed atrocities, including the Allies (the bombing of Dresden, Tokyo, Hiroshima, and other examples). But no inner-directed historian is willing to conclude from this fact that the Allies and Nazis are morally equivalent, for example. Similarly, the United States has committed atrocities in the Vietnam War, the Gulf War, and other wars, but with the exception of some postmodernists, most analysts do not equate the U.S.' cause with those of its enemies. The important point is that in the current Balkan War, Western intellectuals, journalists, and government officials generally refuse to concede that the Serbian cause of establishing an ethnically pure Greater Serbia is morally repugnant and different from the emancipatory causes that drove Croatia and Bosnia-Herzegovina to secede from Yugoslavia. Thus, the West goes through the post-Nuremberg motions of indicting war criminals without the emotional outrage necessary to pursue them and put them on trial.

Second, and perhaps most important, the IFOR mission in Bosnia is designed to minimize U.S. and other Western casualties because of the ghosts of Vietnam and Somalia, even if such conservatism means that the Dayton Accords will not be fully implemented. Here again, we see signs of the conceit of innocence. Chris Hedges exposes these contradictions in an article on Admiral Leighton Smith, the U.S. commander of the NATO mission in Bosnia:

> Admiral Smith dismisses critics who he say would pull his forces into missions that he could neither enforce nor define, like searching out indicted war criminals. But exasperated Western diplomats criticize a series of recent decisions by the admiral as shortsighted and say he is more intent on keeping troops out of harm's way than on building a durable peace. They lambasted the NATO mission, which is to withdraw early next year, for ignoring provisions in the peace agreement, like arresting war criminals, in an effort to mollify the Bosnian Serbs. And they note that displaced people are not returning home, as called for by the Dayton agreement, and that NATO troops have failed to provide freedom of movement for civilians in Bosnia. These diplomats also say that Admiral Smith usually backs down when confronted by the Bosnian Serbs. . . . Admiral Smith says he will not order his forces to hunt down war criminals because it would draw them into armed confrontations, forcing them to take sides in the conflict . . . The Bosnian Serb leaders, for their part, praise the admiral's even-handedness. "Smith facilitated the looting of Bosnian property," a

Western ambassador said . . . "he just refuses to confront the Serbs."[68]

Third, the West has lionized Ratko Mladić and Radovan Karadžić despite the horrible crimes they have committed against humanity. This is demonstrated by Slaven Letica in his contribution to this volume. One should keep in mind that Hitler, Mussolini, and other Fascists were admired by many in the West for their efficiency and other modernist traits. The Bolsheviks and Stalin were also admired in the West. It is beyond the scope of the present analysis to delve further into the reasons that many Westerners find an affinity with barbarians, but this is certainly an important subject that should be pursued in the future.

Finally, the West has erected a vast, bureaucratic machine for handling international war crimes that seems unable to achieve the simple, innocent reaction to any crime that used to be accepted as a normal part of social structure. Consider, for example, the genuinely innocent reaction by a Texan volunteer in Bosnia: "In Texas, we would just go over there and arrest this [Serbian] mob for blocking a lawful assembly, but that's not really an option here . . . We are unarmed. All we can do is observe . . . We have no power to act at all."[69] Contrast this Texan's reaction to the alleged impotence of the West to act on its indictments of international war criminals: "'Not only do most of the accused and all of the commanders stand beyond reach,' said an official with the court who asked for anonymity, 'but the court is being blocked from amassing the necessary evidence to try suspects. No power, whether within NATO or the individual governments, shows any willingness to assist in the operation. And the court alone does not have the clout to see justice through.'"[70]

In general, these are among the postemotional reasons that the West is unable simply to indict international war criminals, seek them out, and put them on trial. Some of the ambiguities, ambivalence, and contradictions that preclude such straightforward moral actions existed at the end of World War II, but they have been greatly magnified in the postmodern 1990s, because postmodernism has enshrined ambiguity and ambivalence as moral virtues. Given this state of affairs, the West goes through the motions of innocence without its heart engaged in the actions necessary for genuine morality. In particular, as of this writing, the West is putting on trial war criminals who were low in the hierarchy of power and responsibility for the crimes that occurred, and continues to refuse to arrest and put on trial the chief architects of the highly visible genocide that occurred. The one high-ranking indicted war criminal that was in custody, the Bosnian Serb general Djordje Djukić, was released and *not* put on trial because he was terminally ill.[71] This policy constitutes nothing less than a reversal of the Nuremberg legacy, which put the chief architects of Nazi policy on trial. If the international war crime trials continue on their present course, they will achieve nothing more than a pale imitation of Nuremberg.

The Inability to Cope with the Future

Postemotionalism is something like a collective neurosis: So much emotional energy is spent on inadequate catharsis of past traumas that the present and future are neglected. Serb-sponsored genocide did not occur in a vacuum, but encouraged dictators elsewhere to defy international rules of law. The most significant development in this regard was Boris Yeltsin's slaughter of the Chechens and the general drift in Russia toward authoritarianism. (It is worth noting that I made such ominous predictions concerning Russia as early as 1993 in my *Habits of the Balkan Heart*.) Yet with the notable exceptions of Richard Johnson and Albert Wohlstetter, most commentators failed to make the connection between Serbian and Russian Fascism in the 1990s. This neglect may prove to be disastrous for the future if Russia achieves a counterrevolution to its much-touted demise of Communist rule.

In addition to these ominous developments in Russia and that country's aims to restore the Soviet Empire, a new world disorder seems be replacing the new world order that President Bush proclaimed. As of this writing, China is intimidating Taiwan; North Korea is behaving belligerently toward South Korea; Saddam Hussein continues to brutalize the minorities in Iraq; and Turkey and Greece came close to war over an island in the Aegean Sea, among other recent developments. In all these cases, the Clinton administration has reacted with a policy derived from the Age of Aquarius, namely appeasement and a call for a peace conference. It is an open question whether such other-directed responses will preserve international peace in the long run or serve as a prelude to yet another phase of international anarchy and war.

America may drift along this postemotional cultural trajectory for a long time to come, thereby influencing the postemotionalism of the rest of the world, or it may suddenly revivify its collective consciousness and its once innocent faith in American civil religion. Boldness, courage, happy confidence, faith, and trust may still emerge from the ruins of Americanism. Until this collectively emotional issue is resolved for Americans, it seems to be the case that America will simulate boldness, fabricate courage, ape confidence, and imitate faith from its once innocent past.

Notes

1. See Norman Cigar, *Genocide in Bosnia-Herzegovina* (College Station: Texas A&M University Press, 1995).
2. James Risen, "Clinton Aides Defend OK of Iranian Arms Shipments to Bosnia," *Houston Chronicle*, Apr. 6, 1996, p. A19.
3. Thomas Cushman and Stjepan G. Meštrović, *This Time We Knew: Western Responses to Genocide in Bosnia* (New York: New York University Press, 1996).
4. Jean Baudrillard, *America* (London: Verso, 1986).
5. Stjepan G. Meštrović, *Genocide After Emotion: The Postemotional Balkan War* (London: Routledge, 1996).
6. The concept of inner-directedness is taken from David Riesman, *The Lonely Crowd* (New Haven: Yale University Press, 1950).
7. Stjepan G. Meštrović, *Postemotional Society* (London: Sage, 1996).
8. David Riesman, "Innocence of the *Lonely Crowd*," *Society* 27, no. 2 (1990): 76–79.
9. Pauline Rosenau, *Postmodernism and the Social Sciences* (Princeton: Princeton University Press, 1994). Émile Durkheim, *The Elementary Forms of the Religious Life* (1912; New York: Free Press, 1965).
10. Durkheim, *The Elementary Forms of the Religious Life*.
11. David Reisman, *The Lonely Crowd* (New Haven: Yale University Press, 1950).
12. See, for example, Anthony Giddens, *Modernity and Self-Identity* (Stanford: Stanford University Press, 1991).
13. See "Bosnia Peace Effort $500 Million Over Projection," *Houston Chronicle*, Apr. 18, 1996, p. A22: "The Clinton Administration now estimates that the peace operation in Bosnia will cost $2.8 billion . . . $200 million to accommodate unanticipated harsh environmental conditions to improve the quality of life of our people . . . costs of intelligence gathering have grown by $200 million."

14. Arnold Toynbee, *America and the World Revolution* (New York: Oxford University Press, 1962).
15. Alexis de Tocqueville, *Democracy in America* (1845; New York: Random House, 1945).
16. Vaclav Havel, "Hesitant West Has Created NATO in Crisis," *Houston Chronicle,* Apr. 28, 1996, p. C1.
17. John Tagliabue, "Balkan Leaders Pledge to Carry Out Dayton Accords," *New York Times,* Feb. 19, 1996, p. A3. Tagliabue writes that "the United States and its allies agreed to begin the process of lifting sanctions imposed by the United Nations against the Bosnian Serbs."
18. Mike O'Connor, "First Lady, in Bosnia, Salutes the Troops, Some Proud, Some Still Perplexed," *New York Times,* Mar. 26, 1996, p. A6.
19. Ibid.
20. Ibid.
21. Philip Shenon, "Pentagon Report Predicts Bosnia Will Fragment Without Vast Aid," *New York Times,* Mar. 20, 1996, p. A1. See also Chris Hedges, "U.S. Led Effort For Bosnia's Army in Danger of Failure," *New York Times,* Mar. 22, 1996, p. A1: "The American-led effort to train and equip the Bosnian Army is in serious danger of foundering because of the failure to attract any significant financial support from either Western allies or oil-producing Muslim countries."
22. O'Connor, "First Lady."
23. Craig R. Whitney, "In Bosnia, Securing a Peace Depends on Roads, Refugees and Elections," *New York Times,* Mar. 26, 1996, p. A6: "5.1 billion in foreign aid would be needed."
24. Alexander G. Higgins, "Sounds of Hammering Beautiful to Bosnians," *Houston Chronicle,* May 5, 1996, p. A34: "With heavy armor and NATO sharpshooters standing guard, U.S. officials Saturday kicked off a much-trumpeted $25 million project to help rebuild Bosnia."
25. Whitney, "In Bosnia."
26. See Robert N. Bellah, "Civil Religion in America," *Daedalus* 96 (1967): 1–21.
27. Chris Hedges, "Bosnia's Checkerboard Partition: Instability More Likely," *New York Times,* Mar. 20, 1996, p. A8: "Yet the peace accords, by allowing the Serbs a semi-autonomous republic, always contained the seeds of division."
28. James Barron, "The Camelot Auction Begins, With the Prices Fit for Kings," *New York Times,* Apr. 24, 1996, p. B1; "Camelot Auction, Day 3: From 'Pearls' to Putters," *New York Times,* Apr. 26, 1996, p. A1.
29. Roger Cohen, "Peace in the Balkans Now Relies on Man Who Fanned Its Wars," *New York Times,* Oct. 31, 1995, p. A1.
30. Stephen Kinzer, "Dutch Complete Inquiry on Bosnia," *New York Times,* Oct. 31, 1995, p. A1.
31. Stephen Engelberg, "Srebrenica: The Days of Slaughter," *New York Times,* Oct. 29, 1995, p. A1.

32. Kinzer, "Dutch Complete Inquiry."
33. Engelberg, "Srebrenica," A6.
34. Ibid.
35. Ibid.
36. Reproduced in *New York Times Magazine,* Apr. 14, 1996, p. 90.
37. Mike O'Connor, "Serb Village Chooses to See Only Flowers Among Dead," *New York Times,* Apr. 19, 1996, p. A6.
38. Kit R. Roane, "U.N. Threatens Serbs With Force Over Convoy Harassment," *Houston Chronicle,* Nov. 30, 1995, p. A27.
39. Craig R. Whitney, "Amid U.S.-NATO Tensions, Troops Prepare for Bosnia," *New York Times,* Nov. 30, 1995, p. A6.
40. Raymond Bonner, "Many Serbs in Sarajevo May Leave," *New York Times,* Nov. 30, 1995, p. A6.
41. Barbara Crossette, "Tough Words Against Serbs From the U.N.," *New York Times,* Nov. 30, 1995, p. A6.
42. See Kit R. Roane, "Serb Refugees Fearful and Wanting Answers as Land Seizure Nears," *Houston Chronicle,* Feb. 25, 1996, p. A21; Kit R. Roane, "Sarajevans Return to Find Only Ruins: Refugees' Old Homes Stripped Bare by Departing Serbs," *Houston Chronicle,* Feb. 29, 1996, p. A16; Kit R. Roane, "Serbs Flee Another Suburb, Leaving Destruction Behind," *Houston Chronicle,* Mar. 12, 1996, p. A11; Kit R. Roane, "Bosnians Return Home to Find Suburb a Ghetto," *Houston Chronicle,* Mar. 13, 1996, p. A20; Steven Erlanger, "Bosnian Serbs Burn Homes Before Fleeing," *New York Times,* Mar. 19, 1996, p. A1; Chris Hedges, "Defiance and Disorder for Another Serb Exit," *New York Times,* Mar. 12, 1996, p. A3; Chris Hedges, "A Fiery Farewell in Bosnian Land Transfer," *New York Times,* Mar. 19, 1996, p. A4; Chris Hedges, "NATO to Move Against Anarchy in Serb-Held Suburbs," *New York Times,* Mar. 11, 1996, p. A3. According to Hedges, "Gangs of Serbian toughs, many brandishing weapons, moved about the suburbs of Ilidza and Grbavica today, lighting fires and threatening Serbs who refuse to leave." See also Chris Hedges, "Muslims Return to a Rubble Called Home," *New York Times,* Mar. 13, 1996, p. A5. Hedges interviewed a Muslim woman who returned after Serbs had destroyed her home: "'Now we are back,' she said. 'But they left nothing of ours behind. They ripped up our parquet floor. They pulled out the plumbing. We lived here 23 years. This apartment held everything we had saved in our lives. But, at least we have finally come home and we were lucky they didn't burn our building.'"
43. Philip Shenon, "A Postwar Shortage in Sarajevo: Space for Graves," *New York Times,* Apr. 21, 1996, p. A3.
44. Stephen Kinzer, "Serbs on Trek: Weighed Down and Terrified," *New York Times,* Feb. 23, 1996, p. A1. Kinzer elaborated: "Before leaving, some smashed their windows, doors, furniture, appliances and whatever else they could not carry with them, not wanting to leave anything of value to the

Muslims who may soon be occupying their houses and apartments. Several set fire to their homes as they left ... Kris Janowski, a spokesman for the United Nations High Commissioner for Refugees, said the refugees were fleeing largely in response to 'propaganda hype in the Pale media.'"

45. Stephen Kinzer, "Bosnian Serbs Pressed to Flee Area Near Sarajevo," *New York Times,* Feb. 21, 1996, p. A3.
46. Dušan Stojanović, "Residents Pillage Town Before Fleeing: Bosnian Serbs Leave Only Bare Walls to Welcome the Enemy," *Houston Chronicle,* Jan. 20, 1996, p. A23.
47. Stephen Kinzer, "Muslims to Take a Sarajevo Suburb Sooner Than Expected," *New York Times,* Feb. 20, 1996, p. A3.
48. "Christopher Rebukes Both Sides," *New York Times,* Mar. 18, 1996, p. A4.
49. "Gangs of Serbs Ravage Suburb Near Sarajevo," *Houston Chronicle,* Mar. 18, 1996, p. A1.
50. Roy Gutman, "Serbs Stone U.S. Ambassador Albright's Motorcade," *Houston Chronicle,* Mar. 22, 1996, p. A20.
51. Kit R. Roane, "NATO Troops Block Muslim Refugees From Returning Home," *Houston Chronicle,* Apr. 29, 1996, p. A7.
52. Mike O'Connor, "New Refugee Conflict Points Up Flaw in Bosnia Pact," *New York Times,* Apr. 29, 1996, p. A3.
53. "3 Muslims in Bosnia Die Going Home: Refugees Attacked by Mobs of Serbs," *New York Times,* Apr. 30, 1996, p. A7.
54. Kit R. Roane, "Serb Violence Greets Returning Muslims," *Houston Chronicle,* Apr. 30, 1996, p. A9.
55. Barbara Crossette, "UN is Slow in Deploying Bosnia Police," *New York Times,* Mar. 21, 1996, p. A6.
56. Stephen Kinzer, "Two Months After Treaty is Signed, Sarajevo Blooms," *New York Times,* Feb. 19, 1996, p. A3.
57. Chris Hedges, "Bosnian Serbs Said to Detain Muslim Men: Sniper Fires on Bus; Two Hurt in Sarajevo," *New York Times,* Feb. 15, 1996, p. A5.
58. John Pomfret, "Night Beatings Strike Fear in Bosnian Town: Attacks Expose NATO's Street Failures," *Houston Chronicle,* Mar. 10, 1996, p. A32.
59. Kit R. Roane, "Latest GI Sabers Rattle Persuasively in Bosnia," *New York Times,* Feb. 19, 1996, p. A3.
60. Morris B. Abram, "Peace and Justice Are Inseparable," *Wall Street Journal,* Feb. 16, 1996, p. A12.
61. "Shrugging Off Indictment, Bosnian Serb General Skiis," *New York Times,* Mar. 11, 1996, p. A3.
62. Chris Hedges, "Bosnia Limits War-Crimes Arrests After NATO Delivers Two Suspects," *New York Times,* Feb. 13, 1996, p. A1.
63. Chris Hedges, "Muslim Detention of Bosnian Serbs Threatens Accord: Contacts Are Suspended, Two Officers Held on Suspicion of Role in War Crimes—NATO Voices Concern," *New York Times,* Feb. 7, 1996, p. A1.

Hedges writes: "Andrew Cumming, the British officer who directs the NATO force's Joint Operations Center, described the arrests as 'provocative and inflammatory.'"

64. Kit R. Roane, "Bosnian Serbs Begin Effort to Ditch Dayton Peace Process," *Houston Chronicle,* Feb. 10, 1996, p. A26; Chris Hedges, "Extradition of Two Officers Angers Bosnia Serbs," *New York Times,* Feb. 14, 1996, p. A4.
65. Mike O'Connor, "War Crimes Officials Say Dead Possibly Were Moved," *New York Times,* Apr. 4, 1996, p. A3.
66. See Cigar, *Genocide,* and also Philip J. Cohen, *Serbia's Secret War: The Deceit of History* (College Station: Texas A&M University Press, 1996).
67. This was the implication in a speech given by David Rieff, "Bosnia After Dayton: Are Peace and Justice Reconcilable?" at the Wilson Symposium, "Conflict and Crisis in the Former Yugoslavia," Wellesley College, Massachusetts, Mar. 5, 1996.
68. Chris Hedges, "Diplomats Fault Bosnia NATO Chief," *New York Times,* Apr. 28, 1996, p. A13.
69. Kit R. Roane, "Texan in Bosnia Finds 'Destruction All Around,'" *Houston Chronicle,* May 4, 1996, p. A24.
70. Chris Hedges, "First Hague Trial For Bosnia Crimes Opens on Tuesday: Obstacles for Tribunal," *New York Times,* May 6, 1996, p. A1.
71. Stephen Kinzer, "Bosnia War-Crime Defendant is Sent Home, Terminally Ill," *New York Times,* Apr. 25, 1996, p. A6.

CHAPTER ONE

Ethnic Cleansing: A Metaphor for Our Time
AKBAR S. AHMED

Although ethnic cleansing itself is not a new phenomenon, developments in the mass media allow it to play a crucial role in influencing people in their perception of culture on an unprecedented scale and with heightened intensity. Hatred of the enemy, defined simply in ethnic or religious terms, is heightened through the use of television. Honor, glory, and ethnic nationalism are extolled, creating a predisposition for extreme arguments. The sex and violence in the media encourage it in real life. Ethnic cleansing of the enemy (usually the minority) appears as a logical and necessary step in the attainment of ethnic glory. Rape or sexual intimidation is extensively employed to terrorize and humiliate the ethnic enemy and explains the bitterness among combatants.

What theoretical and methodological implications does the study of ethnic cleansing in our time have for social scientists? First, we must recognize that all such crises need to be looked at in a global frame, that what is happening in one part of the world has a direct and immediate bearing on events in another part, that those who share the religion or race of the victims of ethnic intolerance in one part of the world are the aggressors in another, that no one group is entirely blameless. Second, we need to recognize that the discrete boundaries between disciplines are redundant. We need an understanding of ethnicity and identity as well as that of the nature of evil; we need to poach on anthropology for the former and religious philosophy for the latter. We need to understand anthropology, the nature of the mass media, and the implications of global geopolitics, and we must possess some idea of the past to construct contemporary paradigms. Third, while we need to study the ethnic death and torture camps (like those in the Balkans) we must also spot other less obvious and more subtle but almost equally tragic forms of ethnic cleansing resulting from racism and immigration policies (as in Western Europe). Finally, we need to recognize that the monopolistic position of the grand narrative is no longer valid. Modernity, for instance, which held sway for so long, is under challenge. We note fragmentation, new mutations, transformations, revivalisms, and revisions. This fragmentation is both cause and effect of ethnic revivalism.

In adopting a global perspective we will attempt to elucidate universal principles, keeping before us the bewilderingly different cultural and political contexts within which ethnic cleansing operates.

I wish to start not with a proposition or thesis but with an autobiographical confession. My analysis and interest in the subject are not entirely of an academic nature. True, as an anthropologist, I am interested in ethnicity and ethnic boundaries, that is, how people define themselves and are defined by others on the basis of genealogy, language, and customs. But I also approach ethnicity as someone who has had to come to terms with it in respect of my own identity, throughout my life.

From early childhood I was aware of the fact of ethnic differences that could lead to ethnic animosity and ethnic violence. Such differences accounted for my parents choosing to live in Pakistan when it was created in 1947. Large Indian provinces, as big as large European countries, were ethnically cleansed with all the attendant rape, torture, and destruction. About fifteen million people crossed each other as Hindus and Sikhs headed for India and Muslims for Pakistan; about two million died. Ethnic cleansing, clearly, is not a new phenomenon, although it is disguised for us under a new term.

In Pakistan where I grew up and worked, although the vast majority of people belong to one religion, Islam, and Islam condemns discrimination based on ethnic background, it matters a great deal which ethnic group you belong to. In 1971 I was in what was then East Pakistan, and became Bangladesh in that year, and saw firsthand the power of ethnic identity, how it could successfully challenge loyalty to a common religion.

Here, in the United Kingdom, I am given yet another identity, one based on color and race: I am seen as black or Asian. Those who do not like Asians call them "Paki," a term that denotes racial abuse. (What they perhaps do not know is that "Paki" derives from the Urdu word *pure,* and it is no bad thing being called pure, even by swearing, snarling skinheads.) Yet others learning that I am a Muslim have reservations, implying that all those with traditional religious belief are fanatics or extremists or what the media call fundamentalists. For some Muslims, suspicious and resentful of the Western establishment, I am a Fellow of a Cambridge College and therefore sullied. Multiple identities have thus been imposed on me.

Viewing the turbulence of South Asia I once envied what seemed the secure and fixed identity of being American or European. The passion generated by race and religion, I read in my American and British textbooks, was a characteristic of backward societies, those that were not modern. I now know that Northern Ireland can be as violent in its ethnic and religious hatreds as the worst affected place in South Asia. In Wales and Scotland ethnic resentment against the English surfaces easily. In parts of London the color of your skin can make you a target for abuse and assault. There are flash points in the United States, Germany, and France ready to explode into ethnic violence. To be an English-speaking male from the West in some parts of the Middle East is to know fear, to be vulnerable to the horrors of kidnapping. I no longer envy American or European identity.

Clearly I was not alone in my ethnic susceptibilities. It seemed that all of us were confronted with the same questions: What is my ethnic identity? How does the past shape it? How does it affect my life and those who are not like me? Why are the hatred and violence based on ethnic opposition so intense and so widespread? What is its relationship with the collapse of the project of modernity and the beginnings of a post–Cold War, post-Communism, postmodernity period? Is the ethnic cleansing in Bosnia a consequence of these changes and is it restricted to Bosnia alone? Has ethnic cleansing become the cognitive and affective symbol of or metaphor for our postmodern age?

In attempting to answer these questions my academic and personal interests in the subject coincide. I need to understand it in all its complexity to make sense of it. I therefore come to the subject with urgency and conviction and, I hope, with academic rigor.

Beginnings and Endings

In examining the worst excesses of ethnic cleansing we are transfixed by Bosnia, which has given the chilling euphemism "ethnic cleansing" to the late twentieth century. It is the suffering of the Bosnians that challenges frontally European self-perception and self-identity, a fact not fully appreciated here in Britain (see Bell-Fialkoff 1993; Meron 1993; Meštrović 1994; Schopflin 1993; Vulliamy 1994). Where, we may legitimately ask, are the much-vaunted European liberal values — humanism, civilization, and the rule of law?

The ethnic killings and hatred are a consequence of the collapse of the Soviet Union, it is argued. There is even some nostalgia for the old certainties. At least there was no mass murder, no ethnic cleansing, people say, forgetting one of the champion ethnic cleansers of history, Stalin. Others argue that the excesses of Bosnia are a reflection of the ethnic violence that took place half a century ago, an inevitable ethnic denouement. Some smugly talk of the conflict in the Balkans as typical of that area; they reflect cultural if not outright racial prejudice.

This is reductionism and simplification of complex historical events that are taking place on a global scale. There are many peoples facing persecution in our world — Muslims elsewhere in the Balkans, especially in Kosovo; Palestinians; Kurds; Kashmiris; the Chittagong Hill Tribes; and the East Timorese, for examples.

But however much it hypnotizes us we need to broaden our frame of reference beyond Bosnia in order to draw universal principles and locate global explanations. We may then begin to understand ethnic cleansing in our time. The explanations we provide are interlinked, some links strong, others tenuous, some fuelling the ethnic violence directly, others contributing more indirectly to it. Cumulatively they ensure that no society is immune, black or white, secular or religious, industrial or agricultural. Our exploration, however, of these explanations is tentative and can only suggest further areas of research.

We note the collapse of the idea of communism, but we need to be also aware of another, more significant collapse taking place: that of the notion of modernity with its cluster of ideas, derived in the main from the Enlightenment, such as freedom of speech, humanism, rationality, and secularism. To this was added subsequently economic and scientific progress. Sociologists like Max Weber placed these ideas firmly in Europe through explanations of a specifically European brand of Christianity. Because modernity was located in and spread from Europe over the last two centuries it allowed Europe to become the standard-bearer of civilization, indeed of the future. Cultural and racial superiority was implied. During the high noon of empire, authors like Jules Verne and H. G. Wells extolled the virtues of modern ways to and for all the world with the naïveté of enthusiastic schoolboys, but its European dimension was clearly assumed.

However, modernity had its dark side even in Europe. Bauman, citing Weber (Bauman 1991, 14), blames it, in part at least, for the Holocaust: "The most shattering of lessons deriving from the analysis of the 'twisted road to Auschwitz' is that — in the last resort — *the choice of physical extermination as the right means to the task of* Entfernung *was a product of routine bureaucratic procedures:* means-ends, calculus, budget balancing, universal rule application . . . The 'Final Solution' did not clash at any stage with the rational pursuit of efficient, optimal goal-implementation. On the contrary, *it arose out of a genuinely rational concern, and it was generated by bureaucracy true to its form and purpose*" (ibid., 17).

Those who believed in modernity saw other systems, Buddhist, Hindu, or Islamic for examples, as anachronistic. They would be obliterated in due course in the triumphalist march of Western rationalism and progress. Modernity has therefore always been viewed with ambiguity by people in Africa and Asia; it is too closely associated with European colonization and the rejection of religious and traditional ways.

We cannot say with certainty when modernity began to falter — there is no dramatic equivalent to the fall of the Berlin Wall in 1989 that symbolized the collapse of Communism. But the process of collapse had been gathering momentum. It became increasingly apparent since the middle of this century that modernity could not solve all our problems. In the last decade or two the loss of optimism combined with other developments: law and order deteriorated in the cities, unemployment grew, families fell apart, and the use of illegal drugs and alcoholism spread. Bosnia, and all it stands for, was perhaps the last straw.

What follows after modernity is still uncertain. Some, like Anthony Giddens, note continuity in modernity and use the term high or late modernity (1991). Others call it postmodernity—the social condition formed by information technologies, globalism, fragmentation of lifestyles, hyperconsumerism, the fading of the nation-state, and experimentation with tradition (the related concept, post-modernism, is the philosophical critique of grand narratives). Some write of a post–Cold War period or post-Communism, yet others see a time of ethnic and religious revivalism. However, in noting the revivalism we point out the yearning for premodernity, a desire to re-create a mythical past and imagined purity. In that sense the revivalism reflects antimodernity. It is characteristic of the age that its names are not original and reflect a relationship to the past.

What is certain is that the changes after Communism, the Cold War, and the failure of Western modernity have universal implications. The cement binding different peoples in the large blocs and uniting them in the grand narratives has cracked. This is most notable in the former Soviet Union. But in France, in Germany, even in Britain, we can also trace the dramatic rise of racism in the last years to the dark underside of modernity. Political opinion polls reflect the growing strength of the racist. By calling the racists neo-Nazis the media acknowledge the Nazi past. We hear louder and louder the voices of racism in Europe: "Expel the foreigners," "They are noisy and dirty," "They mean disorder and drugs," "They are not like us—cleanse our land of them."

A similar process is also to be noted globally. Hindus and Muslims in South Asia, Muslims and Jews in the Middle East, Russians and non-Russians in Russia—those ambiguous about modernity but frozen for half a century in the Cold War structures—are falling back to an imagined primordial identity, to their own traditions and culture. People define themselves in terms of the ethnic other, usually a group that has lived as neighbors.

No one group is entirely isolated from ethnic passions. If Hindus terrorize the Muslim minority in India during communal rioting, in turn, they are terrorized in Bangladesh and Pakistan by the majority Muslims. In Kashmir, Muslims have been killed and tortured in the thousands. Half a million troops are deployed in Kashmir to crush the Muslim uprising. This is a great human tragedy, but there is another human tragedy taking place simultaneously in Kashmir that is not known outside India. Hindus, who have lived in Kashmir for centuries, have fled the land out of fear; Kashmir is thus ethnically cleansed of them. Most Indians only see the plight of the Hindus, most Pakistanis that of the Muslims.

Yet in order to understand ethnicity an objective approach is needed. As an anthropologist I believe my discipline has much to say about the nature of ethnic conflict. Yet somewhat to my bafflement anthropology has been conspicuous by its absence in the commentary on such major international events of the last years as the Gulf War and the conflict in Bosnia.

Yet surely anthropologists need to explain for the general public why in some countries there is relatively little ethnic cleansing (for instance in Fiji in spite of the coups)? Or why it is particularly vicious in a certain period of history? Why have some minorities adjusted relatively well in an alien cultural environment (like the Sikhs in the United Kingdom) while others are less successful (consider the anti-Arab prejudice since the 1970s also in the United Kingdom)? Finally, what role does ethnicity itself play in ethnic cleansing?

Rediscovering Ethnicity

The understanding of ethnicity is therefore crucial to our task. Yet despite the efforts of Western social scientists, the popular imagination and popular media continue to reflect traditional ignorance and prejudice when dealing with ethnicity.

Ideas and arguments about ethnicity are usually based on the assumption that ethnic identity is a characteristic of primordial and tribal societies, that only society in North America and Western Europe represents modernity. Modern society has moved beyond, evolved away from, religion, belief, and custom. In any case there is little nostalgia in the West for religion, which is popularly associated with bigotry, superstition, and intolerance. Only backward societies cling to the past. Progress, science, rationality are the key words, although they are difficult to quantify; tradition, tribe and religion represent the outmoded and obsolete past. Not surprisingly Western anthropologists studying African or Asian peoples once routinely classified them as "savage," "primitive," or "tribal"; you only have to glance at the titles of one of the great London School of Economics names, Malinowski, for confirmation.

Those working in or on communist societies and those of a Marxist persuasion also analyzed ethnicity and religion as remains of the discredited feudal and traditional order. According to their social trajectory, ethnic and religious identity, although present, would in time fade away as people became equal citizens in the modern world. Clearly this has not happened for the majority of the world population, and the failure of these analysts is spectacular.

Indeed the problem of defining key concepts such as ethnicity, race, nation, and tribe that has faced social scientists is symptomatic of this malaise (Ahmed 1976, 1980; Ahmed and Hart 1984; Barth 1969; Godelier 1977; Helm 1971). What, for example, is a group of Scots in the Scottish highlands? With its clans, language, and customs, is it a tribe, an ethnic group, a race, or a nation? While the classic anthropological text on tribes, *African Political Systems* (Fortes and Evans-Pritchard 1940), restricted the definition to groups like the Bushmen and the Zulu, some anthropologists, like Max Gluckman, included as "tribal" along with the Bushmen and the Nuba, the Scots, the Irish, and the Welsh (1971). The debate continues.

Walker Connor contributed to the discussion by combining ethnicity and nationalism and used the term *ethnonationalism* (Connor 1993). He is right to underline the irrational and emotional wellsprings of ethnonationalism—hence the title of his Ethnic and Racial Studies/London School of Economics annual lecture: *Beyond Reason*—and its capacity to influence group behavior. But the category creates analytic problems. Surely in certain places, as in India, we need to accept the religious rather than the strictly ethnic dimension of large-scale confrontation.

Ethnicity in one place and religion in another are the central concerns of our time. Indeed in some areas of conflict "ethnic cleansing" is a misnomer. In most cases it is straightforward religious genocide, as with the Muslims in Bosnia. So to restrict the term strictly to ethnicity is incomplete at best and misleading at worst. When we employ the term we will do so broadly and generally to indicate notions of exclusivity in a group, based around a cluster of symbols such as language, religion, or historical memory, vehemently opposing and in turn opposed by neighbors with similar ideas of identity expressed with corresponding fervor. "Ethnic cleansing" is the sustained suppression by all means possible of an ethnically or religiously different group with the ultimate aim to expel or eliminate it altogether.

Although we are pointing to the widespread nature and intensity of ethnic cleansing we are not suggesting it is characteristic of or exclusive to our age. Elimination, as in Bosnia, and segregation, as in the Occupied Territories of Israel, of the other (hated and weaker) group have been practiced in the past: the *Reconquista* and *Inquisition* in Spain and *Glaubenskrieg* in Germany (reaching a climax with the Nazi Holocaust) are examples of the former; *apartheid* in South Africa and Indian reservations in the United States of the latter.

However, the exercise of grappling with the definitions of tribe, ethnic group, race, and so on may be a red herring. What we really need to analyze is why members of a group — ethnic or religious — want to oppose members of another group with such intensity that they are prepared to inflict the most horrific cruelty on them. We are thus really examining the causes for the radicalization of mass culture and the worldwide growth in and acceptance of extremism, fanaticism, and violence as a solution to the ethnic problem. It is this we need to focus on for purposes of our analysis in the otherwise amorphous and shifting global landscape.

Ethnic hatred has a mimetic quality: the opposed groups mirror the hatred, rhetoric, and fears of each other. It makes everyone an outsider, and it makes everyone a target. Everywhere — in the shopping arcade, at the bus stop, in the cinema, in your living room — you are vulnerable to sudden, random violence. Anger and hatred are easily created.

The hatred is generalized, universal, and maintained at a high level. For those in traditional societies it is engendered by the dangers posed to the core unit of society, the family, whether the extended or nuclear variety. In urbanized and industrialized society this threat is exacerbated as the family is under stress externally and internally: externally from migration, immigration, unemployment; internally from divorce, drugs, alcoholism. All this creates an anger at the world around, and a scapegoat is easy to locate and blame.

Members of the neighboring ethnic group are dirty outsiders, fifth-columnists, disloyal, speak a different language and have different customs. They must be cleansed. This argument can be heard not only in the Balkans but in one form or another in other parts of the world where ethnic clashes are taking place. The mindless cruelty takes in everyone — children, the elderly, the sick — as long as they belong to the other side.

It is this combination of perceived ethnic threat and personal vulnerability that forces people to fall back to community and group. There is logic here. If formal networks fail, then the more informal ones may be able to assist.

With international structures — like the UN — not to be trusted (as in Bosnia, Palestine, Kashmir) people fall back to their own group. The belief provides a security in an age of confusion and uncertainty, protection against the imagined or real conspiracies of the enemy. It also inures us to the stories of cruelty we know exist. By adopting an ethnic position people simplify complex ones, and by talking of national honor and glory they disguise the cruelty of their compatriots.

As a parenthesis I might point out the implications of this line of argument for Edward Said's *Orientalism* (1978; also see 1993). Said's thesis is based on the idea of the other (for Europe it is, famously, Islam). The other is out there geographically and culturally, dark, backward, and mysterious, to be dominated and exploited. In contrast to this external other is the internal other that we are pointing out: it is home-grown, among us, speaking our language and reflecting our customs, and sometimes it is stronger than us. Said's other is only a limited tool of analysis for our post-Orientalism argument.

Ethnic cleansing in one sense has leveled the categories that divided the global community — First World, Second World, Third

World, or North-South, or East-West. In various degrees and in different forms ethnic cleansing is in evidence everywhere, not only in Bosnia but elsewhere from Bonn to Bombay, Cairo to Karachi. Cities such as New York and Los Angeles, where entire neighborhoods are based on color and more or less out of bounds for those of the wrong color, are ethnically cleansed; a similar conceptual strategy to that in Bosnia is at work. Ethnic cleansing has made us all "primitives," "savages," "tribals" — pace Malinowski.

For their insensitivity during the Holocaust many governments made the puerile excuse that they were not aware of what was taking place in Germany. The gory daily news from Bosnia — or with less frequency but equal to it in the spirit of violating human rights, from Israel, Iraq, or India — shown on TV or discussed in print has little impact on the governments of the world; they appear to have developed compassion immunity. These stories are reduced to little more than voyeurism.

As with the Holocaust, many ask questions of a deep and disturbing nature: "Why does God — if there is a God — tolerate this suffering? Why doesn't God punish the aggressor, the rapist, and the murderer? What happened to the idea that good triumphs over evil?" If there is a divine parabolic lesson in Bosnia it has escaped most people.

For a Muslim, events in Bosnia are truly shocking. The holy Koran clearly preaches tolerance and understanding. Indeed, there is an anthropologically illuminating verse that talks of the wonders of the world, the diversity of races, and points to this: "O Mankind! We created you from a single pair of a male and a female and made you into nations and tribes, that ye may come to know each other — not that ye may despise each other" (Surah 49: *Al-Hujurat,* Verse 13). It is this spirit of ethnic tolerance that is under attack in our world.

Perhaps for us as academics the most distressing aspect of ethnic cleansing is the involvement of those who are educated and considered the pillars of modern society, the doctors, lawyers, engineers, and writers (the Jewish mass murderer who killed about fifty and wounded two hundred Muslims kneeling at prayer in Hebron in February, 1994, was a medical doctor). But we need to be cautious here. Although ethnic loyalty tends to be a tidal wave that sweeps all before it, we can cite many courageous people precisely from this class who stand up to and expose their own community (for examples, Meštrović in the Balkans, 1994; the Jewish women who published *Women for Women Political Prisoners* in Jerusalem, December, 1989; Makiya in Iraq, 1993; and Padgaonkar—with too many others to name—in India, 1993). Padgaonkar, chief editor of the *Times of India,* was dubbed the chief editor of the *Times of Pakistan* in Bombay by Hindu communalists when he attempted balanced reporting of the riots after Ayodhya and published the book *When Bombay Burned;* this is the equivalent of the white liberal who earns himself the contemptuous title "nigger lover" from his people for supporting black issues.

Unfortunately these exceptions do not disprove the ethnic rule that members of the other ethnic group are considered aliens or enemies regardless of their merits. Let us now explore some explanations for ethnic cleansing.

The Economic Argument

Perhaps the most commonly cited man-in-the-street explanation of ethnic cleansing is the global economic crisis. It is directly related to modernity running its course, to the loss of confidence in the future for the world community. There is a general economic crisis in the world—call it recession or by some other name. Unemployment figures are high. Even educated people roam the streets looking for jobs. Prospects are poor. The long-term global forecast is pessimistic, keeping in view the continuing population explosion in Africa and Asia. Poverty turns men into beasts. It is in this context that minorities—the Bangladeshis in Tower Hamlets or the Muslims in Bombay—become the target of irrational emotions. Matters are made worse by pointing to those individuals who have prospered. "They are taking all the jobs. They are being given all the housing. They must not be allowed to get away with this pampering."

There is a strong argument to be made correlating economic deprivation and ethnic confrontation. Whether in Gaza or in Kashmir the government has made virtually no economic investment. The neglect is interpreted as ethnic prejudice.

However, it is not only the minority that feels neglected. It is striking that each major section of society views its central problems in a similar light, casting itself as victim, and complains of injustice, blaming its woes on the ethnic or religious enemy, members of which are citizens and neighbors.

While the economic argument is valid to a point it is also limited, for economic statistics and material progress are taken as a yardstick of life itself, an end in themselves. Yet poverty has never been an excuse for violence and intolerance; indeed material austerity and spiritual development are central planks of most Asian religious thinking. This was made clear by the examples of the great spiritual messengers of history — Moses, the Buddha, Jesus, and the Prophet of Islam. In our century men like Mahatma Gandhi and women like Mother Teresa have advocated the message of austerity and simplicity with success. Human beings clearly cannot live by bread alone.

Globalization and the Mass Media

Globalization and the mass media provide us another explanation for ethnic cleansing. Let us explore this idea with the caution that while globalization is a characteristic of postmodernity it is also a direct consequence and in many significant ways a continuation of modernity. Giddens in his definition of globalization draws our attention to the relationship: "Globalisation means that, in respect of the consequences of at least some disembedding mechanisms, no one can 'opt out' of the transformations brought about by modernity: this is so, for example, in respect of the global risks of nuclear war or of ecological catastrophe" (Giddens 1991, 22).

Globalization draws in people all over the world who willingly or reluctantly participate in a global culture (see Ahmed 1993c; Ahmed and Donnan 1994; Ahmed and Shore 1995; Beck 1992; Fukuyama 1992; Giddens 1990, 1991; Huntington 1993; Moynihan 1993; Nash 1989; Robertson 1991, 1992; Turner 1994). Satellite TV, the VCR, communications technology, and developments in transport have made this possible (for an illuminating discussion on ideology and mass communication see Thompson 1990; for the role of the media in disasters and relief see Benthall 1993). McDonald's and Mickey Mouse, *Dallas* and *Dynasty*, Coca Cola and Levis, Toyota and Sony, as much as ideas of mass democracy and human rights are now the universally recognized signs of this global culture, whatever their country of origin. "Globalization," sighs one of the pundits studying it, "is, at least empirically, not in and of itself a 'nice thing,' in spite of certain indications of 'world progress'" (Robertson 1992, 6).

It is still early days for media studies, and the influence of the media on how people behave needs to be explored at greater length by social scientists. There is a tendency to dismiss media studies as an upstart and not take it seriously. This is a mistake because we can learn a great deal about contemporary life through media studies. Besides, it is salutary to recall the derision with which economics, sociology, and anthropology—each in its turn—was greeted by fellow scientists when these subjects attempted to secure a foothold in academe.

Today TV, the VCR, satellite dishes, and newspapers spread information and images more quickly and more widely than ever before in history. The consequences for our argument are enormous. For most of the population on this planet the reductive and hedonist images are a mirage, the hyperconsumerism out of reach. Envy, frustration, and anger result. The need to blame someone, to find scapegoats, is great. Radicalization and violence follow.

We know that the state-controlled TV in Belgrade played a crucial role in manipulating and articulating Serb identity. It showed pictures of atrocities, often of Serb victims, which confirmed in people's minds the necessity to stand together against a hostile world bent on denying them dignity and statehood. Ethnic passions were aroused, and ethnic cleansing appeared justified.

With their tendency to simplify complex issues, the media also allow a false and dangerous argument to circulate, one mounted by the chauvinistic and aggressive middle class, the keepers of the ethnic flame, that there is a "global conspiracy" to keep the nation or race down and prevent it from becoming great and fulfilling its destiny, that the minorities play the role of a fifth-column in this exercise. Across the world this complaint is echoed. Let us examine the situation in India (for the recent high-quality literature on religion and the rise of extremism in India, mainly written by Indians, see Ahmed 1993a, 1993e; Akbar 1988; Basu et al. 1993; Das 1992; Engineer 1984; Gopal 1991; Graham 1990; Madan 1992; McLeod 1989; Padgaonkar 1993; Phadnis 1989; Tully 1991).

The Hindu backlash was almost inevitable and needs to be explained. The vast majority of the population was Hindu, but in the postcolonial rhetoric—secularism, national progress, socialism—Hindu identity was in danger of being submerged. Hindus felt justifiably aggrieved. Among India's founding fathers were men of great piety like Mahatma Gandhi and Sardar Patel, but it was the first prime minister, Jawaharlal Nehru, who influenced independent India the most with his secular, tolerant, and modern ideas. However, in the eyes of the traditional and orthodox, modernity appeared to demean, disempower, and marginalize custom and belief. The Marxist vocabulary of the intellectuals added insult to injury.

By the 1970s, with Nehru not long gone from the scene, Hindu revivalism began to gather momentum, and Indira Gandhi, always a political animal, abandoned her father's position for an openly communal one. The globalization process and its aggressive cultural manifestation, especially of American origin, further alienated and threatened Indians—Hindus and Muslims—and forced them to hark back to the past (a point perceptively raised by Iyer 1992; also see Amin 1994).

The political and cultural atmosphere in the 1980s was charged. The mildest reservation about or the merest hint of opposition to the Hindu cause by a Muslim would risk swift, noisy, and painful retribution. It would be a feeling familiar to a Muslim Bosnian in Serb-controlled Bosnia with reservations about the battle of Kosovo, a Copt about the capacity of the Egyptian state to protect Christian churches and property, a Palestinian about the fairness of the state of Israel, a Kurd about the humanity of Saddam Hussein's regime, a Jew about the Islamic Revolution in Iran, and a Bangladeshi Hindu about Islamic revivalism in Bangladesh.

A glance at the long list of credits of the major and popular TV series depicting a mythical Hindu past, *Mahabharat, Ramayana,* and *Chanakya* (all shown in Britain) will illustrate the position of the Muslims in India today; the names are almost exclusively Hindu. It is assumed that only Hindus can make or contribute to "religious" films. Notions of purity and exclusiveness are implied and ethnic boundaries clearly drawn. This too, it can be argued, is a side of ethnic cleansing. (The process works both ways in South Asia: the popular Pakistani series *Dhoop Kinarey*—also shown in Britain—has almost all Muslim names in the credit list).

This was not always so in Indian films (see Ahmed 1992a). One of the most significant contributions to the idea of a genuinely multicultural and multireligious India was made by the Bombay cinema in the early decades of independence. It may have been an ideal, but it inspired millions. One of the most famous Hindu devotional songs from the popular film *Kohinoor* (1960) provides an example. It was sung on screen by Dilip Kumar (Yusuf Khan), written by Shakeel Badayuni, directed by Naushad and actually sung by Mohammad Rafi, all four Muslims. This was a remarkable comment on Indian tolerance and synthesis. It reflected the spirit of the founding fathers—Mahatma Gandhi, Jawaharlal Nehru, and Maulana Azad. It is this spirit that is under threat and that worries many Hindus, who wish to see it preserved. The minorities are simply terrorized by the new mass violence.

Films like *Mahabharat, Ramayana,* and *Chanakya* did not necessarily aim to have a contemporary political message but were watched by an estimated 600 million people every week, and this, in itself a unique media phenomenon, created a highly religious atmosphere in the 1980s. It generated a nationwide glow of pride and identity—a specifically Hindu pride and identity. The images projected an idealized Hindu past, a society in harmony, in flower.

Had the matter ended there, that is, TV as entertainment, this would be admirable and innocuous. But a subtext could be discerned: the ideal picture was shattered by invaders from outside India; Muslims were to blame. The series assisted in setting a chain of events in motion. Some media pundits in the Bharatiya Janata Party, a party floundering on the verge of extinction, at this point joined the emotions generated by the mass media and a political issue concerning the birthplace of Lord Ram at Ayodhya where a medieval mosque stood. Overnight the party's fortunes changed—from 2 seats in parliament to 119—although the results of the latest state election in north India indicate the support of the Bharatiya Janata (BJP) may have peaked.

So while Hindus thrilled at the doings of the attractive warrior-hero figure of Lord Ram on TV, they were angered by the mosque at Ayodhya. A vigorous campaign daubed the legend "Declare with pride your Hinduism" on walls, posters, and billboards all over India. A not so subtle subliminal message was contained in this slogan: vote for those who identify with Hinduism (like the BJP). The BJP notably, but also the Congress, then recruited the stars from the TV series, who were treated almost like divine figures in India, as their parliamentary candidates. They helped mobilize public opinion in demanding the mosque at Ayodhya be replaced by a temple. Widespread tension all over India resulted in frequent large-scale riots in the name of Lord Ram.

Hindu extremists were now offering Muslims all over India the standard choices of ethnic cleansing: absorption into Hinduism by accepting Lord Ram and becoming "Hindu Mohammedans" or expulsion (to Pakistan or Saudi Arabia or wherever). The third choice was to prepare for the destruction of life and property. From the *Reconquista* in Spain to the Occupied Territories in Israel, subjugated minorities have confronted these dilemmas.

The transformation of what its devout and thoughtful followers see as a philosophic, humane, and universal religious tradition to a bazaar vehicle for ethnic hatred and political confrontation saddens many Hindus. The mosque at Ayodhya was destroyed in December, 1992, and an orgy of killing followed all over India in which the paramilitary and security forces were later implicated (the world saw them on TV idly standing by as the frenzied mob in Ayodhya went about its business). Horror stories circulated of Muslims being burnt alive or raped while video recorders filmed them. In Bombay mobs stopped men and forced them to drop their trousers; those circumcised were identified as Muslim and stabbed. The link between the media and politics, between the religious-cultural assertion of identity of one group and the persecution of another, is suggested.

There were also immediate and serious international repercussions: Hindus were attacked and their temples destroyed in Pakistan and Bangladesh while angry mobs demanded a "holy war" against India in retaliation. In Britain tension was created between the Hindu and Muslim communities and Hindu temples were mysteriously damaged. The span of the responses confirms our other argument that to understand ethnic violence we need to keep its global context before us.

Although commentators singled out the BJP as the main culprit behind the ethnic violence this is incorrect and misleading; indeed elements in the Congress had long compromised on its secular position. Others too — influential opinion makers such as bureaucrats, media commentators, and academics — had been transformed and abandoned their earlier secular neutrality on communal issues. Those who were dismayed by this trend were reduced to powerless spectators.

Let us not make the mistake of the critics of the BJP by simplification of a complex phenomenon. Beneath every case of ethnic cleansing is layer upon layer of history and culture. The movement for a separate Muslim state, the creation of Pakistan (seen by many Hindus in a religious light, as sacrilege, as the division of Mother India itself), the wars between India and Pakistan, the perception of a threatening Islamic revivalism (in neighbors like Pakistan and Bangladesh and also, of course, Iran), and the continuing problems of the Muslim minority in adjusting to the new realities of India all contributed to the ethnic suppuration.

Indeed as early as the 1930s Gowalkar, one of the most influential Hindu ideologues, had argued that if Hitler could finish off the Jews in Germany then the Hindus ought to be able to do the same to the Muslims in India (1938). Hindu extremists even today continue to use the unsavory language of the Nazis. The tradition of virulent propaganda against Muslims disguised as scholarly research continues (Elst 1992; Oak 1990). Muslims in these books are depicted as whoring and pillaging drunks, breaking Hindu temples and buildings. These stereotypes feed into the mass media and neatly reinforce Hindu chauvinism, which is calculated to win the Hindu vote.

The argument will be made that India is, after all, Asia, Third World, backward, a society stuck in the rut of religion and tradition, that the influence on society of TV is a sign of such societies. It would be incorrect. Not only in India but throughout the world what we see on our TV screens helps to form our ideas. The arguments that the sex and violence on TV influence people await long-term statistical findings but on the surface appear plausible. They inure people to cruelty. Children grow up into adulthood convinced that the simple solution is to kill or maim or hurt. Not surprisingly, American pilots, on at least one carrier, about to bomb Iraq the next day during the Gulf War were shown sadistic, pornographic films (Marilyn French, "Dying to Please Nobody," *Sunday Times,* Oct. 10, 1993). Not surprisingly either the young killers of little James Bulger here in the United Kingdom had grown up on a diet of "video nasties."

In December, 1993, half a dozen young men raped for over an hour two young girls barely in their teens who were dragged from a McDonald's in London. About twenty other men stood around and cheered. The inspiration for this is not difficult to guess. Dozens of American films have depicted the same scene. That the gang was predominantly black gave the incident an ethnic dimension (life was also imitating art a few weeks earlier when a black gunman walked along a New York underground train shooting anyone not of his color).

No Heroes Any More

The mass media are also responsible, because of their aggressive irreverence and unceasing probing, for the lackluster leadership of our age. Our age has produced a distinctly mediocre set of leaders. Political scientists need to investigate further into this phenomenon so we are enlightened. Consider the list at random—Clinton in America, Major in the United Kingdom, Kohl in Germany, Yeltsin in Russia, Rao in India, Mubarak in Egypt. Most of us, I am sure, are not even aware of the names of the heads of government in China and Japan.

Charismatic leaders are not always the best leaders, and those like Hitler and Stalin were ardent supporters of ethnic cleansing. But what makes some charismatic leaders extraordinary is their capacity to stand up to majority opinion on matters of principle. We have the example of Mahatma Gandhi agreeing to the creation of Pakistan, however much it pained him, if that is what the Muslims wanted, and then starting a fast to death unless Hindus stopped killing Muslims in India. A Hindu fanatic killed him, accusing him of being too sympathetic to the Muslims. De Gaulle in France took the unpopular decision of giving independence to Algeria. For many French it was the ultimate betrayal and De Gaulle's life was constantly under threat. Churchill's support for Jews overruled the anti-Semitism in the Foreign Office.

In contrast, Rao in India, a year after promising to reconstruct the mosque in Ayodhya, still vacillates. In France North African immigrants are the subject of the crudest form of racism, and the prime minister's office talks openly of smelly and dirty aliens. Charles Pasqua, and others, have powerfully and mendaciously linked crime and immigration. Pasqua talks of returning immigrants to Africa "by the planeload and the boatload." He has tapped a vast reservoir of votes but also added a new and dangerous dimension to both issues.

The Failure of the Nation-State

The failure of the nation-state to provide justice and inspire confidence—as well as the frustrations it engenders—is another consequence of the collapse of modernity and of the rise of ethnic identity. Modernity was expressed by the form and idea of the nation-state. "National identity" emerged as a by-product of the formation of the nation-state, itself impelled by "industrialization" (Gellner 1983; Giddens 1991). But in large parts of the world the nation-state itself is under challenge—in East Europe, in the lands that once constituted the USSR, in the Middle East, in South Asia, and in Africa. Boundaries are being redrawn or rejected. As old states are threatened new ones are demanded or formed.

In their haste to depart, after the international climate changed following World War II, the colonialists took little time or effort when demarcating the new nations. Tribes and villages were sometimes divided between nations (in the case of the Kurds, the tribe was divided among five nations). Half a century of living together should have cemented the new states. This is not so.

One reason is the blatant discrimination the state practices in favor of the dominant group. I am not suggesting that the state legally supports the subjugation or the elevation of a group. On the contrary states are based on modern notions of equality and justice and in some cases appear to favor minorities (as in India where the Constitution in this regard compares favorably to those of the putatively advanced countries like France and Germany). Rather I am suggesting that even state functionaries are now contaminated with ethnic hatred.

Most dangerously for the health of the state the majority has developed a "minority complex" — whether in Serbia, Israel, Iraq, or India. Through a process of Alice-in-Wonderland logic it has come to believe, and proclaims for all to hear, that its population is in danger of being swamped (the minority breed like rabbits); its economy is in crisis (the minority act as a brake); it is the victim of an international conspiracy (the minority are a fifth-column); and the law and order have collapsed (the minority are responsible for the drugs and gun culture). To be a member of what is seen as the pestilential minority by the majority is almost to be a persona non grata, irrespective of the merits of the individual (whether Muslim in India, Hindu in Bangladesh, Palestinian in Israel, or Kurd in Iraq). The minority argue that the nation-state has meant suppression of their identity usually by brute force. Torture and death are common methods. Besides, the majority monopolize economic and political power, they point out. Democracy, they rightly claim, means perpetual subordination and humiliation. Ultimately, they fear, they will be wiped off the face of the earth.

A significant ethnic lesson is drawn from Bosnia. Many are now skeptical about the plausibility of plural or multicultural societies in the future. They wonder, "If the Serbs can do this to the Muslims who even married Serbs what hope is there for integration? Is the idea of integration irretrievably lost?" There were no easy answers, even from the optimists. The only security, it seems, was in reversion to primordial identity, a return to the idea of the tribe, of purity in an impure and menacing world.

An important idea, widely believed, is that international organizations that should have ensured justice, law and order, and the rule of law have failed. The United Nations is the primary example. It has failed the Bosnians, the Palestinians, and the Kashmiris. Resolution after resolution is passed regarding the destiny of these people and blatantly ignored.

For Muslims the world over, Bosnia, Palestine, and Kashmir signify the hostility to Islam in our times, of the persecution of Muslim minorities in particular. Muslims are convinced that fellow Muslims are being raped, killed, and uprooted because of their religion. Muslim anger and anguish echo the heartrending cry of Shakespeare's Jew: "Hath not a Jew eyes? hath not a Jew hands, organs, dimensions, senses, affections, passions?"

The historical past is evoked in each case. For instance, Muslims believe that the West, which was capable of stopping the genocide in Bosnia, would not do so because it did not want a viable Muslim nation in Europe. The last Muslim kingdom was extinguished in 1492 in Granada, Spain, and Europeans, five hundred years later have not changed. Muslims — both in Bosnia and around the world — suggest that European ideas of humanism, freedom, and equality appear to be applicable only to white Europeans with a Christian background (Ahmed 1992b, 1993d; Meštrović 1994; also *Impact International* and *Q News* published in London). It is in this context that commentators construct the global confrontation between Islam and the West (Ahmed 1988, 1992c, 1993b, 1993e; Huntington 1993).

Matters are complicated as ethnic groups across international borders are prepared to assist their oppressed kin (India accuses Pakistan of assisting the Kashmiris, Israel accuses the Arabs of aiding the Palestinians, and so on). Once again the majority feels threatened and talks of fifth-columns. Unless free and fair channels of representation are available and unless the majority genuinely consider the needs of the minority, the democracy in these countries will be incomplete and the nation-state will continue to be challenged as the minorities demand their own state.

We need also to point to the nation-state and nuclear proliferation. In the context of our arguments, until a decade or two ago, the nuclear option did not exist outside the Cold War structure. Today it does. India and Pakistan have fought three wars. They are poised for a fourth. Tension is at a peak following the destruction of the Ayodhya mosque and the revolt in Kashmir. This time experts fear the war will be nuclear, a total war; it will also be total madness. No one can win.

It is not difficult to conjecture what extremists on either side — Serbs or Bosnians in the Balkans, Jews or Palestinians in the Middle East, Hindus or Muslims in South Asia — would do if allowed to decide whether a bomb should be dropped on their enemy. It would solve all their problems, they will say enthusiastically. Holocaust solutions have always been popular by those who believe in eliminating supposedly inferior races.

Ethnocentric perceptions lull us into believing that nuclear weapons are more unsafe in the hands of the North Korean leaders than American or British ones. All fingers, whatever their color, on the nuclear button are dangerous, although the safeguards are greater in a democracy. The fact is that nuclear proliferation poses a major danger to the world. The question of nuclear weapons urgently needs to be addressed on an global level.

Rape as Policy in Ethnic Cleansing

Rape is one of the most infamous acts on man's long list of infamy, one suggesting deep psychological and emotional disturbance. Because rape is so intimately tied to ideas of honor and disgrace, people are reluctant to discuss it. Yet to learn about the true nature of ethnic and religious conflict social scientists need to study rape and sexual intimidation.

We know that in Bosnia rape was used deliberately as an instrument of war, a fact confirmed by innumerable international organizations and media reports. Dogs, HIV-infected men, and gangs were used to rape women in what have been exposed as rape camps. Small girls were raped in front of their mothers by soldiers taking turns. Rape was known as an ugly face of battle committed by soldiers in the heat of war. But in the manner it is used in the Balkans it is chillingly sinister. Civilians, administrators, students — ordinary people — were all involved as active participants or as spectators.

Bosnia is not alone in this regard. There is also considerable evidence gathered by international human rights organizations and by Indian writers that Indian troops in Kashmir are using the same tactics. There may not be official rape camps as in Bosnia, but troops have regularly surrounded villages, expelled the men, and raped their women all night. After the destruction of the Ayodhya mosque the police were clearly implicated in organizing riots involving rape against Muslims in Bombay and Surat. Iraq and Israel, the former in a crude way, the latter in a more subtle manner, also use sexual tactics to intimidate minorities, according to the book *Cruelty and Silence* by an Iraqi expatriate writer (Makiya 1993). Iraqi soldiers force Kurd women from camps, taking them to be raped; Israelis lock up Arab women in security cells for the night with threatening men. An organization of brave Israeli women risked the wrath of the authorities and documented the widespread cases of sexual abuse by the Israeli police (in *Women for Women Political Prisoners,* 1989.)

The woman is twice punished: by the brutality of the act and by the horror of her family. Notions of honor, modesty, and motherhood are all violated. Rape strikes families at their most vulnerable point, especially in traditional societies where, in certain tribes, illegitimate sexual acts are wiped out by death alone (Ahmed 1980). Rape is thus deliberately employed by ethnic neighbors who are fully aware of its expression as political power and cultural assertion to humiliate the internal other.

The sociological implications are clear for purposes of our argument: rape as a final line divides one group from the other; the state, through its forces, becomes the rapist, raping its own citizens, those it is sworn to protect. Bitterness is at a peak. So is the hatred in the response. Blood and revenge follow. A spiral of violence is set in motion. All the key notions of modernity—justice, rule of law, rationalism, civic society—are negated by the criminal nature of ethnic rape. For the victim and her family it is no longer an age of modernity and progress but one of barbarism and darkness.

The Uses of the Past

Finally, to justify the acts of humiliation like rape and as a consequence of the general sense of disillusionment with international and national bodies, the collapse of law and order, and the conviction that the only security lies in one's own people, the perpetrators employ increasingly creative historical-religious arguments, which, in turn, support ethnic cleansing.

History is employed to buttress ethnic and religious polemics and, more important, to reclaim and reconstruct ethnic identity by a whole range of commentators, academics, and politicians (Ahmed 1993a, 1993e). Thus Kosovo in the Balkans, Jerusalem in the Middle East, and Ayodhya in India are not just neutral historical placenames; they are also deeply emotive and affective symbols of identity. They rally the community as they provide it a visible proof of the perfidious enemy by reviving bitter memories from a distant past. In the mass media such history translates into kitsch, sentimentality, and commercialization; it also becomes popular and accessible. In the vacuum caused by the collapse of the grand narratives like Communism the indigenous becomes both relevant and inevitable. Honor, identity, and the media, the past and the future, the rise of what is called fundamentalism or revivalism all relate to the historical reference points.

Historical-religious mythology feeds the ethnic passions of the Russians (like Zhirinovsky) and Serbs (like Arkan) who talk of a Christian crusade, Jews and Muslims in the Middle East and Hindus and Muslims in South Asia who view each other as enemies in a holy war. "God is with us," the faithful pronounce with utter conviction and sincere belief.

It is this zeal that drives men in Bosnia to burn the sign of the cross onto the bodies of innocent Muslims and impale them in crucifixion (Goytisolo 1993; Yusuf 1993). This is not the spirit of Jesus, but it is a crude ethnic justification for the murder and mayhem. The first target is the village mosque. The destruction of these buildings is to be condemned on religious as well as architectural grounds as most of them are centuries old.

Academics who have dismissed the influences of historical mythology as irrelevant to our modern lives do not fully appreciate its power and influence. We are pointing to zealous supporters of ethnic superiority who number in the millions across the world and their governments, which have access to nuclear weapons.

Conclusion: Into the Millennium

Prognosis is difficult for the post–Cold War, post-Communism, postmodern age that is forming, but it is likely that the next millennium will open with limited but intensely messy ethnic conflicts— with vigorous ethnic cleansing—ongoing low-intensity wars in which there are no real winners or losers, no major defeats or victories, no defined battlefields or boundaries. We need to pull back from this nightmare Hobbesian scenario of the future to restore a balance between tradition and modernity, to restore local custom and culture, to restore respect for law and the way of others. Above all, we need more imagination and tolerance in dealing with others.

It can be done. The last years have provided us with some dramatic examples of a silver lining to the dark ethnic cloud. Long-standing ethnic enemies shook hands, an act symbolic of the wish to remove the vast psychological and cultural barriers that divided them and their people—Rabin and Arafat in Washington but also the British and Irish prime ministers in Northern Ireland and the black and white leaders in South Africa. In Germany, in spite of widespread and vicious ethnic violence, Dr. Ravindra Gujjula, an Indian, was elected the first Asian mayor in that country's history. In December, 1993, the Vatican reconciled with Judaism, thus ending the hostility of two millennia. But these significant gestures need to be more than media events and must be followed by concrete steps; the ethnic fires still rage on the ground.

Important steps need to be taken to encourage ethnic understanding. The first and most important is to underline the plurality of our world, that although people are divided by birth, language, and religion, they belong to the same species. To counter narrow nationalism we need to stress the extent of interdependence in today's world. Organizations like the UN, weak and ineffective in the face of ethnic crises, need urgent structural changes and larger budgets. Human rights and minority groups must be protected not only under the law but in the spirit of good neighborliness. The idea of tolerance and understanding needs to be encouraged through the mass media. We have seen the mass media acting as a source of division, let us see its positive side (for example, see Benthall 1993 for its impact on disasters and relief). For a start it can be conscious of and avoid its stereotypes of the other.

Education is another way to discourage ethnic hatred. Ill-defined ideas and prejudices in students' minds are easily developed into prejudice for the other. Islam and Hinduism need to be taught seriously in Britain as regular subjects, Christianity in Sudan and Pakistan, and so on. We need to call for an intensification of interfaith dialogue. There is so much common ground; spokespersons for the different faiths should point to it and act upon it. We need more Christians and non-Christians in Europe, Jews and Muslims in the Middle East, and Hindus and Muslims in South Asia sitting across tables in serious discussion.

Never before in human history have the global and the local, the high and the low, the past and the present, the sacred and the profane, the serious and the frivolous been so bewilderingly juxtaposed and so instantly available to stimulate, confuse, and anger the individual. Violence is almost inevitable, the ethnic victim often at hand. Globally, the disillusioned children and inheritors of modernity live in what the academics have termed "a risk culture" (Giddens 1991, 3) or "risk society" (title of Beck 1992; also see Ahmed 1992c; Ahmed and Donnan 1994; Ahmed and Shore 1995; Giddens 1990; Turner 1994).

I have pointed out the links between globalization, radicalization, sexual intimidation, the mass media, the uses of religious mythology, and ethnic and religious violence in the aftermath of the collapse of modernity. Cause and effect are clearly involved here. We have noted that victims of ethnic intolerance in one part of the world are themselves aggressors in other parts through the acts of those who share their religion or ethnicity. Every group appears to be susceptible to the ethnic virus. Ethnic cleansing ranges from the outright barbarity of death and rape camps to more subtle but also traumatic cultural, political, and economic pressures brought to bear on the minority.

In ethnic cleansing the human race faces a moral collapse leading to the most diabolical acts of cruelty. But we also possess the capacity and resources to tackle other pressing problems that we face, such as hunger and disease. Clearly, the global community is at some kind of dramatic crossroads, a cusp, a critical point in history.

Ethnic cleansing is the dark and ugly side of human nature. To contain it and to combat it we need first to understand it. Therefore to examine ethnic cleansing is not to look at the aberrant or the marginal or the temporary, the specialist's area of interest; it is to come face to face with our age, our nature, and our aspirations; it is to confront the human condition.

Acknowledgments

For their comments on this essay I am most grateful to Jonathan Benthall, Tam Dalyell MP, Professor Anthony Giddens, Professor Martin Bulmer, Professor Charles Keyes, Sir David Lane, Professor Stjepan Meštrović, Dr. Chris Rojek, Shawar Sadeque, Jon Snow, and Gary Waller MP.

References

Ahmed, Akbar S. 1976. *Millennium and Charisma among Pathans: A Critical Essay in Social Anthropology.* London: Routledge.

———. 1980. *Pukhtun Economy and Society: Traditional Structure and Economic Development in a Tribal Society.* London: Routledge.

———. 1988. *Discovering Islam: Making Sense of Muslim History and Society.* London: Routledge.

———. 1991. "Anthropology 'Comes Out'?" *Anthropology Today* 7, no. 3 (June).

———. 1992a. "Bombay Films: The Cinema as Metaphor for Indian Society and Politics." *Modern Asian Studies* 26, no. 2: 289–320.

———. 1992b. "Palestine Revisited." *Newstatesman and Society,* November 20.

———. 1992c. *Postmodernism and Islam: Predicament and Promise.* London: Routledge.

———. 1993a. "The History-Thieves: Stealing the Muslim Past?" *History Today* 43 (January): 11–13.

———. 1993b. *Living Islam: From Samarkand to Stornoway.* London: BBC Books.

———. 1993c. "Media Mongols at the Gates of Baghdad." *New Perspective Quarterly* 10 (Summer): 10–18.

———. 1993d. "New Metaphor in the 'New World Order.'" *Impact International,* March 12–April 8: 24–27.

———. 1993e. "Points of Entry: The Taj Mahal." *History Today* 43: (May): 62–63.

Ahmed, Akbar S., and David Hart, eds. 1984. *Islam in Tribal Societies: From the Atlas to the Indus.* London: Routledge.

Ahmed, Akbar S., and Hastings Donnan, eds. 1995. *Islam, Globalisation and Postmodernity.* London: Routledge.

Ahmed, Akbar S., and Cris Shore, eds. 1994. *The Future of Anthropology: Its Relevance to the Contemporary World.* London: Athlone.

Akbar, M. J. 1988. *Riot after Riot.* New Delhi: Penguin.

Amin, Samir. 1994. "India Faces Enormous Danger from Globalization." *Mainstream* 32, no. 9, (January 15).

Barth, F. 1969. "Introduction and Pathan Identity and Its Maintenance." *Ethnic Groups and Boundaries: The Social Organization of Culture Difference.* London: Allen and Unwin.

Basu, Tapan, et al. 1993. *Khaki Shorts and Saffron Flags: A Critique of the Hindu Right.* London: Sangam Books.

Bauman, Zygmunt. 1991. *Modernity and the Holocaust.* Cambridge: Polity Press; Oxford: Blackwell Publishers.

Beck, Ulrich. 1992. *Risk Society: Towards a New Modernity.* Translated by Mark Ritter. London: Sage. [Originally published in 1986.]

Bell-Fialkoff, Andrew. 1993. "A Brief History of Ethnic Cleansing." *Foreign Affairs* 72 (Summer): 110–210.

Benthall, Jonathan. 1993. *Disasters, Relief and the Media.* London: I. B. Tauris and Co.

Connor, Walker. 1993. "Beyond Reason: The Nature of the Ethnonational Bond." Annual ERS/LSE Lecture, 1992. *Ethnic and Racial Studies* 16, no. 3 (July): 373–89.
Das, Veena, ed. 1992. *Mirrors of Violence: Communities, Riots and Survivors in South Asia*. Delhi: Oxford University Press.
Elst, Koenraad. 1992. *Negationism in India: Concealing the Record of Islam*. New Delhi: Voice of India.
Engineer, Asghar Ali, ed. 1984. *Communal Riots in Post-Independence India*. London: Sangam.
Fernandez, C., and Naresh Fernandes. 1993. "A City at War with Itself." In Dileep Padgaonkar, ed., *When Bombay Burned*. New Delhi: UBS.
Fortes, M., and E. E. Evans-Pritchard. 1940. *African Political Systems*. Oxford: Oxford University Press.
Fukuyama, Francis. 1992. *The End of History and the Last Man*. London: Hamish Hamilton.
Gellner, E. 1983. *Nations and Nationalism*. Oxford: Blackwell.
Giddens, Anthony. 1990. *Consequences of Modernity*. Cambridge: Polity Press.
———. 1991. *Modernity and Self-Identity: Self and Society in the Late Modern Age*. Cambridge: Polity Press.
Gluckman, M. 1971. *Political, Law and Ritual in Tribal Society*. Oxford: Basil Blackwell.
Godelier, M. 1977. *Perspectives in Marxist Anthropology*. Cambridge: Cambridge University Press.
Gopal, Sarvepalli, ed. 1991. *Anatomy of a Confrontation: Ayodhya and the Rise of Communal Politics in India*. New Delhi: Penguin.
Gowalkar, M. S. 1938. *We or Our Nationhood Defined*, Nagpur, India: Bharat.
Goytisolo, Juan. 1993. "Terror Town." *Newstatesman and Society* (December): 17–31.
Graham, Bruce. 1990. *Hindu Nationalism and Indian Politics: The Origins and Development of Bharatiya Jana Sangh*. Cambridge: Cambridge University Press.
Helm, J., ed. 1971. *Essays on the Problem of Tribe*. American Ethnological Society. Seattle: University of Washington Press.
Huntington, Samuel P. 1993. "The Clash of Civilizations?" *Foreign Affairs* 72 (Summer): 22–49.
Iyer, Krishna. 1992. Review (of Ahmed 1992a). *Economic and Political Weekly*, November 7.
Madan, T. N., ed. 1992. *Religion in India*. Oxford in India Readings in Sociology and Social Anthropology. Oxford and Delhi: Oxford University Press. [Originally published in 1991.]
Makiya, Kanan. 1993. *Cruelty and Silence: War, Tyranny, Uprising, and the Arab World*. London: Jonathan Cape.
McLeod, W. H. 1989. *Who is a Sikh? The Problem of Sikh Identity*. Oxford: Clarendon Press.

Meron, Theodor. 1993. "The Case for War Crimes Trials in Yugoslavia." *Foreign Affairs* 72 (Summer): 122–35.
Meštrović, Stjepan G. 1994. *The Balkanization of the West: The Confluence of Postmodernism with Postcommunism*. London: Routledge.
Moynihan, Daniel Patrick. 1993. *Pandaemonium: Ethnicity in International Politics*. Oxford: Oxford University Press.
Nash, Manning. 1989. *The Cauldron of Ethnicity in the Modern World*. Chicago: University of Chicago Press.
Oak, P. N. 1990. *Some Blunders of Indian Historical Research*. New Delhi: Bharati Sahitya Sadan.
Padgaonkar, Dileep, ed. 1993. *When Bombay Burned*. New Delhi: UBS.
Phadnis, Urmila. 1989. *Ethnicity and Nation-building in South Asia*. New Delhi: Sage.
Robertson, Roland. 1991. "The Globalization Paradigm: Thinking Globally," in D. G. Bromley, ed., *Religion and Social Order*. Greenwich, Conn.: JAI Press.
———. 1992. *Globalization: Social Theory and Global Culture*. London: Sage.
Said, Edward. 1978. *Orientalism*. London: Routledge.
———. 1993. *Culture and Imperialism*. London: Chatto and Windus.
Schopflin, George. 1993. "The Rise and Fall of Yugoslavia," in John McGarry and Brendan O'Leary, eds., *The Politics of Ethnic Conflict Regulation*. London: Routledge.
Thompson, John B. 1990. *Ideology and Modern Culture*. Cambridge: Polity Press.
Tully, Mark. 1991. *No Full Stops in India*. London: Viking, Penguin.
Turner, B. S. 1994. *Orientalism, Postmodernism and Globalism: Intellectuals in the Modern World*. London: Routledge.
Vulliamy, Ed. 1994. *Seasons in Hell: Understanding Bosnia's War*. New York: Simon and Schuster.
Women for Women Political Prisoners. 1989. Jerusalem: n.p.
Yusuf, Feyyaz. 1993. "Christian Radicalism Stirs the Serbs." *'Q' News* (December): 10–17.

CHAPTER TWO

The Pinstripe Approach to Genocide
RICHARD JOHNSON

My thesis here is a simple one: senior U.S. government officials knew that Serb leaders were waging genocide in Bosnia but would not say so in plain English because this would have raised pressures for U.S. action.

Beginning in late summer 1992, the executive branch of the U.S. government, under the both the Bush and Clinton administrations, came under significant pressure to make an unequivocal determination that the Serb campaign in Bosnia constitutes genocide under the 1948 United Nations Genocide Convention.[1]

External pressures came from the U.S. media, human rights organizations, American Jewish and Muslim advocacy groups, prominent foreign policy experts, members of Congress, the Bosnian government, and from states friendly to Bosnia at UN fora including the UN General Assembly, the UN Commission for Human Rights, and the June, 1993, UN World Conference on Human Rights in Vienna.

Internal pressures came from lower-and mid-level foreign service officers (FSOs) with line responsibilities for U.S. policy on Bosnia, other FSOs who have used the State Department's dissent channel mechanism to press their views, and the four FSOs who subsequently resigned to protest U.S. policies.[2]

These pressures triggered a number of statements by senior

State Department officials and by the president, particularly after December, 1992, that implicitly or explicitly addressed the issue of whether genocide was under way in Bosnia.

Some of these came very close to saying yes. However, none made a clear and unequivocal determination that Serb leaders were waging genocide in Bosnia, and that the moral and legal obligations of the Genocide Convention apply. Instead, administration statements typically asserted that the Serb campaign "borders on genocide," or that "certain actions" by "Bosnian Serbs" have been "tantamount to genocide" or constitute "acts of genocide."[3] There are two hypothetical explanations for such equivocation.

One is that further collection and assessment of evidence was needed before a clear determination can be made, particularly with regard to *intent* (that is, do Serb leaders and their forces seek to destroy a substantial part of the Bosnian Muslim population, or rather to displace it, or does the mass murder by Serb forces stem from a systematic plan or from a coincidence of local decisions by local commanders?) and *responsibility* (can responsibility be traced up to Bosnian Serb political and military leaders, and to Serb leaders in Serbia, and with what degree of conclusiveness?).

Several State Department and National Security Council (NSC) officials gave me this explanation, in more or less explicit terms. These officials also often asserted that the genocide issue may be of moral and historical interest but is not of operational importance in terms of pursuing justice (war crimes are easier to prove than genocide) or ending the killing in Bosnia (through a "negotiated settlement").[4]

However, some of these as well as other State Department officials also acknowledged that policymakers at the White House and in the State Department have shown little interest in clearing up the questions that supposedly stand in the way of an unequivocal finding of Serb genocide in Bosnia. There was never a presidential or NSC directive to the State Department and other intelligence agencies to conduct research and analysis aimed at establishing whether there is a good case against Slobodan Milošević et al. for genocide in Bosnia. Nor was there any mobilization of resources to this end. The human resources applied to the Bosnia war crimes issue at the State Department and in the CIA were minimal, and declined in the State Department in 1993. The personnel involved were tasked more with recording specific war crimes than with tracking the responsibility for such war crimes to the Serb leadership.[5]

The other explanation is that policymakers opted for equivocation because an explicit, unequivocal determination that genocide was under way in Bosnia, and that Milošević, Radovan Karadžić, and their military commanders are responsible, would produce more political pressure to take effective action, including the use of force, to end and punish the genocide. At a minimum, such a determination would undermine the credibility of Western policies that rely on UN/European Community–mediated "peace talks" to reach a "voluntary settlement" between "warring factions"—who would now be defined as the perpetrators and victims of genocide. This explanation is supported by the following elements of the executive branch's treatment of this issue since autumn of 1992.[6]

The most explicit, forward-leaning administration positions were never followed up with consequent actions. In August, 1992, the State Department confirmed that Serb-run "detention centers" in Bosnia featuring systematic killing and torture were a significant problem.[7] The State Department then initiated a process of submitting data on war crimes in Bosnia to the UN War Crimes Commission. However, lead action on compiling these submissions was assigned to an FSO in the Human Rights Bureau with no prior knowledge of Balkan affairs and a short-term State Department intern just out of college—hardly a commitment of personnel and expertise commensurate to the recognized gravity of the issue.[8]

In mid-December, 1992, Acting Secretary Lawrence Eagleburger broke new ground in drawing parallels between Serb behavior in Bosnia and Nazi behavior, naming senior Serb leaders as bearing responsibility for war crimes and crimes against humanity in Bosnia, and citing some of the questions they should face. However, his public statements were not followed up by any internal taskings within the State Department or the CIA to build up cases against these leaders.[9]

In that same month the United States also voted for a UN General Assembly resolution on Bosnia that, among other things, stated that Serb "ethnic cleansing" in Bosnia is a form of genocide.[10] However, the executive branch never followed up by citing or using this determination as a basis for Western policies. Similarly, in June, 1993, the United States supported an appeal of the UN World Conference on Human Rights to the UN Security Council to take "necessary measures to end the genocide in Bosnia and Herzegovina." However, the U.S. took no subsequent action on the basis of this appeal and its finding of genocide. Indeed, as of December, 1993, an official at State Department Bureau of Human Rights was unable to locate a copy of the Conference appeal in office files, and described it as something the department viewed as "not really an official act of the Conference."[11]

More equivocal statements tend to be made by more senior officials in high-profile fashion. Less equivocal statements are made by lesser officials in lower-profile fashion. The president has, largely in response to questioning, repeatedly drawn some degree of analogy between the Holocaust and the present mass extermination of Bosnians. But he has chosen never explicitly to address whether Serb leaders are engaged in genocide. Warren Christopher volunteered during his confirmation hearings that the Serb campaign of "ethnic cleansing" was resulting in "near genocidal or perhaps really genocidal conditions."[12] But he never raised the issue after becoming secretary of state, and his most extensive comments on the matter as secretary, under questioning on May 18, 1993, before the House Foreign Affairs Committee, were also the most equivocal presentation by any administration official since the beginning of the war in Bosnia.[13] These comments triggered an extraordinary memo to the secretary from the acting assistant secretary for Human Rights reminding the secretary that Serb and Bosnian Serb forces were responsible for the vast majority of war crimes in Bosnia.[14]

The most straightforward statement by a senior official of the Clinton administration has also been the most obscure: a mid-November, 1993, written submission to a House subcommittee in response to a question taken by State Counselor Timothy Wirth five months earlier, stating that "the Department of State does believe that certain acts committed as part of the systematic Bosnian

Serb campaign of 'ethnic cleansing' in Bosnia constitute acts of genocide."[15]

Secretary Christopher opted out of the Bosnia genocide issue after May, 1993. Persistent questioning by Congressman Frank McCloskey was the primary trigger of administration review of this issue after April 1, 1993, when McCloskey got Christopher to promise him a clear determination as to whether the Serb campaign in Bosnia is genocide under the Convention.[16] How to respond to McCloskey's question (and his repeated follow-ups) was a recurrent issue among the Bureaus of European Affairs, Human Rights, Intelligence and Research, International Organizations, Congressional Relations, and the Office of the Legal Advisor, and between these offices and the "seventh floor" (that is, the secretary and his senior advisors) from April to October, 1993. On October 13 the secretary finally approved an action memo that had been redrafted numerous times, and which would have authorized the assistant secretary for congressional relations to sign a letter to McCloskey using the language subsequently used in the State Department's mid-November submission to the House subcommittee cited above. However, the secretary annulled his approval of the proposed letter to McCloskey after the latter called for his resignation in mid-October, 1993.

In a subsequent exchange with McCloskey during an early November, 1993, House Foreign Affairs Committee hearing, Christopher chose not to respond to McCloskey's question on the genocide issue. Instead, the secretary charged that McCloskey's views on Bosnia would require several hundred thousand U.S. ground troops, asserted that McCloskey's emotions were clouding his judgment, and rejected any further "debate" with McCloskey on Bosnia.[17]

Seventh-floor policymakers at the State Department have repeatedly rejected efforts by the bureaus to have them make less equivocal statements on genocide in Bosnia.[18] On April 1, perhaps in response to McCloskey's questions to Christopher, outgoing State Department spokesman Richard Boucher instructed then Bosnia desk officer Marshall Harris to draft a strong statement by the secretary on genocide in Bosnia. Harris's draft, dated April 2, was cleared by all the relevant bureaus and submitted to the Office of the Spokesman. It included the assertion that "the United States Government believes that the practice of 'ethnic cleansing' in Bosnia includes actions that meet the international definition of genocide as well as constitute other war crimes." The statement was never issued; Harris believes it was killed by incoming State Department spokesman Thomas Donilon, in consultation with the secretary.

Similar language was again cleared by the relevant bureaus in September in one iteration of the proposed response to McCloskey's April question to the secretary; this draft was also rejected by the seventh floor.[19]

Senior policymakers do not have better information about realities in the Balkans than do the lesser officials who have sought to bring them to make clearer statements on genocide. Comments made by Undersecretary Peter Tarnoff and Counselor Wirth at an April 28, 1993, State Department luncheon for Elie Wiesel shed some light on their thinking.

Weisel argued that whether or not genocide was under way in Bosnia, the Serb concentration camps and mass murders there constituted a moral imperative for decisive outside intervention. Tarnoff took Weisel's point but noted that failure in Bosnia would destroy the Clinton presidency. Wirth agreed with Weisel that the moral stakes in Bosnia were high but asserted that there were even higher moral stakes at play: "the survival of the fragile liberal coalition represented by this Presidency."[20]

Conclusion

This is a story of many failures. Senior policymakers have failed to level with the American people on the nature of the moral and security challenge the United States faces in the Balkans. Lesser officials have failed to resist the obfuscation of their seniors. Outside the executive branch, the broad range of interested observers who see Milošević's campaign for a Greater Serbia as an instance of genocidal aggression that the United States must confront have failed to apply coherent and sustained pressure to force at least a straightforward executive branch statement on the genocide issue.

I draw no constructive lessons from these failures except that avoiding them requires a series of moral choices by individuals. Those made by senior policymakers with the most influence in defining the challenges America faces are most momentous. But all, cumulatively, make a difference.

Notes

1. Under the 1948 Convention on the Prevention and Punishment of the Crime of Genocide, to which the United States, the successor states to former Yugoslavia, and some one hundred other countries are parties, "genocide" is defined to include any of the following acts committed with intent to destroy, in whole or in part, a national, ethnic, racial, or religious group: (a) killing members of the group; (b) causing serious bodily or mental harm to members of the group; (c) deliberately inflicting on the group conditions of life calculated to bring about its physical destruction in whole or in part; (d) imposing measures intended to prevent births within the group; (e) forcibly transferring children of the group to another group. The Convention is a specific response to Nazi extermination practices during World War II.
2. I am personally aware that in December, 1992, three FSOs who had shared responsibility for Yugoslav affairs between 1990 and 1992 used the dissent channel to press for a State Department determination that Milošević was engaged in genocide in Bosnia; that in April, 1993, twelve FSOs actively engaged in Bosnia policy submitted a letter to the secretary that, among other things, described the conflict in Bosnia as Serb genocide; and that the four FSOs who resigned in protest—George Kenney in August, 1992, and Marshall Harris, Steve Walker, and Jon Western in August, 1993—have all defined the war as genocide.
3. Several officers with experience in the State Department's Office of the Legal Advisor have told me that there is no legal difference between saying starkly that "what has happened is genocide" and saying less starkly that "what has happened is *tantamount to* genocide" or "what has happened are *acts of* genocide": The "tantamount to" formulation appears to have originated on the "seventh floor" (the secretary and his senior advisors).
4. From author's December, 1993, interviews with sixteen current and former State Department employees ranging from desk officers to deputy assistant secretaries, and with NSC European Affairs director Jenonne Walker in May, 1993. In December, 1993, Walker declined to discuss U.S. policy process on the issue of genocide in Bosnia with the author, on the grounds that it was "too sensitive."
5. Ibid.
6. This explanation was also advanced by many of the sixteen current and former FSOs interviewed by the author for this essay.
7. See President George Bush's August 6, 1992, remarks on "Containing the Crisis in Bosnia and in Former Yugoslavia" and Acting Secretary Lawrence Eagleburger's August 5, 1992, statement "Detention Centers in Bosnia-

Hercegovina and Serbia" in *Dispatch,* U.S. Department of State Bureau of Public Affairs, Aug. 10, 1992; and George Kenney, "See No Evil," in the *Washington Monthly,* Nov. 1992. Kenney underlined senior State Department officials' resistance to investigating, confirming, or publicizing Serb atrocities in Bosnia and their efforts to minimize U.S. media attention to them.

8. From author's interview with the State Human Rights Bureau action officer and the former intern in question.

9. See Secretary Eagleburger's December 16, 1992, statements in Dispatch, U.S. Department of State Bureau of Public Affairs, Dec. 28, 1992. The absence of follow-up taskers was confirmed to the author in interviews with the current and former FSOs cited above.

10. See UN General Assembly Resolution A/47/92 of December 17, 1992, passed 102 for (including the U.S.), 57 abstentions, and none against, which holds Serbian and Montenegrin forces responsible for aggression and for "the abhorrent policy of 'ethnic cleansing,' which is a form of genocide."

11. From author's interviews with State Human Rights Bureau officers, December, 1993. Notwithstanding the State Department's unofficial view as to the unofficial status of the Conference's appeal, it was in fact forwarded by Alois Mock, president of the World Conference on Human Rights, to the president of the UN Security Council on June 16, 1993, as a decision of the Conference.

12. For typical statements by the president and secretary, see *New York Times,* Jan. 14, 1993.

13. See Christopher's May 18, 1993, comments before the House Foreign Affairs Committee, including the insinuation that Bosnian Muslims are suspected of genocide themselves. Several State Department officials told the author that they were flabbergasted by Christopher's remarks on atrocities and genocide in Bosnia in his May 18 House Foreign Affairs Committee Hearing and that these remarks bore no relationship to expert and consensus views within the department on those issues. One State Department official told me that late on May 17, the secretary's office sought urgent information from the Human Rights Bureau on Bosnian *Muslim* atrocities only.

14. Author's interviews with current and former FSOs.

15. The text of Wirth's statement, responding to a question put to Wirth by Congressman McCloskey on June 10 at a House Appropriations Subcommittee meeting, is presumably available from that subcommittee.

16. McCloskey's April 1 question and Christopher's initial response are available in transcripts of House Foreign Affairs Committee hearings for April 1, 1993. The author's account of the reaction to McCloskey's pressures within the State Department is based on interviews with current and former FSOs in December, 1993.

17. See transcripts of November 4, 1993, House Foreign Affairs Committee Hearing.

18. This and the following paragraph are based primarily on author's December, 1993, interview with Marshall Harris, foreign policy advisor to Congressman McCloskey.
19. Ibid.
20. The author witnessed this Wiesel/Tarnoff/Wirth luncheon discussion.

CHAPTER THREE

How the Conscience of the West Was Lost
GEORGIE ANNE GEYER

All that spring of 1991, you could see the "Yugoslav situation" coming ever closer to collapse. So it was not totally by accident that I arrived from East Berlin the night before the fighting started in Slovenia. The Belgrade airport was hushed and confused; passengers and crew milled around without speaking, and long lines waited for passport control. In one of those Kafkaesque little dramas that so often attend the opening acts of tragedy, I sat down on the floor with two Yugoslav journalists and, while we waited, we drank their whole bottle of Slivovitz, their famous and lethal brandy. In the days to come, we would need more than that.

"Floundering amid turbulent tides . . . no visible rescuers?" Washington Times, July 9, 1991.

The war had started. After arriving there on its eve, I spent some days in Belgrade, watching helplessly as the tides of conflict engulfed the country, the people, the mentality of the times. Before moving on, I paused to write this column recounting Secretary of State James Baker's "at least we tried" policies that effectively did nothing to halt the progression of terror.

BELGRADE, YUGOSLAVIA

Only two weeks ago, I watched Secretary of State James Baker wage deft diplomacy in Berlin. At the Conference on Security and Cooperation in Europe (CSCE), he was for the first time in history instrumental in bringing together the United States, Europe, the Soviets, and even Albania into one group.

But only two weeks later, one sees here a different American diplomacy under the same Bush and Baker hand. This diplomacy toward a rapidly disintegrating Yugoslavia is confused, contradictory, and tremulous in its indecision.

First, immediately after the American triumphs in Berlin, Mr. Baker rushed to Belgrade for only a few hours to proclaim with obvious sincerity that the United States supported a united Yugoslavia. Fine, if a little late! But once Slovenia and Croatia declared independence from Yugoslavia on June 25 and once fighting began two days later, the State Department all but gave its blessing to the two republics' independence.

At this point, one of the major outcomes of the Berlin meeting came into play in the violent and unruly Yugoslav scenario. In Berlin, CSCE had pioneered by creating an undefined new "mechanism" for dealing with precisely the prototypical ethnic conflicts within nations that we now see erupting. This CSCE mechanism—which probably means diplomats trying to negotiate away the conflicts, although no one exactly knows—was a struggling attempt to deal with this new form of Balkanization. And so European negotiators were soon headed toward Slovenia and Croatia to do something, no one being sure just what.

It would be easy, perhaps, to be overly critical of the American and European diplomacy toward Yugoslavia. Both dithered too long, while it was clear for the past two years that Yugoslavia was breaking up into least six republics.

By the time the United States acted to support Yugoslav unity and reversed its actions to support the dissident republics, one had to wonder: What exactly was the real interest of the United States and Europe here, unity or democratic separation? And why did these very limited outside forces, exemplified by the CSCE's new ethnic-conflict mechanism, even think there was really something outsiders with such restricted power could do in such divided and fanaticized situations?

As Milovan Djilas, the great Yugoslav scholar, told me here of the outside pressures: "We see that the economic pressure from the

European Community and the U.S. was absolutely without effect. These people are obsessed fanatically with nationalism."

Indeed one wonders exactly what outside forces could do in a country whose newest "president," the Croatian Stipe Mesić, announced for months before finally being accepted by the Serbs that he would only supervise the disintegration of the state of which he was now president. Or where is it reliably reported that the presidents of Serbia and Croatia, the two major rivals, nevertheless only during these lasts months discussed dividing up between them the third republic of Bosnia? Or where the demagogic president of Serbia, Slobodan Milošević, is probably correctly described as moving to destroy Yugoslavia in order to pick up the pieces for a "Greater Serbia" under his authoritarian hand?

So the question is not a simple one, either for the United States or for Europe. American policy for the last three years, as Yugoslavia headed down the disintegration path, has been to want unity (at least thirty other independence groups wait in the wings). But if unity was too expensive in terms of Yugoslav federal intervention, then the United States would choose democratic separation.

An ideological problem also underlies this bedeviling situation. American history gives little moral guidance on these matters. Independence of Nations? Sure! Just look at our Revolutionary War. Unity of nations? Of course! We fought a sanguinary war of brothers to preserve the Union.

We are faced in Yugoslavia with a watershed "politics of devolution." Different from the traditional diplomacies of the Berlin meeting and different from the old exigencies of revolution (where at least we know what we are dealing with), devolution presents the world with the question of how to push the contradictory values of democracy and unity all at once where centralized power is devolving to smaller groups.

The American policy here so far has been "at least we tried," that hapless expression heard across many forms of American diplomacy, and it has always been disastrous. Here it symbolizes the fact that American diplomacy today can deal brilliantly with the largely consensual needs of the big countries but that we are in for a new period of chaotic and to-date ineffective and vacillating diplomacy in these new and troubling situations.

Memphis Commercial Appeal, *October 5, 1992.*
I met the "imam" of the Zagreb mosque in the lobby of the modern and pleasant Incontinental Hotel in Zagreb. It was an incongruous picture. Zagreb was quiet and peaceful, although we knew that the war was only miles away, and here, this sincere man, who worked most of the time in America, gave me an impassioned warning of what was to come. I knew that I was hearing a plea for help-before-it-was-too-late, one of those historic pleas that at least I could pass on through my column. But none listened.

ZAGREB, CROATIA

The last desperate appeal for help as a whole people is about to be destroyed usually comes in loud, angry, despairing screams. I myself heard Free Radio Hungary go off the air in October, 1956, when the Russians poured into Hungary — and the voices were that way.

So could it be possible that this pleasant, cultured, meticulously dressed man before me is actually voicing such a genocidal fear? Can it be that soft-spoken Dr. Mustafa Cerić, in his Northbrook, Illinois, English, is telling us something we need badly to hear?

"My message to the Western world is that we Bosnian Muslims want to live in Europe, and we want to be Europeans," Dr. Cerić, the imam of the Zagreb mosque, said to me, in a steady but urgent voice, as we sat in the coffee bar of the Intercontinental Hotel here.

"But after what is happening in Bosnia-Herzegovina, it seems that Europe does not want us and does not want us to be Europeans.

"I would appeal to my colleagues across the world — those who still have Christian and humanitarian values — to do something, anything, to stop the concentration camps, the 'ethnic cleansing,' the random massacres of civilians, mostly Muslims.

"And please, please, don't kill us on the pretext of Islamic fundamentalism!"

At this very moment, the Bosnian Muslim community's worse nightmares are being brutally realized. Despite all their pious agreements with the United Nations and with naively trusting negotiators, the Serbs are intensifying the destruction of the innocent Muslim communities, purging, killing, shelling, torturing, moving them out and burning their homes. That the peaceful two-million-member community could actually be wiped out as a people this winter is no longer unthinkable.

Moreover, and incredibly, the Western sanctions were and are imposed against both Serbia *and* Bosnia. So the Bosnians are deliberately being left as helpless animals to the Serbian slaughter. They cannot even obtain weapons from outside to protect themselves, while the Serbs have a huge backup arsenal of weapons left from the Cold War.

But the story worsens.

The savage Serbs and the indolent and cowardly West are now excusing the massacre of the Muslims by the same astounding excuse: that Islamic fundamentalists are about to take over Bosnia!

"What is striking is that both sides [Serbian and Croatian] are beginning to be afraid of the Muslims," Cedric Thornberry, the UN's leading political adviser here, told me. "I've seen propaganda on both sides warning of a jihad [holy war]."

Now, these are truly miraculous developments. Here you have a tiny community left over from those Slavs that converted to Islam under the Turkish Ottoman Empire. Here you have blond, blue-eyed Slavic Muslims who historically have been far more Europeanized than the Serbs. Here you have an imam who has a Ph.D. from the University of Chicago and who served at the Islamic Cultural Center in Northbrook, Illinois. And nearly all are now prisoner, dead, or refugee.

These surely are people who are going to rage out of the hills of Bosnia and threaten Europe, just like the Turks at the gates of Vienna!

There is the reality that probably between two and five hundred "Mujahadin" fighters have joined them, many of them Arab students who had studied earlier at Bosnia's rich educational institutions. Some arms have come in from Islamic countries, largely through the recently freed Croatian port of Split.

But every single source I talked to—and there were many—agreed that this aid from other Islamic countries was peanuts. Besides, is there something wrong with people, because they're Muslims, trying to save themselves from being slaughtered?

What is happening to the Muslims of Bosnia is not going to go away historically. Books will be written about it, songs will be sung, legends will grow like implacable vines about the corpse. Small peoples have imperishable memories.

It will also stand as a monument, in the Islamic countries and elsewhere, to the fact that Europeans and Americans just don't care much about Muslim deaths—even, ironically, when they are their own race and even when they so avidly have embraced the tenets of European rationalism and humanism.

One good thing will come out of it, though: Islamic fundamentalism now will never get to Rostock.

Washington Times, *October 21, 1992.*
By now, I was trying—really trying—to analyze this from its roots up. Actually, that was not hard at all, given the tools of sociological, political, and psychological knowledge that we have. But the West, and in particular the European defense ministries, were utterly refusing to look at the war for what it was: a cynical play by the Old Communists in Belgrade for land and for power, using the primitive passions of the "mountain Serbs" and the criminal classes. Instead, the Western Europeans persisted in seeing the wars in terms of World War II: "valiant Serb guerrilla fighters, Croatian Nazis, Bosnian Turks." Europe was returning, too, to its pre–World War II neutralism: Neville Chamberlain would have loved Bosnia.

BELGRADE, YUGOSLAVIA

The Yugoslav war is not the inexplicable quagmire that it has so often been portrayed as. Instead, the war has a key that could easily have unlocked all the tightly closed doors to a successful policy.

That key is the Serbian gunmen who even at this moment burn and ravage Bosnia while Western "statesmen" ostentatiously fiddle in New York and London. That is the nature of this frightful war.

From the beginning of the war in June, 1991, both European and U.S. diplomats and officials have repeatedly refused even to send air cover for hundreds of thousands of innocents being slaughtered. Why? Because the Serb gunmen were courageous "World War II–style guerrillas" like those who fought the Nazis to a standstill.

Here, in Belgrade and Zagreb, in Sarajevo and in what is left of Vukovar, that analysis—the core of all Western thinking—is generally thought too ridiculous to consider. Diplomats, military men, and journalists here know what this war is about, if diplomats and officials in Western capitals do not.

This was and is a war of Serbian gunmen in Bosnia and Croatia and their mountains of artillery guns and ammunition, all left behind by the well-endowed Yugoslav army when it collapsed a year ago. Over and over, their military "style" has been only one: to bomb the Vukovars and the Sarajevos to death—from a safe distance—and never, ever fight hand-to-hand or commit infantry.

Indeed those mixtures of old Yugoslav army (few), local warlord armies (many), and uncontrolled "wild mountain Serbs" or "wild irregulars" (too many) have repeatedly refused to enter the cities as infantry. There is wide agreement here that they are largely thugs, psychopaths, and would-be World War II "Chetniks," whose specialty is slitting throats and cutting off limbs while the victims are still alive. Some are "weekend warriors" from Montenegro who go in for "fun" and are paid in deutsch marks.

All are basically cowards when it comes to any traditional ideas of military engagement or the honor of the battlefield. But they have also been fighting a war of the countryside and the mountains against the city and the plains. Indeed the intellectuals, journalists, and public figures of the city have with total deliberateness been the first to be killed.

Unquestionably, Miloš Vasić, the courageous Serbian editor and military analyst of the leading antiwar journal *Vreme*, the equivalent of our *Time* magazine, has the correct key to the gunmen's character. "This war is definitely anthropological," he told me, sitting in *Vreme*'s busy offices here. "We always divided our population more by altitude than by language or ethnic group.

"First, there is the mountain cattlemen approach. The other is the farmers' approach. The cattlemen perceive the world in terms of space for their herds; the farmers in terms of time for their crops.

"That is why the wild mountain men with no sense of humor are the driving force of this war. And that is why Sarajevo and Mostar were so savagely destroyed. These cities are a different civilization to guys frustrated by not being able to settle in them."

He might have added that that is why churches and cultural monuments were the constant and cynical targets of the Serbs. Four hundred Croatian churches have been destroyed; the Serb gunmen have consistently used UN Educational, Scientific and Cultural Organization (UNESCO) flags, supposedly protecting historic monuments, as markers to destroy those monuments. Over and over in the smitten cities, the gunmen would hit a church steeple with artillery, and journalists at the scene could hear the "yea, yea" in the background.

But if this entire analysis is true, and it is — and if the Yugoslav tragedy is a war fought almost entirely by artillery, and it is — then the initial and continued reasons for nonintervention are absurd.

Of course Western forces could have bombed the artillery sites around these ancient cities: of course they could have used smart bombs and counterbattery fire weapons; of course they could have put an air cap and sea cap on the massively equipped Serbian forces.

"Most of the artillery could have been taken out by air," General Slobodan Praljak, vice defense minister of the Croatian army, told me. "Why, you can see it, and everybody knows where everything is, anyway. We know every piece of ground. The West is lying because there is no answer as to why they didn't stop this in time."

Indeed, we now have sufficient time into this war to look back at the equally flawed diplomatic policies. Military sanctions were imposed on both Serbia and Bosnia, although Serbia had mountains of arms and Bosnia had none. A no-fly zone was declared in the Banja Luka area — and then never enforced. UN troops were sent in but without the ability to fight, so they and innocent, idealistic relief workers became the tools of the gunmen.

History is not going to be kind to the West, and in particular to the Europeans, whose cowardice rivals that of the gunmen. Again it has been shown, unfortunately, that without U.S. leadership, Europe regresses to a 1930s paralysis — and there was no U.S. leadership.

So what happens when the roll is called up yonder, and Yugoslavia has been destroyed, and four million have died, and the Balkans are in flames, and Europe and Central Asia have both been poisoned by this new Balkans tragedy? Well, the West will come out of its cave to discover that those great World War II guerrillas were simply ugly thugs who could have been halted right in the beginning. Then, perhaps, the West will realize that it has helped greatly to cause, by sheer cowardice, the greatest tragedy since World War II.

Furrowed brow at the UN. Washington Times, *June 4, 1993.*
My overseas peregrinations for my column soon took me to Brussels to meet with North Atlantic Treaty Organization (NATO) Secretary-General Manfred Woerner. It was strategic "love" at first sight; his clear and classic view of the uses of force and his willingness to be unequivocal about how Western force should be used in the former Yugoslavia stood as an enormous relief to me from the "neutralist" doubletalk of the Western Defense Ministries over Bosnia. I would stop by in Brussels to talk to him every once in a while, if only to remain sane.

BRUSSELS, BELGIUM

If there is an angrier man in all Europe than NATO secretary-general Manfred Woerner, it would be hard to find him.

First, he sees the time to act over Bosnia is being fatally dribbled away. Second, he still cannot find a defined mission for NATO action in any quarter. And third, he is convinced that the organization he so loves will in the end be blamed for "losing" Bosnia.

After a stormy meeting May 24–26 of NATO defense ministers here, in which the ministers refused to endorse President Bill Clinton's latest plan of basically unprotected "safe havens" for the beleaguered Bosnians — Mr. Woerner discussed the open questions that are driving him crazy.

"What is the meaning of 'safe havens'?" he demanded, in an interview in NATO headquarters here. "What happens to access for humanitarian aid? Does 'safe haven' mean defense by United Nations troops, by themselves? What are the rules of engagement?

"What happens if cities are shelled? Will we allow it? If shells hit only the UN troops, will we allow it? What are the Americans prepared to do? Protect only UN troops — or the population? If only these zones are declared safe, does that mean everything else is not safe?

"What is the relation between these new concepts and a peaceful settlement? Does that mean you have turned back the Vance-Owen plan? But how would you even implement that, if no one is prepared to push them out of the zones — and nobody is prepared to do that!"

Mr. Woerner — a man of direct thrusts, common sense, and elegant speech — has been one of the few leaders in Europe to be consistent about the wars in the former Yugoslavia since they began in June, 1991. He believes that early use of force, combined with a tough embargo against Serbia, would surely have driven the Serbs to realism and peace.

He is a "new German" who was ten at the end of World War II and who is determined that "it" should never happen again. Yet today he heads the most powerful military organization in human history and can do nothing as 135,000 people are slaughtered like cattle only an hour's flight time from Frankfurt.

Underlying his angry words is the idea that all these multifaceted, wildly (and perhaps intentionally) imprecise plans of the West define leaders who are not serious about doing anything. It's hard to argue with him.

Then there is his baby: NATO, the North Atlantic Treaty Organization, since 1949 probably the most successful alliance the world has ever seen; the Western defense grouping that protected Europe from the Warsaw Pact without ever the semblance of a war and that effectively won the Cold War.

NATO is now involved in Bosnia in a small way, with ships waiting in the Adriatic and a more-or-less order to enforce the long dithered-over "no-fly" zone over Bosnia. But typical of the incredible stupidities that in the West seem to have attended every step of this war, at the United Nations in New York the French, because of their own sympathy for Serbia, have been holding up a resolution (820) to allow NATO troops to fire back if fired upon.

"The final assessment is too early," said Mr. Woerner, a former German defense minister, "but what I see with great concern is that somehow they will blame NATO, as though NATO had any responsibility for managing this conflict. We offered our support, but we can only do what they ask us to do. To use an instrument, you need political will."

Night of the long knives in Belgrade. Washington Times, June 8, 1993. Constantly of consternation to me, particularly as a journalist, was the fact that there was so little reporting being done inside Yugoslavia, and particularly inside the increasingly bizarre political cabals of Belgrade. Once the war really started, there was a good deal of brilliant reporting from the war zones — indeed, extraordinarily courageous reporting, particularly from besieged Sarajevo. After 1992, I did not myself go back to Belgrade. After what I had written about the leadership and the military there, I did not think it "wise." But, as with any story, there were excellent "listening posts" all around the peripheries: thus, this column from Zagreb, where eventually you could hear every whisper from Belgrade. (So, yes, I do predict here that Milošević will be overthrown — nobody's perfect.)

ZAGREB, CROATIA

Americans who were raised on "sticks and stones may break your bones but words will never hurt you" will never understand what was happening in Belgrade last week. It was the "night of the long knives" for the proud and poisonous men of words who really started this war.

On the television screens of the world, Belgrade was exploding with street riots against the government of Slobodan Milošević. Riot police beat up Belgraders in the heart of opposition territory. Journalists duly and soberly announced that all of this was a move against those elusive Serb "moderates."

Indeed it reminded me forcefully of the dire predictions of Serbian intellectuals when I was in Belgrade last October. "The radicals talk privately about the day they will march on Belgrade and destroy all the moderates," Miloš Vasić, the remarkable editor of *Vreme*, the *Time* magazine of Yugoslavia, told me. "They believe their day is coming."

But this week was far more confused than that. For the removal of Dobrica Ćosić, the famous, white-maned storyteller and writer of grand Serbian epics, was the ostensible reason for the riots this week. As president of what was left of the Yugoslav Federation, he had been seen as a kind of moderating influence.

But, just who was this grandfatherly-looking man who seemed of late to be standing up to the wild-eyed Milošević? Why, he was no less than the very ideological author of the entire Serb holocaust. It was the writings of this "kindly" gentleman that inspired an entire generation of Serbs to believe they were the oppressed of the Earth — but that they deserved to be the monarchs of it. "Serbs gain in war and lose in peace," he used to like to say, in the old days, before it became rather obvious that some Serbs also lose in war.

The prominent Slovenian writer Svetlana Slapšak writes of him:

"Mr. Ćosić holds up a mirror to the Serbian people that reflects a gloomy collective portrait of warriors who think only of glory, national aims, and generally abstract achievement, but who are surrounded by tricky 'Westerners' who manipulate them."

Another leader who was felled by the final fanaticization of the country this week was the melodramatic Vuk Drašković, leader (now) of the democratic movement. With his flowing black hair and beard and noble nose, Mr. Drašković walked arm in arm with the demonstrators—until the police took him, broke his nose and cheekbones, and left him comatose and half-alive in the hospital. Before that, he had said of Mr. Ćosić's fate, "The children arrested the father." He could have said those same words of himself, for he, too, was one of the early radical haranguers.

They thought they were just playing grand word games, you see, manipulating the dangerous emotions of their compatriots for the fun of the intellectuals' special kind of power. When they saw it had come to 150,000 dead and a country destroyed, they and others less famous than these two tried abortively to pull away—that wasn't what they had in mind!

But the clever, odious politicians know how to manipulate their words. Since 1987, when he took power as president of Serbia, the darty-eyed Mr. Milošević immediately began to use the words of such as Messrs. Ćosić and Drašković to form fanaticized Serb militias to convince the Serbs that there were enemies all about, and finally to wipe out those "others," those Croats, those Muslims. . . .

This week, then, marked the final radicalization of the regime. Standing alongside Mr. Milošević now are only Vojislav Šešelj (who says he would like to carve out Croats' eyes with rusty spoons) and Željko Ražnjatović (the bully, wanted for armed robbery in Sweden, who terrorized Bosnia and Croatia as the terrorist "Arkan").

In a grotesque kind of way, this is good for the West. It tears away any last fig leaf that may be left for the naive Western leaders who dreamed that Belgrade might change. The total criminalization of the regime is now complete, clear, unequivocal. What you see is really what you get.

I will make you a couple of bets. One, in six to ten months, Slobodan Milošević will be out, probably murdered by one of these swell guys he now has around him. (We know that he has already been practicing desperate getaways from his underground bunker.) Two, this total radicalization of the regime, buoyed by the Western failure to engage here, means that further violent and brutal expansionism is now inevitable.

Men such as Mr. Šešelj and Arkan cannot stop. They are driven to ever more desperate and diabolical acts. Indeed, Arkan is already in the southern Albanian-majority province of Kosovo, strutting about the Serb police-controlled streets and predicting a bloodbath.

So if the leaders of the West think the Serbs will win in Bosnia, and that will be that, they are misunderstanding words even more badly than did poor old white-thatched Mr. Ćosić and black-bearded Mr. Drašković. This conflict is not about to end; it is really only beginning.

Perils on the peacekeeping frontier. Washington Times, *June 19, 1993.*
It was in 1992, and then into 1993, that I began to see that we were dealing with something very new in these post-Yugoslav wars. As the United Nations and the humanitarian organizations got more and more involved, particularly in Bosnia, any idea of using force to defeat aggression — which has been, after all, the modus vivendi of war for the world for centuries — was giving way to a moral "neutralism" and to using ostensibly military forces as "peacekeepers." Later, I would begin to try to analyze this tragic new mindset that was taking over the Western and the international mind; but at this point, I was still looking primarily at what the troops were actually doing on the ground. That turned out to be horrifying enough.

ZAGREB, CROATIA

The very possible next phase in the post-Yugoslavia wars — the deliberate involving of American ground troops in the quicksand that the United Nations has watered here — was outlined to me recently by Cedric Thornberry, the leading UN civilian authority here.

"We really need to get the Americans involved in peacekeeping here," he said, sitting in his simple office in the United Nations' base. "If we don't fully engage the major powers in it, we are in danger of becoming peripheral and being given brush fires in far-away countries.

"I detect a new interest in the U.S. administration and Congress in peacekeeping. Instead of high-risk areas, wouldn't it be good for the U.S. response to be in less controversial areas—like policemen, logistics experts, elections observers? We need to tap creative idealism and to use force, but sparingly."

As I write this, I hear that the United States has decided to send three hundred Americans as "peacekeepers" to Macedonia to defend against a Serb attack. It sounds good, but it establishes a dangerous precedent that we must analyze.

The question of Americans on the ground—both as peacekeepers and as ground forces to protect "secure enclaves"—is becoming ever more vociferous, both in Bosnia and prospective Bosnias. Secretary of State Warren Christopher was just in Luxembourg for the European Community foreign ministers' meeting where he repeated the Clinton administration's commitment "to provide ground forces in connection with an agreement negotiated in good faith."

Should the United States consider putting American peacekeepers on the ground in Bosnia? No, no, a thousand times no! Let's glance at some of these idealistic outside interventionists who are already busy, each plowing his own little humanitarian garden plot in the soil of the former Yugoslavia.

Everyone thought it was great, really avant, when several thousand Russian "peacekeepers" joined the UNPROFOR (UN Protection Force) that was set up as of April 7, 1992. How very end-of-the–Cold War it all seemed, as the Russkies took up position in the Eastern Croatian city of Osijek, ostensibly to protect the Croats from the rampaging Serbs.

Not so fast. The Russians have had a historical religious and geopolitical liking for the Serbs. Rather than protect the Croat victims, first they let the Serbs take oil out of the Croatian oil fields. In the end, the Russians were doing maneuvers with the Serbs, helping them in their "ethnic cleansing" of Croats and even flying helicopters (forbidden by the UN no-fly zone) for the Serbs. The Russian commander is now training the Serb militias. He has left the United Nations, but the UN has taken little action against these dedicated Russians who are so loyal to their old friends.

The Ukrainian soldiers in Sarajevo, meanwhile, have kept the

Black Market afloat. They were so dedicated to their No. 1 task that they would stop escorting humanitarian convoys in order to change money. But it has surely been the Nepalese soldiers, stationed for UNPROFOR in the sensitive Bihać area of Western Bosnia, who illustrated the only real artistic sensibility. They are now known as the best dealers in gold the United Nations has ever had in its ranks.

Still, not even these disgraceful depredations on the part of these peacekeepers would be enough to argue totally for keeping Americans out. The British and the Canadians have done splendid and effective work in their sectors, simply because they had the confidence, the command structure, and the guts to use force when needed.

To put Americans on the ground in the middle of that hapless, hopeless mess, then, would endanger our own young men (and perhaps women), and even more, give validity to a doomed and foolish ineffective use of power.

Ironically, from the very beginning of this disaster of Western legalistic intervention in Bosnia, with troops that cannot even shoot back at the aggressors, America has been stout about "no American ground troops." This was and is absolutely correct. Now, the Europeans and the United Nations and other are trying to bring us in, on the most dangerous grounds, through the treacherous, unworkable plans of more peacekeepers of the insecure havens and the equally unworkable Vance-Owen Plan.

I have a better idea. Get everybody out and start over.

Washington Times, *September 3, 1993.*
A few courageous individuals were there from the start, trying, often at incredible risk to their physical being and to their sanity, to tell the world what was going on. One of them was an old friend of mine from Chicago, the immensely respected international criminal law scholar, Professor Cherif Bassiouni. He went to Bosnia; he dug up and documented the bodies and the war crimes. Bassiouni's work was, to put it mildly, extraordinary. But when the time came to name the prosecutor for the war crime tribunal in The Hague, UN bureaucracy chimed in and the post went to a South African judge. Nevertheless, Bassiouni's name will stand in the lineup of the great seekers-of-justice of mankind.

CHICAGO

Cherif Bassiouni has had thirty years of practice in international criminal law, which is unequaled by probably any other legal scholar in the world. Besides being a man of impeccable integrity and a respected professor of law at De Paul University here, he is also head of the DePaul Human Rights Institute.

For the last nine months, this dedicated, Egyptian-born American has been in and out of Sarajevo, Bosnia-Herzegovina, meticulously documenting more than three thousand cases of war crimes. With a small, largely volunteer staff, he has developed a database system in his busy offices that truly could realize the United Nations' threats of bringing war criminals to trial in an international tribunal.

So Mr. Bassiouni, the man who has done all this dangerous and heartbreaking work (three "close calls" his last trip to Sarajevo alone) is the man to be named prosecutor of the war crimes trials that would take place in The Hague, right?

Well, don't move so fast. You see, no matter which way you look in Bosnia and elsewhere in the former Yugoslavia, you find the poison of Western guilt and complicity in mass murder. Many of those Western "observers" — in particular the British, who ironically gave the world the Western system of law — are so compromised that the last thing they want anywhere around them is a man of strong will who would actually *do* things.

Here is where the case stands now. As Mr. Bassiouni has been doggedly digging through graves and assembling grim facts of death and torture, the United Nations has been moving slowly toward a tribunal. Late in August, the Security Council held a straw vote on the prosecutor and the vote broke down seven for Mr. Bassiouni (including the United States), seven for a Briton, John Duncan Lowe, and one undecided. It was also suggested by some that a Brazilian attorney general would be put forward, although he clearly knew nothing about the case.

The unpalatable fact here is that any of the suggested candidates except Mr. Bassiouni will assure that nothing gets done. Not only have the British, under the equivocal negotiator Lord David Owen, taken a wholly un-British, amoral "moral equivalence" position in Bosnia ("everybody's guilty, so we're not guilty for doing nothing");

but to have the British be prosecutors of the Serbs would be such a conflict of interest that the entire process would be better scrapped.

While the United States did support Mr. Bassiouni in the straw poll, American messages have been mixed. At one point, Secretary of State Warren Christopher indicated strongly he did not want an American prosecutor because it would indicate the United States had "taken sides." (If that seems a rather weird contrast to you, compared with the last time the United States "took sides" in the Nuremburg war crime trials after World War II, well so be it!)

Our U.S. ambassador to the United Nations, Madeleine Albright, has courageously supported Mr. Bassiouni, but there are outright and subtle blocks at every turn of the road. In The Hague, for instance, the United Nations has refused to make any plans for safe houses for the victims, who would have to go there at great danger to testify. The United Nations is planning on housing them at wide-open bed-and-breakfasts, where they would have no protection at all from their tormentors.

Meanwhile, Lord Owen and the other hapless negotiators of the West — who by assiduously refusing to use Western force to contain the Serbs have given them undeserved stature — every day in Geneva treat men responsible for mass murders as respected negotiators. How, then, for the world to try them? No one quite knows.

If all of Mr. Bassiouni's careful work is now set aside, the simple fact is that no one else can start again and retrieve this evidence of barbarism in our time. The evidence is slipping away in the dust and destruction of Bosnia. No paper trail there!

The conduct of the "peacekeeping" forces in the negotiating process has been a practical and a moral horror: the whole world knows that. So this new situation is really the last chance for the United States in particular to regain even a modicum of credibility and honor. Obviously, many are afraid of a strong-minded, committed man such as Mr. Bassiouni. He does not believe that all the atrocities are balanced so that the slaughtered Bosnians are as guilty as the rampaging Serbs. He does not want to see "de facto impunity" negotiated in Geneva, so war criminals walk free. He is a man of principle.

It is time the United States really pushed for him as prosecutor, for he is the only hope of achieving any remaining moral high ground at the end of this evil interlude in human history.

Reality check: Why the war in Bosnia wasn't "inevitable." Chicago Tribune, *February 16, 1994.*
Finally, I tried to put everything together that I knew to date: it was my attempt to keep my own balance in these strange days.

WASHINGTON, D.C.

By the beginning of 1994, there was no question in my mind that we were at a crucial turning point regarding the diplomacy, politics, and security responses of the "civilized" world, and that the war in Bosnia was the herald of changes that would affect us on every possible level. I had been there at least every six months since that first fateful trip in the fall of 1989, and now I sat down and put together in one long column what I saw happening to us all.

Lurking always just behind the day-to-day realities of the war in Bosnia is a controlling presumption that will contort military and political thinking in the Western world for years to come. It is the dangerous assumption that the murderous post-Yugoslavia wars were "inevitable" and that the "ethnic hatreds" simply "spontaneously" bubbled up from historic underground caverns that not even the greatest social paleontologist could predict.

If you accept these assumptions—as virtually all of the European governments and much of the Clinton administration do—then the policies they have followed and are still following this week are not only acceptable but (always that word) "inevitable."

But the assumptions are not only wrong, they are tragically wrong, because the defining basic analyses of the "nature" of these post–Communist era wars are so woefully wrong.

Far from inevitable, the Serbs' brutal wars against their former neighbors were meticulously planned, cynically orchestrated, and realized not because of historically immutable ethnic hatreds but because corrupt Old Communists for years nurtured them in every possible way in order to hold onto a power they knew they were losing. The wars were totally avoidable.

But let us back up a bit to 1989. That fall, I traveled in those prophetic times from East Berlin to Belgrade, my determination forged by the instinct that Yugoslavia was about to become the model and paradigm for post-Communist breakdown. I was not to be disappointed.

In fact, every single analyst there placed the disintegration already well advanced, not in ethnic terms but in sheer political power terms. As Budimir Košutić, a respected professor of political systems at the University of Belgrade, told me, "The differences in our country are not consequences so much of difference in 'nations' but more the consequences of bad politics."

Had the economic paralysis that had begun with the death of Marshal Tito in 1975 and the resulting economic breakdown, which had humiliated Yugoslav men unable to care for their families, led to the ethnic problems? "Absolutely," he averred. "And what is happening is that each of the political leaders is presenting himself as the defender of the interests of his own nationality." So these "leaders" have to create differences in order to hold onto political power? "Exactly!"

Dr. Vladimir Štambuk, secretary-general of the Communist League of Serbia, told me on another day, "The fights are not between nationalities, you see, but between political leaderships. When you are going downhill, you try to grab from others as much as you can. The Serbian leadership is split, so the idea of 'Greater Serbia' is put forward as an attempt to stop the changes."

Indeed, as early as that fateful and prophetic fall of 1989, the American ambassador to Belgrade, Warren Zimmermann, told me, "What does Slobodan Milošević want? He wants to destroy Yugoslavia and pick up the pieces in a 'Greater Serbia.' That is the only theory that explains all the facts. For the last few years, most of his actions were against the unity of Yugoslavia.

"He gave aid to the autonomous Serbs in Croatia. He tried twice to destroy the Yugoslav presidency. He formed and unified groups of Serbs in Bosnia to gain autonomy. Even when the Croats and Slovenes were willing to work out a loosely federated Yugoslavia, Milošević said that would 'not be Yugoslavia,' and so Serbia should just 'look out for the Serbs.'"

While unemployed, frustrated, and eventually violent young

men were being paid to travel around Serbia, Kosovo, and Vojvodina to participate in hysterical "Greater Serbia" rallies, Serbian president Milošević was waging one of the most extraordinary propaganda campaigns in modern history.

Using the wildly irresponsible "Memorandum" of the Serbian Academy of Sciences of 1986, which extolled the grandeur of "historic Serbia" and presented extravagant historic claims to the region of Kosovo in the South, Milošević began brilliantly and terrifyingly propagandizing the Serbs. With virtually total control of television even then, he orchestrated fear and loathing of the outside through hour upon hour of mournful Orthodox Church music and of films of Serb graveyards and churches and battlefields. The mesmerizing and propagandizing use of television cannot be overemphasized here.

In southern Kosovo, the 90 percent Albanian-occupied province of Serbia that the Serbs claim because of their historic monasteries and battlegrounds, I sat one day before Serbian TV watching the surreal picture of Serb soldiers being "thanked" by Bosnian Muslims for "liberating" them. George Orwell is alive and well in Yugoslavia.

Finally, the "ethnic wars" of post-Yugoslavia, as well as those in other Caucasus and Central Asian areas, are wars of criminals, psychopaths, and "mountain Serbs" or "wild Serbs" (their terms) who inhabit a wholly different world from both the urban and educated Serbs of Belgrade and the Bosnia Muslims and Croats of the once-sophisticated cities like Mostar, Vukovar, and Sarajevo.

What we are seeing renascent in the former Yugoslavia is not the courageous World War II Serb guerrilla fighter that the Western militaries imagine there but a return to the national mythology of the mountain outlaw—the "hajduk" common to the peoples of the Dinaric Alps, which cross the former Yugoslavia. Far from heroic guerrillas, these are brigands and bandits.

It is these irregular forces—which have spearheaded what is not really a war and not a civil war but a war of conquest and extermination—that believe the preposterous Milošević propaganda.

As Zlatko Dizdarević, editor of the remaining newspaper in Sarajevo, told me on a visit to Washington in December, 1993, "It is true that before the war there were large economic, cultural, and psychological differences between the cities and the countryside. If some radio repeats many times in one day that the 'Mujahadin' from Sarajevo are giving Serbian children to the lions in the zoo for supper, to us that is a joke. But, believe me, 80 percent in the countryside believe that. And if you keep repeating that, they soon want to get guns and go out and kill."

"The war in Bosnia-Herzegovina is not a civil war," he went on thoughtfully, "and it is not between nationalities and religions. It is a war produced by third-class Communists elected in our first elections in 1987 who are using the past and using historic myths against people who want to go to the future. They had to produce the hatred; in Yugoslavia in the last forty years, hate was not something natural."

In the mountains around Sarajevo, he and other analysts say, where artillery has for nearly two years bombarded the city with destruction, there are approximately one hundred men from the cities and five thousand from the countryside. It is their hatred of the exquisite cities of Bosnia and Croatia—and their deliberate destruction of every church, mosque, and historic library—that is the sociological mark of the primitive and vicious mountain men, along with criminals, and that is the true mark of this war.

So, let us look at the pattern and not at all the uninformed chatter about "inevitability" and "spontaneous ethnic hatreds":

First, the end of the secular ideology of communism. Second, the economic collapse that soon attended it. Next, the Old Communists, determined to hold onto power through the deliberate and cynical manipulation of old ethnic differences. Finally, their use of the worst criminal and psychopathic elements, along with the naive, manipulatable, and brutal city-hating mountain people.

And Yugoslavia was not alone. If we look at the confluence of events that led to the similar ongoing wars in Armenia/Azerbaijan, in Tajikistan and in Soviet Georgia, we find nearly exactly the same pattern and chronology of event. But none of this was "inevitable." Take only as a counterweight the case of little Bulgaria, the one country in Eastern Europe that is doing well. Bulgaria is peaceful, its economy is gradually liberalizing, small shops fill the busy streets of Sofia.

But only a few years ago, Bulgaria, too, was in a pre–"ethnic war" stage. The Communist government was expelling and killing the Turkish minority, forcing them to change their names and threatening war with Turkey.

But instead of ethnic war inside and/or conflict outside, because of the coming to power electorally of democratic president Zhelu Zhelev, Bulgaria today is a peaceful and prospering country; the Turkish minority is back in Bulgaria and prominently in politics and in the parliament; and even the Gypsies, always despised throughout Eastern Europe, were being reasonably well-integrated into Bulgaria.

And so, it turns out that these "inevitable" ethnic wars are not so inevitable at all. This fact is at the very core of the problems that the world faces from Bosnia to Azerbaijan to Georgia to Tajikistan — and will face. It means that these wars are stoppable. It means that the policies carried through by the West were pitifully wrong because Western leaders did not see that these were fanatics and thugs who could have easily been stopped in the beginning by any determined show of force.

Instead, we have mass murder, and all in the name of determined unreality that now dominates the thinking of the foreign ministries and militaries of the Western world.

Soldiers in a war but not at war. Washington Times, *July 28, 1994.*
This day, as no other, exemplified to me the absurdity of the Western and the international response to Bosnia.

ZAGREB, CROATIA

We had left this beautiful old Hapsburgian city at dawn, sure and eager to be in Sarajevo before noon. I was, frankly, both excited and apprehensive, for Sarajevo was the city whose suffering personified this terrible war.

When our small group of journalists arrived at Pleso air base just outside of Zagreb, I wondered, "Where have I seen this before?" But comparing the milling soldiers, flak jackets and helmets in hand, with almost any other war in our generation just didn't seem right.

Here, in place of any one national army there were Brits and Nigerians, French and Nepalese, Russians and Ukrainians — and they were, as UN officials put it, "in a war, but not at war." If that seems a little hard to sustain, you're all too right. Perhaps that is why the Norwegians, who run one of the myriad jerry-built air forces here, call theirs "Maybe Airlines."

As we waited at Pleso, with these "multicultural" troops milling around us, we were issued bright blue flak jackets and helmets. Having nothing better to do, I made a silly sarcastic remark, "What do we do with these?" I sniped. "Sit on them?" No one laughed (cranks).

Soon we were sitting in the dark in a huge Russian troop carrier, ready for the hourlong trip to Sarajevo. We waited . . . and waited . . . and waited.

"Damn Croats," one soldier snapped. "They're always holding the planes back — just to be important."

Then the soldiers around me, Swedes, Norwegians, and Canadians, began to talk. "This is a ridiculous war," one said. "None of us can figure out why in God's name we're here." "In our area," another added, "we hear shooting all the time, but we are forbidden — get that, forbidden! — to know who is shooting. UN rules!" Even in the darkness, I could sense him shaking his head.

At that point, the voice from the pilot's seat came on again. "No flight today," it was saying. "Sarajevo's under fire."

And so we stumbled and heaved and grumbled our way off, clumsy flak jackets and helmets in hand, to find that the Serbs had "expressed" their utterly predictable feelings toward all of us. Only the day before they had contemptuously rejected the "take-it-or-leave-it" Western and Russian peace plan. These actions were meant as their exclamation point at the end of the "no."

We soon learned what had happened in Sarajevo. Two incoming planes — a Russian Antonov and a U.S. Starlifter, had been hit at 10:10 and 10:30 A.M. that Thursday, July 21, as we waited in the darkness. Without question, it was Serb machine-gun fire. One American security man was hit from below as he sat in the plane. The machine gun fire went right through the Russian plane's floor!

"You see," I said triumphantly to one of my colleagues. "We *should* sit on our flak jackets and helmets!"

But there was nothing funny about what was going on. That same day, at 10:45 A.M., the Serbs attacked a French mission trying to put up antisniping barriers on Sarajevo's "Sniper's Alley" along the recently reopened tramways. Five French and Ukrainian peacekeepers were seen on CNN across the world, throwing themselves on the ground under the Serb bombardments. The French commanding general in Sarajevo, General Andre Soubirou, was heard, as his men fell on him to protect him, shouting words that in previous generations would not have been proper for even young soldiers' ears.

When I asked our UN Protection Forces or UNPROFOR press hosts why the enraged general and (one would suppose) angry "peacekeeper" troops did not fire back, the answer was vintage neutralist UN-speak. "Because the Serbs were firing *over* them," one official said. "They can only fire back if they are firing *at* them."

At that moment I was very grateful to whatever gods still watch over anybody in this terrible place that our plane did not "make it." We would, after all, have been the very next plane in. Or, as the UN spokesman, my respected friend Michael Williams, put it, "If you hadn't got shot in the plane, you might have got shot on the street."

Before we turned in our flak jackets for good, it suddenly hit me how similar this situation of being "in a war" was to Vietnam. Here, too, are many of the finest civilians and soldiers in the world — placed in an impossible situation by impossible restrictions. There is stultifying micromanagement from afar that effectively destroys any chance of "winning." There is the same lack of clarity about outcome that the Serbs continue contemptuously to manipulate, while they go on killing.

Given these realities, sitting on one's flak jacket seemed one of the day's more reasonable suggestions.

Mired machinery of peace in Bosnia. August 4, 1994.
Every once in a while, as I covered both Bosnia and the paradigmatic "bosnia" for our times, I sat down and tried to put everything together instead of writing about it in pieces and scraps. Here, I realized where we were and wrote it that way.

ZAGREB, CROATIA

It's all over. The first multilateral experiment of the post–Cold War period — the first attempt to show that the civilized world can and will solve ethnic wars—has failed. In the end, this utopian experiment in neutralism didn't work for a very simple reason: It couldn't work.

Everybody here—from the UN headquarters to the troops on the ground to the foreign ambassadors—privately acknowledges that peacekeeping in Bosnia is finished, but it probably will not disappear completely for some months, during which time the situation here will unravel even further.

"The UN and collective mechanisms have not worked" was the way one of the city's leading foreign diplomats put it during the week I was traveling with the United Nations all over Croatia, Bosnia, and Macedonia. "After the Cold War, the mechanisms were just not mature, but if the UN forces [the UNPROFOR] withdraw now there will be all-out war here. It will most closely resemble World War II."

What will happen during a pullout of the thirty-eight thousand UN forces? "There are some frightening scenarios," one UN spokesman told us, "like British troops being shot at by both sides."

I get no pleasure out of carrying such messages. The people who designed this key post–Cold War policy of non-use of power, with its strategy of not using force, are good, intelligent people. This makes it all the more astonishing that they have done what they have done.

At one point, for instance, I posed a question on the "logic" inherent in the mission here to the top UN representative, the dedicated Japanese diplomat Yakushi Akashi. Was there not, I asked, perhaps some gigantic mistake over human nature underlying the policy the United Nations has pursued here?

"Your question is a haunting one," Mr. Akashi replied, "and it might lead to the conclusion that people might fight a bit more to have a better moment to make peace. But we UN people have a professional stake in stopping bloodshed."

He explained why the use of force—in particular, the much threatened NATO air strikes against the Serbs—was impossible. "We would be perceived as the enemy and that would endanger our carefully constructed relations with the parties. We are impartial; we are in a war but we are not at war. Once we became a party to the war, we would have to liquidate our efforts—withdraw or cut down."

Suddenly I understood a crucial part of the picture. As the rampaging Serbs took over 70 percent of Bosnia, leaving (at that point) two hundred thousand dead behind them, the United Nations last winter finally appeared to agree to NATO strikes against the omnipresent Serb artillery positions. In Sarajevo, the threat worked and the Serbs withdrew.

But it was in the besieged city of Goražde that the "UN mentality" revealed—and neutralized—itself. After air strikes were threatened there, Mr. Akashi refused to call for them and is proud today that he finally negotiated a kind of standoff. But UN officials never really intended to use NATO force at all. They innocently thought that the threat would be enough. The Serbs called their bluff, a moment when superior force could have halted the victories of the Serbs was lost, and now a big war beckons.

One could capsulize the UN intentions this way: They offered something that the Serbs didn't want in exchange for their doing what they had no interest in doing. To synthesize further the impossible UN mentality: In this mission, well-meaning "neutrals" threw away every maxim of warfare and insight into human nature that various cultures have discovered through the centuries. Apparently nobody here has read Shakespeare, much less Machiavelli or Suntzu.

And so now, three years after this nasty terroristic war started in this summer of 1991, the nicest people in the world have thrown away the best promise of the post–Cold War period. This was the first period since the end of World War II when, with a little wisdom and leadership, the world could have been created anew.

Instead, largely because Europe and the United States did not want to act, the superlegalized and overbureaucratized United Nations took over this first test-case mission—with a rigid moral neutralism, a non-use of force, and a utopian idea that fanatics like the Serbs can be won over by rationality. With this mentality, the approach soon became devoid of any sense of justice or any element of truth.

Not surprisingly, it failed. In truth, it could do nothing else.

Woerner's unheeded warnings. Washington Times, *August 21, 1994. Manfred Woerner was dead. He died of a cancer that he fought up to the last days and nights, appearing gaunt and sepulchral but still attending at NATO meetings, no matter what the hour. His colleagues wondered how he held up to the end, and others wondered what an increasingly "neutralist" Europe would do now, with her most valiant spokesman for her better-self gone. I have always thought that one of the small things that we columnists can do is to give recognition to courage.*

When he walked briskly into his modern office in Brussels a year ago, NATO secretary-general Manfred Woerner sat down with a flourish, then said angrily, "Miss Geyer, I am fed up!"

And as that impassioned man went on to speak of Europe's and the United Nations' debacle in the former Yugoslavia, he became ever more angry. "What we are doing is simply a cover-up for letting the Serbs win — and NATO will be blamed for it!"

Before this remarkable interview was over, Mr. Woerner had told me two of the most arresting and disturbing stories I had heard in a long career of journalism.

"Yesterday, I had the British defense minister sitting exactly there where you are sitting," he began, "and I was trying to convince him that the arms embargo against the Bosnian Muslims should be lifted. He said, no, that would only extend the war. I said to him, yes, just like bringing the Allies into World War II extended the war."

At one point, he reminisced sadly about his own life — and how he saw the Bosnian conflict eating away at the hard-won, post–World War II hopes of Europe.

"I was ten years old when the war ended," Mr. Woerner said then, leaning back against the spartan couch. "I saw the pictures of the concentration camps for the first time, and I physically attacked my parents . . . And they were not even political, they were religious people. Still, I vowed that that must never happen again."

"Now, Miss Geyer," he said, looking at me with a steely gaze, "I am head of the most powerful military organization in world history — and I can do nothing."

Those revealing comments were off-the-record as long as Secretary-General Woerner was alive. But Mr. Woerner died in his Europe on August 13 of colon cancer. The world lost one of the most courageous and coherent men of our time. Indeed, his passing leaves a vacuum of thought and of action in the crucial North American Treaty Organization that will threaten the defense of the Western world.

In my several interviews with Mr. Woerner, he was always foremost an impassioned believer in NATO's historic role as defender of the West. A suave former fighter pilot and former German defense minister, he was a lean, dark-haired man with a compelling stare. In his varied positions, he had overseen crucial parts of the democratization of the German military, coining the popular new name of "burgher-in-uniform" or "citizen-soldier."

But it was the disgraceful failure of first Europe and then the United States, and finally the United Nations, to respond to the massacres in Bosnia that clearly haunted him during his last three years.

"Europe simply didn't have the determination or the unity," he told me at one point, "so they only used diplomatic means, and then turned to the UN. Soon the Serbs were allowed to conquer whatever they wanted. The situation soon deteriorated to a weapons' embargo unique in man's history. If we compared it to the Second World War, it was as if the League of Nations had declared a weapons embargo on Norway, Belgium, and Denmark. Today we have created and accepted a situation where the aggressor has any weapon he wants, and the civil populations and defenders are helpless."

Over and over, he told me that NATO must not be blamed; that the putative "leaders" of the Western world and the United Nations were seriously threatening NATO with their pusillanimity; that "to use an instrument, you need political will"; and that "dictators understand only the language of tanks and weapons."

Now the West is impoverished indeed. For the challenges are increasingly frightening.

Mr. Woerner oversaw the partial incorporation of Russia and the Eastern Bloc nations into levels of NATO membership, but now NATO faces direct challenges by Russia to water it down by empowering the CSCE, which it could control more. And the poisons unleashed by Western impotence over Bosnia surge through the bloodstream of Europe ever more virulently. Bosnia is neutralizing and paralyzing Europe.

Mr. Woerner saw all of this coming. Indeed, his was a voice imperative and persistent in the wilderness that is Western policy making today. When I saw him in Brussels in 1991, he had said to me, "I don't think that in all European history such a moment existed — we have the chance of stabilizing more than half the globe!"

But by last year that moment had passed. As he spoke again about Bosnia, he told me, his voiced etched with sadness: "If this goes on, there will be no global stability and no security in Europe. We will have to fight again. You cannot take holidays from history."

Washington Times, *October 6, 1994.*
This satire on the diabolical Sir Michael Rose would have been a lot of fun to write — if it were not so awfully serious.

WASHINGTON, D.C.
Who killed Sir Michael Rose? It is a bedeviling question, of importance not only to Mrs. Rose but to the entire world.

For what a guy he was! Lean, mean, and handsome, the fifty-four-year-old British lieutenant general always looked quintessentially the part of the commander who brought Great Britain victory in the Falklands War. When we arrived in Bosnia last January, wearing his jaunty beret and his sure swagger, he seemed just exactly the man to command UN troops and put the whole mess in order. He had, after all, been commander of the "unconventional-warfare unit" of the British Army, the legendary SAS, or Special Air Service.

During his first months in Bosnia, he strode like a lithe god across the world's newspaper headlines and TV screens. In February, backed up by a NATO ultimatum to silence the Serbian artillery and thus lift the yearslong siege of the beautiful old city of Sarajevo, he declared grandly: "I want to restore electricity, collect the garbage, establish a postal service, open up routes out of the city." (Journalists noted with close to uniform praise the determined glint in his pale blue eyes.)

He was going to open Sarajevo's Brotherhood and Unity Bridge and — by God! — get the UN trucks and forces into the stricken city. He was going to use sophisticated electronic surveillance that would allow swift use of air strikes. He was going to turn around the pacifist UN mode of dealing with the rampaging Serbs.

And now that man is gone. And nobody really knows where he went, or why. (The body was never found.) Diplomats, analysts, and military men and women sit around coffee tables and bars from Zagreb to New York to London, and ask with sadness and with wonder: "Whatever happened to Sir Michael Rose?" And nobody has any real answers, except that many feel instinctively that his strange disappearance will surely, someday, explain many of the horrible absurdities of the Bosnian War.

Some of those who revered the early Sir Michael say the man they knew began to die when he realized it was not going to be so easy to bring in NATO air strikes against the Serbs. The UN representative in Bosnia, Yakushi Akashi, was stoically intent on not using force even in the face of a European genocide.

Cynics in Zagreb whispered that they could begin to see the signs of mortality when, during the awful Serb siege of Goražde, several British soldiers alone got out among many foreigners there. Had Sir Michael made a deal with the Serbs that later came back to haunt him?

The *New York Times* wrote that he had suddenly become an admirer of Serbian general Ratko Mladić, often called one of the main "war criminals" of modern times. Had the valiant general of yore let his admiration for military power overcome the better angels of his nature? And the more philosophical among the onlookers opined that he had, like so many of the military sent to an impossible mission in Bosnia, succumbed to the "Stockholm Syndrome." Unable to use force against a clear and brutal aggressor, his only way out was to learn to love that aggressor.

Whatever the actual reasons, that man is gone. The war he could probably in large part have stopped goes on at top speed, with six hundred Bosnians being "cleansed" by Serbs every day.

Now, we must note at this time, only so readers are not confused, that there *is* a "Sir Michael Rose" still in Sarajevo. Indeed, the Brits and others are actually discussing whether he should go home in January. But this man is clearly an imposter and only a bad joke to the memory of the real, courageous military man.

This charlatan marches around Sarajevo and postures for the cameras, but has nothing to say, while thousands suffer and die every week in what is now becoming a "twenty years' war." This man excuses every depredation of the Serbs and actually blames the Bosnians apparently just for "being there." This man clearly cannot be the Sir Michael Rose that the world so lauded.

It is a strange story—indeed, in many ways, a nightmare. For no one can quite determine how this imposter (who looks so much like Sir Michael Rose physically, except that the once valiant facial expression has now changed to fury) gets into the picture at all. Was it Bosnia? Was it the British military? Was it the strange pacifism of the United Nations? Was it all of us, for letting a Bosnia happen?

And so, we are left with the emptiness of his passing and of the final mystery of where his body is buried. Some people who knew him in his early years have a still more profound question: They wonder where his soul has gone.

Feckless humanitarianism just doesn't work. Chicago Tribune, *November 18, 1994.*
As I covered the various "ethnic" and "small" wars of our times — our military now calls them ambiguously and imprecisely "Operations Other Than War" or (with their love for acronyms) OOTW — I began to see that the various ones were not unrelated at all. In fact, all had similar roots, reasons, and resources. I began to see that their ethnic roots were not at all the real cause. Rather, in each situation you had unscrupulous men trying to hold onto power for power's own sake; they then deliberately reawakened and employed the old ethnic hatreds for their own purposes, using every modern propaganda tool from radio to television to those of the "information revolution." In contrast to what many idealists have thought, democracy was no solution here; indeed the new tyrants usually started out by using the new democratic elections to come to power. Here, I tried to bring together some of these new crises and show the links among them.

WASHINGTON, D.C.
Somalia was surely a humanitarian disaster, but it was unique, anomalous, something not to be repeated again. The problem was not

with the humanitarian aid but with the fact that the United Nations and the United States changed the mission in midstream.

Bosnia just hasn't worked out, but is still just a blip of history. You see, the Europeans and the UN should never have put "peacekeeper" troops into a conflict that, far from dying down, was actually at its murderous and persistent height.

Haiti took a long time to ripen, because President Clinton couldn't make up his mind. But our policy may just succeed, even though the American troops there have not solved the problem of the military murders.

Those conflicts, our leaders here and in the UN would like us to accept, are anachronisms. They are part of the "working out" of policy in the post–Cold War world, as men and women of goodwill scratch and scramble for new ways of doing things, as we stumble toward the twenty-first century.

But are they? The question we need to answer — and urgently — is this: Are the many mistakes in all of this essentially well-meaning new policy part of a learning process that will indeed lead us somewhere? Or do they only contribute a tragic series of quite documentable errors that are going to be repeated over and over?

To answer that question, let us look at still another case, that of Rwanda in Central Africa. It would seem that that benighted country must be totally different from the others in its tragedy — and in the world's reaction to it. The operative word is "seem."

After the mass tribal murders earlier this year — 500,000 is a conservative estimate of the dead — and after tens of thousands of refugees fled to hellish refugee camps, it at first did seem that the humanitarian approach might work. The initially rampaging Hutu militias had, after all, been defeated by a new Tutsi government, or so it seemed.

And today? The *Los Angeles Times* just reported in depth from the Zairean border camps that "relief supplies to the estimated 750,000 Hutu refugees have come under the direct control of former Hutu government leaders and militias . . . accused of systematically slaughtering at least half a million Tutsi civilians inside Rwanda before they fled here in July."

And who and what elements of power are allowing them to do this? The food, blankets, and water of the international community.

"It's outrageous," said Samantha Bolton, spokeswoman of the respected organization "Doctors Without Borders," one of the eighty-five aid groups there. "It's gotten to the point where we're aiding and abetting the perpetrators of genocide."

Nicola Dahrendorf, acting director of the UN refugee agency there, spoke to the question of how to aid an impoverished refugee population (of between 750,000 and two million) led by mass murderers.

"We shut our eyes" to helping the murderous Khmer Rouge in Cambodia in the early 1980s in exile, she was quoted as saying, "and we're shutting our eyes here. There's no doubt we're strengthening them." She then cited UN reports that the defeated Hutu Rwandan army is recruiting in these camps, especially among children, so it can resume the war.

Somalia is far away from Bosnia. Bosnia is far away from Haiti. Haiti is really far away from Rwanda. Physically. But, in truth, the experiences are closely linked.

Is it not time to drop all the ridiculous pretense that the well-meaning world is doing so much "good" by rushing in humanitarian supplies and then letting the murderers of the world use them to live to murder again — and more efficiently? (The "well-fed dead," the Bosnians call themselves.) Is it not past time to just stop and see that intentions (our moral problem) are far less important than results (their life-or-death problem)?

The post–Cold War reality is one of ethnic warfare brought about directly by the collapse of the old East-West power structures. The West and the international community don't want to fight any more — or even plan, for that matter — and so we rationalize our failures and our cowardice by sending blankets and canned meat.

If we were the decent people of Rwanda, would we prefer guns or this new price of the world's "humanitarianism?" Of course *we'd* prefer guns. Are the people of Rwanda any different?

UN secretary-general believes in negotiating. Chicago Tribune, *June 16, 1995.*
More of Boutros-Ghali's philosophy. I always enjoyed talking with him and his charming wife, Leia, even when I did not agree with him. This is tough:

he had to know where I stand, and I often politely offered demurrers to UN policies, but I liked him. He was surely right on one major area that is little reported in the American press: that the United States never once used its veto in the Security Council, while no fewer than eighty-five hapless and hopeless resolutions on Bosnia were blithely approved, without any hope — or threat — of their being carried out. In this sense as in so many others, the United States had become third-worldized; in its actions in the Security Council, or nonactions, it was reflecting the modality of the Third World, which so often voted to do something and then never carried through.

NEW YORK

It was a sultry Saturday afternoon, and Boutros Boutros-Ghali was enjoying a rare lunch of relaxation in the garden of his exquisite townhouse overlooking the East River. It looked serene, but it wasn't; indeed, if "frustration" could have another name these days, that name would be "Boutros."

In several hours of intense conversation — with some humorous moments — the UN secretary-general showed clearly the main current of his thinking. Indeed, he returned again and again to one point.

"Either you fight or you negotiate," he said. "If there is no political will to fight, then what can you do? If nobody wants a war, then we have to negotiate."

Later, we sat in the coolness of the antique-filled home he shares with his wife, Leia. I asked him if the UN's "neutralist" policies were not paradoxically providing the Serbs with the courage to go on.

"All right," he said, "the Serbs are the aggressors. Then, punish them, like the Iraqis. I receive instructions from the Security Council. I am a good general.

"And so we have only three options: use force, negotiate, or pull out. I'm saying, I want to negotiate because I believe that, even if the chances of success are limited, negotiating is less dangerous than the other possibilities."

Several times during the afternoon, while by his own admission the fate of the UN in Bosnia hung in the balance, he stressed — rightly, I might add — one point. This was that the members of the Security Council, in which the United States has a veto, are the ones who have approved resolution after resolution giving the United Nations the responsibilities it has in Bosnia. Yet, for all the talk of "enforcement" (United Nationese for fighting), when it comes down to it, none of them want to do it.

And he is left with only a few cards to play.

At times, this usually super-diplomatic man, who weighs every word, mused about his own feelings, revealing himself in ways he habitually avoids.

Why did the United Nations go ahead with the air strike if it knew, as he now says, that hostages would be taken? "We were put under such pressure," he stated. "'You have to do it . . . you have to.' I said, 'No, it will be a disaster.'"

A possible withdrawal of UN troops from Bosnia, then? He smiled weakly. "Here, the egos of the member states come in," he said. "Withdrawal means defeat."

Have the Serbs won, then? Worse, has the UN helped them to win? The secretary-general became somewhat impassioned at these questions. "You might say that, in Bosnia, the Serbs have won," he averred. "But if you take all of Yugoslavia, they have lost. They were the leading group in a country that had Serbia, Slovenia, Croatia . . . They lost everything."

And the negatives of Bosnia for the United Nations? "A great price is our credibility," he said. "Maybe a short surgical operation would be better than people suffering for two or three years. Also on the negative side, both are preparing for an escalation during this period of intermezzo, of transition. But, again, if I put it all on a balance, negative and positive, I'd still say negotiating was best."

Finally, I asked whether—with the UN itself now virtually a hostage of the Serbs in Bosnia—negotiations still could work? He avowed that they could. "Through negotiating, you discover the way," he said. "The Serbs want negotiations in order to get consecration of what they have, to obtain recognition of the international community. They know they are sick—that is why they accepted the negotiations. You have this all over the world: People who have gained on the ground but have no international recognition.

"The result of the negotiations may not be equity, but it may be peace. Then you have a problem: what is more important, peace or peace at the expense of certain principles of equity? My theory is that what happens in a war is so terrible that peace is better, even if it is not a just peace."

The secretary-general delineated his idea about "wars of the rich" and "wars of the poor," which doubtless comes from his earlier diplomatic work for Egypt, particularly in now largely forgotten Africa.

"You are rich when people pay attention to you, and you are poor when nobody pays attention to you," he said. "In Bosnia, despite the suffering, people outside are paying attention . . . But there are also 'orphan nations' in wars . . . in the 'poor wars' which don't attract the attention of the international community. My ambition is to pay attention to the marginalized."

Finally, I asked him what the UN had learned in Bosnia, which he agrees has, for better or for worse, become the paradigm of international action in the post–Cold War period.

"What we have learned is that Bosnia has created a distortion in the work of the UN. We are paying less attention to what is going on in Burundi, in Georgia . . . There are distortions in dealing with other peacekeeping operations, with other activities of the UN. Seventy percent of our activities deal with economic development, with human rights, with democratization."

He seemed to consider what would happen if the United Nations did pull out of Bosnia. "Who is paying attention in the press today to Somalia?" he said. "Nobody. And it was in the headlines for months. In six months, nobody would talk about Yugoslavia . . . and they would continue killing themselves for years."

Clinton's policy pirouette: Backward on Bosnia. Daily Times (Farmington, New Mexico), *July 6, 1995.*
At times I realized that I was becoming a little obsessed with what I was coming to see as "the" American foreign policy question of the post–Civil War world: how to use American power effectively and morally in this "new" world that seemed so strange and untenable to so many. The Clinton team, led by a man with marked "peacenik" and neutralizing tendencies, was simply abdicating the traditional uses of power in the world, and all in favor of the "new neutralism" as a "philosophy" and peacekeeping as its handmaiden. They talked about things being so different, so unsure, that

we could only operate through "trial and error." I ended up in one sure spot: that in terms of human nature and its maladies and thus in terms of how power could be used to cure them, the post–Cold War world was essentially no different from any human world.

WASHINGTON, D.C.

This past week represented far more than just another move in the evil power game of Bosnia. It showed definitively how bizarre Bill Clinton's ideas about the uses of power have become.

Once again—as though obsessed with a need to appear ever more impotent in the eyes of the world—the president played right into the Serbs' hands. If Slobodan Milošević or Radovan Karadžić were alcoholics instead of merely mass-murderers, the president would be described by his many therapy-minded friends as still another "enabler."

First came the daring, courageous use of NATO airpower. (Thank God! many of us initially said.) The president had argued for the use of airpower for some time now, against the essential pacifism of UN officials in Bosnia and against the timid European Defense Ministries. But when the big attack came, there had not been any minimal forethought on getting the vulnerable UN troops into safe deployments. And the attack, incredibly, was on an unmanned ammunition dump!

Anyone who knows anything at all about human nature—and, in particular, about the paranoid, cruel mentalities of men like the Serb fighters—knows that such an "attack" only inflates their sense of their own power and simultaneously whets their appetite for humiliating others. Weakness in others brings forth rivers of bloodlust in such people.

It had taken months of talking, arguing, and haggling before the "great air attack" of May, 1995, was made on the Serbs. If that were not bad enough, when the single attack on the ammunition dump was made, UN soldiers and observers of their own volition remained in the Serb headquarters in Pale. Indeed, foreign parliamentarians who visited there just after the bomb-prick were incredulous and demanded of the essentially pacifist UN representative there, Yakushi Akashi: "You still had men in Pale when bombs were dropping on Pale?"

But Mr. Akashi and the others replied calmly, unconcernedly revealing their unthinking bureaucratic mindset at its very worst, that they "had to be there," that "they were liaison with the Serbs," that they were needed, even in the Serb den "for reassurance to the Serbs and for keeping channels of communication." (They might have mentioned that, that way too, when the Serbs decided to take UN hostages—four hundred as of this writing—they didn't even have to bother to move away from their headquarters.)

The Clinton group then admitted that the air strike idea was wrong, even though it was not. Never ones to lose momentum, they spared no time in moving brightly backward. The president then went campaigning out to the West, where he greeted a world that was looking to him for leadership on the first genocide in Europe since World War II . . . on a horse. With a multi-gallon hat. But perhaps I am being unfair: He did enunciate somewhat of a new policy toward Bosnia.

The new policy, as of last Wednesday, was somewhat to renounce his old policy that American ground troops would never be put into Bosnia. Now he said they could be sent to help the UN redeploy or reconfigure (that means, I think, helping them move around, but not leave). By Friday, all of that was somewhat unsure too. And at this moment? Well, who can keep up with everything the man says?

There are things that can be done. I have argued on many occasions that arming the Bosnians, with a strong and decisive bombing and a counterartillery threat from NATO, would change the situation within weeks. (This, indeed, is exactly what such thoughtful and moral Republicans as Senator Richard Lugar argue.) But that is not what this president is going to do, so we have to keep coming back to the core of the problem with our "somewhat" foreign policy.

Henry Kissinger argues that members of the Clinton group fear American power; that they are above all trying to ameliorate the effects of the Cold War, for which essentially they blame us. (Indeed, with their slavish policy toward Russia, they were even asking the Russians, who unashamedly support the Serbs, for help in Bosnia this week!)

A perceptive retired American ambassador last week characterized Mr. Clinton's psychology to me thusly: "He is very smart about certain things and knows a lot. But he has no system and he has no character."

Sadly, Bill Clinton is—and here I don't use the word "somewhat" at all—a very passive man. Only toward the one cause that in the soul of his generation has replaced religion and nation, the "global economy," does he show zest and pugnacity. Politically, militarily, and morally in the world, the man is, bewilderingly, without the courage to act—and, one fears, also without the capacity.

Mentality of top UN official in Bosnia matters. Chicago Tribune, August 2, 1995.
As the world fell back more and more on "internationalism," which by now was more commonly called "multilateralism," it soon struck me that even a powerful country like the United States was putting its prestige and its power, not to speak of the future of the world, in the hands of a relative handful of men and women whose character and agendas we knew not at all. They were now making the big decisions for the Big Powers on war or peace, and the Big Powers, out of lethargy and cowardice, were letting them make it. But who were/are these little bureaucrats of the UN and the humanitarian organizations, and what did/do they bring to the international picture?

One of the problems in knowing them is the fact that so few foreign correspondents cross regions of the world in their work. Because of my virtually unique position, I can and do do that. So it was that in Tokyo in the summer of 1995, I looked up our little "friend" Yakushi Akashi, who made so many smug and disastrous decisions in Bosnia. Even I was stunned at what I found.

TOKYO, JAPAN

As the war in Bosnia descends day after day deeper into a dark hell, the man who "commands" the representative armies of the world, Japanese diplomat Yakushi Akashi, remains mysteriously unknown.

Most Americans in the theater of war will describe the dapper, determined man as a secret "pacifist" who leads armies he never intends to use. They say he makes a show of being morally neutral while he is actually immorally pro-Serb. When I spoke at some length with him a year ago in Zagreb, Yugoslavia, he spoke of being a kind of patient and impassioned UN "neutralist" who believed so deeply in making peace through negotiation that "if we had to use force, we would have to leave."

But are these the real interpretations of the mentality of a man who has become the pivotal player in the paradigmatic post–Cold War case of Bosnia? Do they explain the secret pacifist who humbles himself and the UN to the Serbs, seemingly grateful for every little crumb they proffer?

The truth is so amazingly different — at least as told consistently by his friends and admirers here in his home country — that it should shake the United Nations and the Western world.

The first interpretation of Akashi comes from former Japanese UN ambassador Yoshio Hatano. "As a Japanese, Akashi may still retain some of the Japanese character, which places peace above justice," he told me. "I was in New York at the time of the invasion of Kuwait and the Gulf War. What did the UN achieve by military intervention? It achieved peace with justice. Even if the UN hadn't intervened, there would have been peace.

"But in Japan, peace tends to equal justice. Because of Japan's experience in the last war, justice tends to be sacrificed. Most Japanese tend to be pacifists — peace at any cost."

Another friend, Yukio Matsuyama, former head of the powerful editorial board of the newspaper *Asahi Shimbun*, sees Akashi as "not militant but not pacifist either; instead, his way of thinking is very Japanese although very loyal to the UN. As the UN representative in Bosnia, he hopes to have Japan make more of an international contribution. But his political activity is tied to the Japanese military. He was always pushing here for Japanese military participation in the UN."

Indeed, the friend who probably knows him best, Takahiro Oda, a top editor and columnist for *Asahi Shimbun*, sees Akashi as a man very open to things military — the Japanese military. "He was one of the strong advocates of sending Japanese troops [to UN trouble spots]," Oda told me. "He wants to see Japan as a permanent member of the Security Council. He tried to persuade the Japanese government to send troops to Macedonia.

"He is not pacifist — never. Every time he comes to Japan to meet with Japanese officials, he tells them that Japan must get very active in these conflicts. In Japan, he is regarded as a kind of hawk, not a dove. He is accused in the papers as being too hawkish."

Perhaps most amazing, in these conversations Akashi, who has always vehemently denied being pro-Serb, comes out as—but of course—unashamedly pro-Serb with his friends.

"You want to know why he sides with the Serbs?" Oda asked me, as we sat in the newspaper's elegant restaurant having coffee. "He says it is because the Serbs are much stronger. He coordinates, and has to bring a solution to the conflict. He used to say to me that of course he is very kind to the Serbs. He told me that the stronger party has to compromise to bring peace. So he has to be friendly with the Serbs."

I mentioned here that many on the spot in Bosnia consider the mysterious Akashi, who only recently again assured the Serbs that even the new European military force would not act against it, viscerally anti-West and particularly anti-American.

Oda though for a long while before responding. "He's not anti-American," he finally said, "but he's very Japanese. Remember, he's sixty-two to sixty-three years old. He respects the U.S. as a great country. But he has to feel America was the aggressor here—as a child here during the occupation, that would be his memory."

So the entire story of Bosnia revolves around the mindset of a man whom surely the United States and the other UN member countries at best do not know and at worst whose agenda they totally misread. Yakushi Akashi, career UN bureaucrat throughout his entire adult life, has set up his own strange satrapy in Bosnia, where he is surrounded by "yes-men" and where he is playing out the dramas of his lifetime. The power of the world has been put in the hands of this man who has called the murderous Serbs "a young people—like the Japanese in 1945."

Where in history can one find a parallel to this incredible situation?

For the media, Bosnia complexity is a big photo-op. Chicago Tribune, December 22, 1995.
Of course, one *had* to *do one on the press.*

WASHINGTON, D.C.

Out of Tuzla in Bosnia, America's newest "Omaha Beach," comes alarming news: There are already more journalists than GIs there. Just listen to the first correspondent's dispatch from the *Washington Times:* "The Big Wait for the arrival of the 1st Armored Division in Bosnia has produced a media monster whose tentacles have spread far beyond Tuzla in a never-ending search for news stories. Until the main force begins arriving . . . there are many more American journalists than soldiers in the country."

Correspondent Richard C. Gross then goes on to tally up the limbs of the looming "monster." For instance, a total of seven TV networks immediately built wooden platforms for their cameras, setting them up so that the American "base" will provide a dramatically bleak background for all those tanned New York anchormen — a veritable TV village. Swedish United Nations troops fired tracer bullets in the air so CBS could get "live" coverage.

Oh my.

For the military in the years after World War II, the cry was "Remember Pearl Harbor!" For us in the press, as the whole process starts again, perhaps we ought to yell in unison every dawn and dusk as we file our copy, "Remember the Gulf War!"

So what am I complaining about?

Well, first, despite brilliant and courageous coverage of the immediate war — the siege of Sarajevo, for instance — there was virtually no American press at all in the rest of the "former Yugoslavia" in 1989, 1990, and 1991, when only a few of us were trying to call the world's attention to the fact that Slobodan Milošević was well into preparing for a Serbian "Anschluss." Since then, there has been virtually no overall geopolitical coverage of the area.

Pathetically little journalistic analysis has been done of what kind of war it was, coverage that would clearly have revealed the true character of the murderous but miserably incapable Serb fighters, the vulnerability of the Serbs to airpower and SerbNet, the dangerous Serb propaganda arm in the United States.

One of the most dangerous legacies from "Bosnia" will be the way it has corrupted so many who have touched it, particularly the Western militaries, who were left with no chain of command to watch over them. For instance, Canadian general Lewis MacKenzie, the former UN commander in Bosnia, traveled throughout the United States after his tour of duty speaking for ten thousand dollars a speech for SerbNet. Yet he was once again on American morning shows this fall, giving not any dispassionate view but that same cynical propaganda.

Much of this is just sloppy journalism, which doesn't check out men like MacKenzie and which is interested in "getting" people, destroying reputations in adversarial carnivals, and basking in the mood of evil playfulness that one sees everywhere in modern journalism. Related to that is the sad decline in numbers of overseas-based foreign correspondents, who knew their countries intimately, and the concomitant rise of the "parachutist."

You say you thought the weather was so bad in Tuzla that no one could parachute in? A reasonable question; but I mean the primarily young journalists who drop in to countries or war zones, unprepared and inexperienced and thus almost always without the tools to cover such complicated stories as the Bosnian war and (we eventually hope) the Bosnian peace.

This genre of new "correspondent" made his and her mark in the Gulf War, where there were no fewer than 1,600 of them. Unfortunately, most of the "marks" were "D." Right after the war, remember, "Saturday Night Live" did a spoof on the suave and with-it military briefers in "Desert Storm." The show had the naive young parachutists innocently querying the experienced military briefers, "What is the password for tonight?" Enough said.

There is every evidence that the hundreds of press people pouring into Tuzla and elsewhere do a repeat of the Gulf War. They will do a good job of covering American troops; indeed, they will overcover them. And the rest of this complex human, military, and geopolitical story will again be ignored, which is a shame, since that is what took us there.

Yet the saga of Bosnia should be a warning shot to us in the press of the kinds of stories that are coming and the kind that we will be asked to cover. As always, the nation depends for its future on understanding those parts of the world that will form that future for us. This story was—and is—replete with neutralist agendas, moral confusion, human degradation, military absurdities and tawdry but powerful ambitions. A Tolstoy or Dostoyevsky would love it.

Instead, even while the world around us becomes immensely more complicated, our journalism is becoming more simplistic.

Washington Times, *February 25, 1996.*
Of all the columns I wrote on Bosnia, I think this was the most important. What we have to deal with, above all else, is the extremely dangerous fact that our military is being "demilitarized" and that "Bosnia" shows the degree to которой we need desperately to clarify what is morally and practically worth using our power for at the end of the twentieth century.

WASHINGTON, D.C.

For the past four years, the greatest mystery for me here in Washington has been the stunning incapacity of the American military on the central military question of this era. I simply could not grasp how these talented people could be doing such a shameful job of analyzing the war in Bosnia.

Indeed, Les Aspin, the late defense secretary, speaking at my own Northwestern University several years ago, laid out their analytical haplessness for all to see. Asked to analyze the Serb soldiers, he said, "We don't know if they're Iraqis or Viet Cong."

Yet not having the faintest idea who the enemy really is never once has stopped the Pentagon from presenting horrendous scenarios to the White House. President Bush himself told me last year that "the Pentagon never told me that artillery or bombing could do the job; they said it would take 250,000 men on the ground. Sometimes the number soared to 500,000."

Indeed, the NATO evacuation plan known as 40104, which was theatrically leaked last year, predicted 5,000 dead — a number that seems extraordinarily inflated until one remembers that the military predicted thousands dead in the Gulf War, where just more than 140 died.

All along, the Pentagon showed such a profound ignorance of the nature of the Serb gunmen or of the type of war it was that it was disturbing for historically knowledgeable people even to talk to them. The Serbs were "World War II guerrilla fighters"; they were "tough fighters"; they would "never retreat." In truth, the Serbs were a bunch of murderous, rampaging mountain men and urban criminals who would have turned back at the first whiff of real opposition.

For a great military like ours to be so willfully ignorant, so persistently wrong, about another fighting force is an embarrassment. And many of us kept asking, "Why?"

Well, I think I finally understand. Recently, I was seated at a dinner with several of our top military men from the Pentagon, who shall go unnamed, and I raised this whole question. They looked at me and simply said, in so many words, "But you don't understand. We didn't want to analyze the war—because we just didn't want to go in."

And the next day, when I discussed this conversation with Zalmay Khalizad, the brilliant military analyst of the Rand Corporation here, he said: "The U.S. military saw getting into Bosnia, even arming the Bosnians, not as an alternative to getting into the war, but as a prelude to it. That is why they held back."

Ah, but one of the few things I really know is that, except in the movies, faulty analysis leads always to unexpected consequences, and very often to disaster. In this situation, it has led to exactly what the American military commanders were trying to avoid. For today, we do have 20,000 American troops in Bosnia. Through its self-imposed incapacity and ignorance, the military has ended up exactly where it didn't want to be!

The Pentagon might have truthfully and accurately analyzed the Bosnia war situation, and then told the president something like this: "The Serbs are thugs and roughnecks, who would be easily defeated by allowing the Bosnians to fight for themselves and backing them up with airpower. They are at the service of an opportunist in Belgrade who pretends to be an ideologue but who will cave in the minute he senses defeat. We should supply the victims with arms and back them up with airpower. We are not succeeding what we want on policy grounds."

Had they done this, the war in Bosnia would have been over in months, if not weeks (indeed, the Serb leaders now admit this). Because they waffled and dissembled, they are now stuck in the mud of Tuzla, feigning "neutrality," all so no one will hurt us.

We know, of course, where this odd, contradictory military thinking comes from. It is the result of the Vietnam syndrome and of the "politicization of the military" under General Colin Powell. Indeed, General Powell who did not want to go into Bosnia, has said of his years as head of the joint chiefs: "Our military advice was shaping political judgments from the very beginning. . . . We were able to constantly bring the political decisions back to what we could do militarily."

Besides having the Pentagon essentially drive political policy, we have the notably peaceable intentions of the Clinton military team. Defense Secretary William Perry is obsessed with winning the Russians and even Chinese over through military cooperation — and we have a security policy that is in conceptual chaos.

We keep coming back to one point. What the American military needs today, more then ever, is the capacity truly to analyze these conflict situations — and what kinds of power can be brought to bear upon them. In the past four years, the Pentagon has been so consumed by trying not to fight that now, through its faulty recommendations, it has to.

Georgie Anne Geyer columns © Universal Press Syndicate. Reprinted with permission. All rights reserved.

CHAPTER FOUR

"We Had To Jump Over the Moral Bridge":
Bosnia and the Pathetic Hegemony of Face-work

KEITH DOUBT

The more the individual is concerned with the reality that is not available to perception, the more must he concentrate his attention on appearances.

— Erving Goffman,
The Presentation of Self in Everyday Life

But, the evil observed, what is its cause and what can be its remedy?

— Émile Durkheim,
The Division of Labor in Society

This study employs Erving Goffman's early accounts of face-work to examine the moral issues that arise from the war in Bosnia and the responses of Western leaders to this war. Concepts like "face" ("the positive social value that a person effectively claims for himself by the line others assume he has taken during a particular interaction"), "face-saving" ("the process by which the person sustains an impression for others that he has not lost face"), and "face-giving" ("to arrange for another to take a better line than he might otherwise have been able to take") are applied to the media descriptions of selected performances on this stage.[1]

Bosnia has become a theater. It has become a stage on which the tensions among as well as within various ideologies like nationalism, modernity, democracy, liberalism, postmodernism, and morality are sharply dramatized.[2] Bosnia, however, is also more than a stage. It is a social entity. It is a reality that "the theater analogy" alone cannot grasp. For this reason, Bosnia refuses to be either defined by or counteracted with the "face-work" of Western leaders or its participants.

On November 16, 1995, in the *New York Times,* Roger Cohen reported the following banal comment by a Western official observing the peace talks at Dayton, Ohio: "But there comes a time, when you have to chose between some absolute justice and moving forward in peace." The comment echoes a refrain frequently heard and widely discussed in the media. The statement creates a dichotomy; the dichotomy asserts a truism. On the one hand, to seek justice means to abandon the possibility of establishing peace. On the other hand, to work toward peace means to ignore justice as a necessary standard for social relations. Peace, the Western official asserts, is established when people stop insisting that justice be the appropriate measure of social and political structure. "Perhaps," Goffman explains, "the main principle of the ritual order is not justice but face, and what any offender receives is not what he deserves but what will sustain for the moment the line to which he has committed himself, and through this the line to which he has committed the interaction."[3]

The official's comment distributes status and distributes status unequally. Those who seek peace are more aware, more worldly; those who demand justice are living in an unreal world, shall we say, a metaphysical or idealistic realm. The comment creates a hierarchy and disabuses those whose commitment is to justice.

To add some details to the setting within which this comment is made, the Bosnian delegation (in the peace talks at Dayton) insisted that the towns of Srebrenica and Žepa be returned to the Republic of Bosnia and Herzegovina. Their end is justice. As Cohen writes, "By every standard of morality or justice, Bosnian control of the towns makes complete sense because they were the scenes of Serbian atrocities against Muslim communities in eastern Bosnian towns." Srebrenica and Žepa (like Bihać, Goražde, and Tuzla) were designated "safe areas" by the United Nations Security Council. The

UN promised to protect these people from violence.[4] As part of this promise, UN forces removed the heavy weapons that the Bosnian government held in the town of Srebrenica. Removing these weapons made the inhabitants more vulnerable to attacks and more dependent upon the UN for protection. When the UN removed the heavy weapons of the Bosnian government soldiers (but not the heavy weapons of the nationalist Serb army in the surrounding area), the Bosnian government focused on the promises of the UN Security Council to protect the civilians in Srebrenica if attacked by the Serbian army. Disarmed, the safe havens fell in July of 1995 to the attacks of the Serbian army, and mass killings, rapes, and sadistic actions (a grandfather was forced to eat his grandson's liver; a mother was forced to drink her dead son's blood) were inflicted on the people living in these towns.[5] "By every standard of morality and justice," these towns should be returned to the Bosnian government.

The Serb delegation, however, is insisting that they be allowed to keep the towns. Their end is peace, more specifically the peace that they see achieved in the creation of a Greater Serbia, that is, an apartheid state where non-Serbs have neither political nor civil rights, no right to worship, own property, vote, or live. Cohen writes, "The Serbs will not relinquish the towns because they are determined that their territory adjoining Serbia be as cohesive as possible." "Put bluntly," Cohen continues, "Bosnian control of Srebrenica and Žepa now makes no sense politically or diplomatically, because the towns would be vulnerable islands surrounded by Serbs and the likely seeds of renewed violence."

What, then, is being said with the statement "But there comes a time, when you have to chose between some absolute justice and moving forward in peace"? The comment exemplifies several important features of "face-work," the practice of sophistry in everyday life, as formulated by Goffman. For one thing, the official asserts "the positive social value" that governs the interactions at Dayton and the behavior of its participants (whether successfully or not). The official draws the "line" that the parties are expected to respect. This line, Goffman adds, "tends to be of a legitimate institutionalized kind."[6]

The dramaturgical point is not whether this line is true or correct. The point is not even whether the parties agree with this line or whether any party agrees. The point is that this line identifies "the basic structural features of interaction, especially the interaction of face-to-face talk." "It is typically a 'working' acceptance, not a 'real' one, since it tends," Goffman writes, "to be based not on agreement of candidly expressed heart-felt evaluations, but upon a willingness to give temporary lip service to judgments with which the participants do not really agree."[7]

With the comment "But there comes a time, when you have to chose between some absolute justice and moving forward in peace," the official is "giving face." He is giving face to the Serb delegation. Given the unconscionable injustices that the nationalist Serb army and its paramilitary groups have inflicted against non-Serbs, given the nationalist Serb policy of genocide, euphemistically called "ethnic cleansing," and given the will of the nationalist Serb leaders to establish an apartheid state, it would seem difficult for the Serb delegation to maintain face with leaders from democratically governed, citizens' rights-based countries. The Serb delegation is therefore dependent upon Western leaders. It is dependent upon Western leaders to provide a line through which they may participate in these interactions. "One can say," Goffman writes, "that 'to give face' is to arrange for another to take a better line that he might otherwise have been able to take, the other thereby gets face given him, this being one way in which he can gain face."[8]

Here is the strategy of U.S. diplomats leading the Dayton talks: "Give face" to the Serbian delegation and, in particular, the Serbian leader, Slobodan Milošević, who controls the Serb delegation. It is widely known that Milošević is the person most responsible for the war for a Greater Serbia and its brutalities throughout former Yugoslavia, starting perhaps with the attack on Vukovar in 1991.[9] In this setting, Milošević, however, is cast as a peacemaker. He is pictured as someone who is different, genuinely different. U.S. diplomats gainsay Milošević's well-documented infamy and in this way arrange for Milošević to take a better line than he might otherwise have been able to take.

The "carrot" used to compel Milošević to assume this "face" is the promise of lifting economic sanctions against Serbia. Serbia has been deeply involved and highly supportive of the war for a Greater

Serbia. Indeed, Milošević gave birth to and nurtured the war. Economic sanctions have caused many in Serbia to live an impoverished and limited life. Lifting economic sanctions helps Milošević maintain his power.

The "stick" used to compel Milošević to put on this "face" is the threat of releasing U.S. intelligence reports to the International Tribunal for War Crimes at the Hague, which is investigating war crimes in former Yugoslavia and which has brought indictments against the Bosnian Serb leaders, General Ratko Mladić and Dr. Radovan Karadžić, as well as others. These intelligence reports would implicate Milošević as a war criminal in the same vein as the others. Richard Goldstone, the Tribunal's prosecutor and a judge from South Africa, who was "a dogged opponent of apartheid," has asked the United States to turn over any such documents in its possession.[10] International law, Francis Boyle points out, requires that the U.S. government do so. If Milošević were indicted, the United States would be required to apprehend Milošević and place him in the custody of the War Crimes Tribunal.

Despite his record, Milošević is the recipient of the "face-giving" treatment of U.S. diplomats, and given his own dramaturgical skills, Milošević carries the line given him perhaps farther than his benefactors intended, which is how Milošević achieves a certain autonomy in these interactions. Goffman calls such behavior "tact regarding tact," that is, Milošević insures that U.S. diplomats continue their face-giving treatment toward him by reciprocating their tactfulness with his own.[11] The more tactful Milošević's behavior is toward Western leaders, the more tactful Western leaders are with Milošević. Milošević, despite igniting the flames of Serbian nationalism that brought hell to so many people in former Yugoslavia, is trusted. He is trusted to play the face-giving game and play it well. "Trouble," Goffman writes, "is caused by a person who cannot be relied upon to play the face-saving game."[12]

What else is being said with the comment "But there comes a time, when you have to chose between some absolute justice and moving forward in peace"? The comment puts the Bosnian delegation in "wrong-face." Insofar as the Bosnian delegation does not defer to "the institutional line" that structures these negotiations, the Bosnian delegation can be said to be "out of face." "A person may 'be out of face' when he participates in a contact with others without having ready a line of the kind participants in such situations are expected to take."[13] The Bosnian delegation, from the point of view of U.S. diplomats, cannot always be relied upon to play the face-saving game. (Think here of the apprehension of the Bosnian Serb general Djordje Djukić and the embarrassment that it caused the Implementation Force [IFOR] and IFOR's "face-work" with respect to implementing the Dayton Accord.) The Bosnian delegation seeks justice; the Republic of Bosnia and Herzegovina, a sovereign nation, was invaded by a foreign force; an arms embargo prevents its soldiers from protecting its land and people; the arms embargo was requested by the invading force, which holds an overwhelming superiority. Many Western leaders want to continue to respect this request.

At Dayton, the more the Bosnian delegation insists on justice, the less the Bosnian delegation is viewed as being interested in peace. The interest in justice is viewed as "out of line." The interest in justice is reduced to a desire for revenge, a desire that is antithetical to the attainment of peace. By insisting upon "some absolute justice," the Bosnian government is "not playing fair." It is viewed by U.S. diplomats as exemplifying an injustice toward the "line" that organizes this setting. "A person may be said to 'be in wrong face' when information is brought forth in some way about his social worth which cannot," Goffman writes, "be integrated, even with effort, into the line that is being sustained for him."[14]

What else, in terms of face-work, is the official saying? The statement "But there comes a time, when you have to chose between some absolute justice and moving forward in peace" saves face. It saves face for Western leaders, most of whom have lost face, given the numerous ways in which they have responded to, tolerated, appeased, and exacerbated the conflict in Bosnia.

There are various methods that Western leaders employ to "save face." For instance, as the towns of Srebrenica and Žepa were falling to the nationalist Serb army, Western leaders of the Contact Group (France, Germany, Great Britain, the United States, and Russia) met at an emergency meeting in London organized by the British government. Western leaders concluded their gathering by replicating a promise that had already been made to the people living in Srebrenica and Žepa. This time, however, they promised to protect the people living in Goražde, a third enclave to the south of Srebrenica and Žepa, which remained under control of the Bosnian government, although it, too, had suffered fierce attacks against civilians and even its hospital by General Mladić's forces. Western leaders concluded their emergency meeting by promising to protect Goražde if, after completing their work in Srebrenica and Žepa, the Serb army proceeded to this third enclave.

In terms of face-work, Western leaders are maintaining poise. "Through poise," Goffman writes, "the person controls his embarrassment and hence the embarrassment that he and others might have over his embarrassment."[15] Western leaders give the appearance of keeping their promise to Srebrenica and Žepa even as they are not. They keep their promise by repeating the promise in another context. (Žepa was still defending itself as this announcement was being made, and the military commander of the Bosnian government forces defending Žepa, Colonel Audo Palić, was thereafter murdered by Serb soldiers while trying to negotiate a surrender.) Western leaders, by transferring to Goražde the promise they made to Srebrenica and Žepa, maintain face. Hyperreality, the hypothetical situation that Goražde would be overrun, displaces reality, which is that Srebrenica and Žepa have been overrun. What is happening in Srebrenica and Žepa becomes unreal and so unnecessary to deal with.

After overrunning Srebrenica, Serbian soldiers ordered UN Dutch soldiers stationed at Potočari just north of Srebrenica to surrender their uniforms and vehicles. (Potočari was an area around which thousands of unarmed civilians herded themselves for protection from the Serbian army, only to be lied to, abused, and murdered by Serb soldiers within earshot of UN soldiers.) Wearing UN uniforms and driving UN vehicles, the Serb soldiers called out to civilians hiding in the forests. After enticing civilians to come out, Serb soldiers murdered these people, many of whom were women and children.

Dramaturgically, Serb soldiers were playing the "discrepant role" of shill or claque, designations, Goffman writes, "employed in the entertainment business, [that] have come into common use."[16] A shill is a member of the audience who works directly against the interests of the audience in league with the performer, unbeknownst to the audience. The shill exploits the audience's trust that he or she is one of them. In this context, Serb soldiers (who were on "the opposing side") deceived the civilians under the guise of being UN soldiers (who, in theory, were "on the same side"). The fraud helped Serb soldiers murder more people and murder more people more efficiently—people whose ethnicity was Muslim.

Within the microcosm of this interaction, Serb soldiers parody the macrocosm of the Western leaders' response to their long-planned attack on a "safe area" and the idea of "ethnic cleansing." Serb soldiers parody the Western leaders' betrayal. Serb soldiers mock the possibility that there are UN soldiers in the area willing to protect the people who have been attacked and under siege for years. Serb soldiers exploit their victims' trust, a trust that Western leaders insisted was warranted and that grounded the relationship that these people have to Europe. The evil in the Serbs' performance is that it erases the possibility of sincerity in human discourse. Drawing evil's conclusion, Goffman writes, "There is, then, a statistical relation between appearance and reality, not an intrinsic or necessary one."[17] Wearing UN uniforms and driving UN vehicles, Serb soldiers simulate the possibility that the UN is collaborating with these murders of non-Serbs, which nationalist Serb leaders call "ethnic cleansing." The question, which paralyzes the world media and enrages academic discourse, is whether this simulation is a statistical possibility or an intrinsic and necessary one. In Srebrenica, UNPROFO (the UN Protection Force) complied with whatever demands General Mladić made of them, for instance, the demand to turn over the Bosnian translators working for UNPROFOR, and these men were thereafter murdered by Serb soldiers.[18]

The actors and circumstances in Bosnia seem to change constantly. New sets are displayed, and different actors play the same role. Face-work, however, remains a ubiquitous feature of the performances on this stage. What is needed to transcend these descriptively interesting but ultimately unsatisfying accounts? Are the insights gained from what Roland Barthes would call the attitude of sarcasm sufficient for understanding this subject, or any subject?[19]

"What I claim" Barthes writes, "is to live to the full the contradiction of my time, which may well make sarcasm the condition of truth."[20] Is sarcasm the best relation that the theorist can have to truth?[21]

Let us analyze another example (still in terms of face-work) with an eye to the ontological assumptions that frame the material. What do Western leaders think such that they act the way that they do in relation to Bosnia? On July 11, 1995, on *The McNeil-Lehrer News Hour,* the U.S. secretary of state Warren Christopher was interviewed as Srebrenica was falling to the invasion of the Serbian army. At one point, the secretary of state said, "So for the time being in a situation where the parties apparently still are not ready to solve the matter themselves, I think that the UN presence is the best of the available alternatives." What is Christopher saying and why is he saying it at this time? He is saying that for him to change his behavior toward the injustices occurring in Bosnia, the parties first must be ready to solve the matter themselves. Until this point is reached, Christopher is unwilling to do any more than he already is. What, though, will make the parties ready to solve the matter themselves? How will this come about?[22]

Christopher believes that, after experiencing enough pain, the parties will begin to do what he expects, namely, solve the matter themselves. Christopher's opinions are governed by his understanding of the Hobbesian theory of social order. In the eyes of Christopher, Bosnia is a Hobbesian jungle. In Bosnia, it is every man and woman for himself and herself. Force and fraud are the only two cardinal virtues. Life is short, nasty, and brutish.

Christopher reasons that, after experiencing this kind of life for a sufficient length of time, the parties will be ready to solve the matter themselves. The parties will be willing to sit down and talk, that is, form a social contract. They will make agreements that they can count on.

Christopher's belief is that only the establishment of a social contract can stop the violence in Bosnia. After creating a social contract, the parties, in the interest of a longer and more peaceful life will suspend their use of force and fraud against each other. "I would have to say, Jim [Lehrer], after having worked on this problem for two and a half years, until the parties get ready to resolve it, it probably won't be resolved." There is no more or less willingness among people in Bosnia to solve the matter themselves than there is in any other place in the world where there is conflict. Think of the talks over the federal budget between President Bill Clinton and the Republican-led Congress. References to the conflict in Bosnia as a unique place where tribal hatreds reign are specious, to say the least.[23]

Christopher's comments on *The McNeil-Lehrer News Hour* are meant to save face. Goffman openly acknowledges how Hobbes's understanding of social order is the basis for his analysis of face-work. The light of reason, which Hobbes assumes will arise out of the Hobbesian jungle and which Christopher believes will arise out of Bosnia, is represented, Goffman says, in the individual's willingness and ability to take on the chores and duties of face-work. Goffman writes: "A person's performance of face-work . . . represents his willingness to abide by the ground rules of social interaction. Here is the hallmark of his socialization as an interactant. If he and the others were not socialized in this way, interaction in most societies and most situations would be a much more hazardous thing for feelings and faces."[24]

There is something amiss, however, in the Hobbesian understanding of social order, whether it appears in the reasoning of world leaders or the inquiry of sociology. While it is possible to turn to the work of Talcott Parsons at this point, it is better to work out Parsons's points in terms of this context.[25]

What would it take for the Bosnian delegation to get ready to solve this matter themselves in talks with the nationalist Serbs? (Notice Christopher's reductionism when he equates the Republic of Bosnia and Herzegovina, which fights for an open, pluralistic society and a rights-based government, with the nationalist Serb party, now recognized by the Dayton Accord as the Republika Srpska, which stands for an ethnically cleansed community and legally sanctioned apartheid state.) Must the Bosnian government accept the right of nationalist Serbs to maim, rape, degrade, and murder its citizens with impunity? Must the Bosnian government accept the power of the Bosnian Serb army in collusion with the Yugoslav People's Army (JNA) to deny its people the right to live either because its people are non-Serbs or because its people are Serbs who chose not to live in a fascist state?

At first glance, Christopher's reasoning is Hobbesian. After experiencing enough pain, the parties will be ready to solve the matter themselves. Christopher's reasoning, however, is more Darwinian than it is Hobbesian, and the Darwinian part, while latent, is the more powerful part. Like his European counterparts, especially in Britain and France, Christopher is upholding the notion that the strongest prevail, the principle that spurs on the nationalist Serbs.

In *The Division of Labor* Émile Durkheim writes: "To be sure, the strongest succeed in completely demolishing the weakest, or in subordinating them. But if the conquered, for a time, must suffer subordination under compulsion, they do not consent to it, and consequently this cannot constitute a stable equilibrium. Truces, arrived at after violence, are never anything but provisional, and satisfy no one. Human passions stop only before a moral power they respect. If all authority of this kind is wanting, the law of the strongest prevails, and latent or active, the state of war is necessarily chronic."[26]

Durkheim's writing provides an apt critique of the Dayton peace agreement. At Dayton the parties were never ready to solve the matter themselves; they were, however, ready to let the United States solve it. Durkheim says that a "truce," basically what Hobbes means by the social contract, lacks the weight required to counter the law of the strongest prevail. The social contract qua truce lacks the power to command respect and win agreement. Human passions do not willingly defer to a truce, which is not to say that there is nothing to which human passions defer.

Impartiality is not itself a moral position despite the pretense of UN officials that it is. Impartiality is simply what Goffman would call a front, a dramaturgical performance of bogus and hypocritical fairness, which may sometimes carry weight with respect to the achievement of objectivity in scientific inquiry. The impartiality of the UN officials, however, has neither commanded respect nor established significant limits.

Western leaders do not want to lift the arms embargo against former Yugoslavia, and Western leaders rely upon the Hobbesian understanding of social order to justify their decision. What is needed in Bosnia, Western leaders argue, is not more force (there is enough force already), but more reason. Reason will be exemplified in the willingness of the parties to establish a social contract, a social contract that limits the use of force and fraud for the safety of all. Lifting the arms embargo, Western leaders reason, hinders this development. It prevents the light of reason from arising out of the Hobbesian jungle. Lifting the arms embargo leads to more fighting and even worse atrocities. It empowers the Bosnian army and enables it to match, if not defeat, the Serb army.

There is a flaw with this argument even in terms of its own frame of reference. The Hobbesian solution, which comes so highly and exclusively recommended, works only when there is an equality among the participants, when, as Hobbes says, no one, given the fragility of human nature, is capable of overpowering another for any sustained length of time. In the state of nature, given the equality of human beings in terms of power and cunning, people surmise that their situation is senseless. People see that nobody wins and everybody loses. Reason prevails, and a peaceful society is established.

The situation in Bosnia, however, is different. As long as there is a significant power imbalance and one party believes itself to be invincible, it is thoughtless (to say the least) to argue that the strongest will establish an agreement with the weaker or that the weaker will trust whatever agreement it is forced to make with the stronger. The situation in Bosnia is unnatural, and the arms embargo insures that the situation remains unnatural. As long as the arms embargo holds, the Hobbesian solution cannot take hold.

"No one," Saul D. Alinksy says, "can negotiate without the power to compel negotiation."[27] (In the Hobbesian jungle, what compels negotiation is that nobody can compel negotiation, which means all can compel negotiation.) Given the lack of military arms vis-à-vis the Serbian army, the Bosnian government cannot compel serious negotiation with the nationalist Serbs on any issue. The Bosnian government depends upon the UN, North Atlantic Treaty Organization (NATO), or the United States to compel negotiation.[28] Western leaders exercise this power only sporadically and only when it suits their interests rather than the interests of the Bosnian government. For instance, to justify the recent deployment of NATO troops in Bosnia, Western leaders argue that it is required in order to hold NATO together and preserve NATO's integrity. What about holding the Republic of Bosnia and Herzegovina together and preserving its integrity?

The times Western leaders are most willing to employ their power to compel negotiation is when the Bosnian government itself is on the verge of realizing this power for itself, for instance, when, in August of 1995, its military forces threatened Banja Luka, the Serbian stronghold in Western Bosnia, or when, given the advice of the U.S. international lawyer Francis Boyle, its government considered filing law suits at the World Court against UN Security Council members for abetting genocide.

Frequently, the Bosnian government is subject to double standards. It is remarkable that the Bosnian government has acted with as much probity as it has. For instance, the corruption and nepotism in the current government is criticized as if it were tantamount to the genocidal practices of the nationalist Serbs.[29] This treatment by Western leaders pressures the Bosnian government in that, to be treated fairly, it is as if the Bosnian government must be morally pure. Paradoxically, the fairer the Bosnian government is toward its citizens as well as its enemies, the more abused the Bosnian government is. Likewise, the unfairer the nationalist Serbs are toward non-Serbs as well as Serbs, the more respected and admired the nationalist Serbs are for their audacity.

The assertion by Western leaders that the Hobbesian solution (and only the Hobbesian solution) must be given a chance justifies the arms embargo. The lopsided advantage of the nationalist Serbs, however, insures that the nationalist Serb leaders never have to think in terms other than might is right. Experience teaches the nationalist Serbs that, with respect to achieving their interest in a Greater Serbia, force and fraud are very "efficient." It is difficult to see why, therefore, the nationalist Serbs would begin to consider abandoning these methods given the gains that are reaped.

"Universal human nature," Goffman writes, "is not a very human thing. By acquiring it, the person becomes a kind of construct, built up not from inner psychic propensities but from moral rules that are impressed upon him from without."[30] With this statement, Goffman shows his dependency upon the Hobbesian understanding of human nature. Why should the nationalist Serbs take on these "moral rules which are impressed upon them from without"? The nationalist Serbs are rational. It would be irrational for them to adapt a Hobbesian logic when the Darwinian logic appears to be to their advantage. For instance, while negotiations were taking place in Dayton (and a cease-fire was in effect), the Bosnian Serb army in Banja Luka, which might have been defeated in August of 1995, was refurbished and resupplied by the Serbian federal army in Belgrade, which Milošević (who was in Dayton) controls.[31]

The vainglory of the nationalist Serbs is that they are both stronger and more cunning than the UN and NATO together, who, logically, ought to be stronger and smarter given their size and strength. The Western press sensationalizes this perception, which helps nationalist Serbs save face. From the point of view of nationalist Serbs, the only authority of the social contract, as proposed by Western leaders, is sheer number. (The rationalization that nationalist Serbs use to explain their murders of non-Serbs is that they are afraid to live in a community in which non-Serbs are a majority.) Nationalist Serbs wonder why U.S. diplomats insist that Bosnian Muslims and Bosnian Croats form a federation as if the two groups have nothing in common except their need to be powerful vis-à-vis the nationalist Serbs? From the point of view of the nationalist Serbs, U.S. diplomacy simply reinforces the nationalist Serbs' own point of view. Is there any difference between the "purported" war crimes of the nationalist Serbs and NATO bombings of Serb targets? From the viewpoint of nationalist Serbs, the actions are the same in that both are committed to the same notion—might is right.

Do Western leaders have to meet force with force, asocial behavior with asocial behavior, to change the situation in Bosnia? Clinically, the behavior of the nationalist Serbs is described as "asocial" behavior. It is then said that asocial behavior is untreatable because it is incorrigible. Neither reason nor punishment can change asocial behavior. Only behavior that is itself asocial "redirects" asocial behavior. The face-saving argument against military intervention in Bosnia is that intervention is as "uncivilized" as the behavior it is meant to confront. To meet force with force means to enter the Hobbesian jungle and to be no different from the animals already in it. Whenever NATO bombs Serb military targets, nationalist Serbs play up this argument to their people and the media. While nationalist Serbs find the use of NATO military force abhorrent, they also identify with it and employ it for purposes of self-justification and self-confirmation.

In the *Structure of Social Action,* Parsons laments the innocence of the Hobbesian understanding of social order. "There is nothing in the theory dealing with the relations of ends to each other, but only with the character of the means-end relationship. . . . For the failure to state anything positive about the relations of ends to each other can then have only one meaning—that there are no significant relations, that is, that ends are random in the statistical sense."[32]

To understand Bosnia in terms other than the theater analogy, it is necessary to locate what is absent in the Hobbesian understanding of social order. "There has been [in the Hobbesian account of social order] . . . a common standard of rationality and, equally important," Parsons adds, "the absence of any other *positive* conception of a normative element governing the means-end relationship."[33] Can we state something positive about the relations of ends to each other? What positive conception of a normative element governing the means-end relationship is there? In Goffman's dramaturgical account, ends are random. They are statistically related. Ends reflect the self-interests of individuals. Parsons calls it atomism. Without a positive notion of the relations of ends to each other, it is impossible to oppose the exceptional dramaturgical behavior of the nationalist Serbs. The best Western leaders can do is match that behavior.

Plato helps. In the *Gorgias* Socrates appears to lose face, as Goffman would say, when he takes an indefensible position. The sophist Polus laughs when he hears Socrates' "bottom line." Socrates says that the person who does wrong with impunity is more unhappy and more miserable than the person who does wrong and is justly punished. Polus (like nationalist Serbs) believes that the person who does wrong without being punished is the happier one, even happier than the righteous person. To Polus, Socrates' comments are "out of line," "unreal," "irrational."

Let us say Socrates' comment represents a parameter of morality that is relevant in every community, albeit in specific ways. If so, his comment generates telltale points for Bosnia. Notice that Socrates' comment imagines a positive conception of a normative element governing the means-end relationship.[34] It surpasses the Hobbesian understanding of what governs the means-end relationships because it points to a foundation upon which the social contract commands respect, which is what limits as well as transforms human passions.

Intervention is necessary in Bosnia not only for the sake of the Bosnian government and its citizens but also for the sake of the nationalist Serbs. Without intervention, the nationalist Serbs remain the most unhappy and most miserable people in the world.[35] Why else is the observing world so interested in these hidden lives? Why else is the media prevented from viewing these concealed regions? What are the consequences of sadistic actions for sadistic actors? When an individual, no longer cloaked in the "crowd" mentality of a paramilitary group, reflects and feels extreme guilt, one possible consequence is suicide. Intervention is necessary to relieve the nationalist Serbs of their misery (a misery that they seem too proud to share but cannot avoid sharing). Relief for wrong actions comes only from being punished justly for wrong actions. The souls of the nationalist Serbs are ill, wretched with the disease of injustice, and justice, absolute justice, is the only medicine that can cure these souls.

This argument is not esoteric. Nor is it archaic. In an interview cited by Anthony Lewis on November 20, 1995, in the *New York Times,* Judge Goldstone points out that "if individuals are not brought to book then there is collective guilt. The victims and their survivors cry out for justice against a group." To support his point, Goldstone adds that "I'm not sure the re-integration of Germany into Europe would have been achieved as it was if those trials [the Nuremberg trials of Nazi leaders after World War II] had not been held." Unless justice is achieved, peace is impossible. Here is the anterior but abused idea in the official's comment "But there comes a time, when you have to chose between some absolute justice and moving forward in peace." No one can move forward in peace and, simultaneously, accept injustice as not requiring punishment. The comment reflects ignorance; it speaks of a time that has never and will never exist. This is a fact as powerful as any fact of nature. Peace and justice are as interdependent in social discourse as life and light are in nature.

The Western official's comment conceals not only how necessary but also how pragmatic it is to achieve justice. Justice is attained when it is achieved absolutely, that is, categorically. Goldstone observes, "I can't believe that many Serbs would condone the kinds of atrocities with which these men [General Mladić and Dr. Karadžić] have been charged. The evidence, if it is upheld, shows that they are people who should not be leaders of any society." Few Serbs want to be forced at gunpoint to murder their non-Serb neighbors, whom they have lived with their entire lives and befriended.[36] It is necessary and pragmatic to achieve justice because it is necessary that justice governs Serbs as a collective. Serbs realize that no justice is exemplified in the notion that might is right.

Catering to Milošević the way that U.S. diplomats do prevents the Serbs throughout former Yugoslavia from becoming who they are. Western leaders are condemning this group of people to a life far worse than the life of the citizens of Bosnia, who have enjoyed the freedom and richness of an open and pluralistic society. Serbs are being forced to live in a community governed by barbarians who have committed unspeakable crimes (and can no longer live with themselves). These barbarians now dominate the communities in which they live, and the political and economic support of Western leaders help them do so.

In the *Gorgias* Socrates says that it is better to suffer wrong than it is to do wrong, and Polus, like the nationalist Serbs, thinks that Socrates is crazy. While no person, Socrates says, willingly suffers wrong, if the choice is only between suffering wrong and doing wrong, the best choice is to suffer wrong. Polus cannot believe that anyone would seriously make this argument. Still, the position explains much of what is true in Bosnia. The people to be most pitied in Bosnia are those who are responsible for war crimes, whether Serbs, Croats, or Muslims. Many citizens in Bosnia know this, which accounts for their contemptuous attitude toward Europe and for their integrity. As Jean Baudrillard says, the people in Sarajevo are to be envied, not pitied, and, while Baudrillard would not formulate it this way, the reason is because the people in Sarajevo understand Plato's insight as a fundamental truth: it is better to suffer wrong than to do wrong. What surprises people in Sarajevo is that nobody else in the world seems to understand this truth.[37]

The reason the nationalist Serbs persist in breaking agreement after agreement and violating truce after truce is that they, too, know what they need. They do not need Western leaders to tolerate their unconscionable actions. Western tolerance only spurs on the nationalist Serbs. The nationalist Serbs need justice not for the sake of their victims but for the sake of themselves and the people who follow them. The nationalist Serbs lack the will to stop themselves. Their wills are ill. By not only continuing but also increasing the degree of their injustices, they seek not unconditional acceptance but a just response. Their souls are stunned, deeply stunned, by the unexpected tolerance of Western leaders. Nationalist Serbs cross moral line after moral line because their souls cannot rest with their actions and because their souls cannot allow others to rest with their actions. Here is the small but unbreakable thread of shared values in the souls of the nationalist Serbs that will insure that they are brought to book. An essential feature of evil is evil's need to be witnessed. The greater the evil is, the greater the need to be witnessed.

Whether or not Admiral Leighton Smith, NATO's commander in Bosnia, wants IFOR, the NATO Implementation Force, to apprehend indicted war criminals and help investigate grave sites is not the point. Admiral Smith can ill afford to evade this responsibility. If he does, the guilty gleefully coopt his collusion. The cost will be high for IFOR and the rewards great for the guilty. The desire of the guilty to show that those who have power over them are, morally speaking, no different from them is a far greater motivation than the fear of apprehension.

What ought to be the motivation of Western leaders? Again, Plato helps. Socrates would say that U.S. assistant secretary of state Richard Holbrooke is anything but Milošević's friend. Indeed, in Holbrooke Milošević could not have found a worst enemy. It is a crime for Holbrooke to help Milošević avoid punishment for his crimes against humanity.[38] If Holbrooke were truly concerned for the well being of Milošević, the Serbian community, and the world at large, Holbrooke, as a friend, would empathetically insist that Milošević "force himself and others not to play the coward, but to submit to the law with closed eyes like a man, as one would to surgery or cautery, ignoring the pain for the sake of the good result which it will bring."[39] Otherwise, Holbrooke insures that Milošević lives the most wretched of lives and that all those subject to him live an equally wretched life. The one way that Holbrooke can atone for his ignorance is to do everything within his powers to place Milošević in the hands of the prosecutor at the International War Crimes Tribunal.

Western leaders need to intervene in Bosnia for their own sake. If Western leaders do not, they allow the nationalist Serbs to determine their own self-concept. They allow the nationalist Serbs to encourage all citizens to assume that the law of the strongest prevails rather than the principle of justice.[40] That is, they allow the nationalist Serbs to determine their citizens' values, which will then determine their citizens' behavior. Intervening in Bosnia is not only in the national interest of Western nations; it is in the highest interest of Western nations.

If, say, the racist leaders of the Ku Klux Klan were able to gain control of every TV and radio broadcast in the United States, what would prevent what happened in Bosnia from happening in the United States? "You must imagine a United States with every little TV station everywhere taking exactly the same editorial line — a line dictated by David Duke. You too would have war in five years."[41] If Western leaders cannot bring justice to bear on the nationalist Serbs, how do they expect to bring justice to bear on the people in their own countries who model their thinking and their actions after the nationalist Serbs? Intervening in Bosnia is in the vital interest of the world.

Notes

"We had to jump over the moral bridge" is a statement attributed to Charles Redman, the U.S. State Department official charged by President Clinton to come up with a peace plan for Bosnia. See David Rieff, *Slaughterhouse: Bosnia and the Failure of the West* (*New York: Simon and Schuster, 1995*), *27*.

1. Erving Goffman, *Interaction Ritual: Essays on Face-to-Face Behavior* (New York: Pantheon, 1967), 5–15.
2. For a thorough and incisive discussion of these complex matters, see Stjepan G. Meštrović, *The Balkanization of the West: The Confluence of Postmodernism and Postcommunism* (London: Routledge, 1994).
3. Goffman, *Interaction Ritual*, 44.
4. UN Resolution #819 passed on April 16, 1993.
5. See the *Human Rights Watch/Helsinki Report* 7, no. 13 (Oct. 1995), on "The Fall of Srebrenica and the Failure of UN Peacekeeping."
6. Goffman, *Interaction Ritual*, 7.

7. Ibid., 11.
8. Ibid., 42.
9. See Laura Silber and Allan Little, *Yugoslavia: The Death of a Nation* (New York: TV Books, Inc., 1996), as well as the television series by the same name produced by Brian Lapping Associates.
10. See Robin Knight in *U.S. News and World Report*, Dec. 4, 1995, cited in *Bosnews*.
11. Goffman, *Presentation of Self*, 234–37.
12. Goffman, *Interaction Ritual*, 31.
13. Ibid., 8.
14. Ibid.
15. Ibid., 13.
16. Goffman, *Presentation of Self*, 146.
17. Ibid., 71.
18. See also Rieff's description of the assassination of Dr. Hakija Turljic, vice president of the Republic of Bosnia and Herzegovina, while riding in an armored personnel carrier under the protection of French and British UN soldiers (*Slaughterhouse*, 150–51).
19. See Zlatko Dizdarević, *Sarajevo: A War Journal* (New York: Fromm International, 1992). The most poignant descriptions in this text are not the ones narrated with sarcasm, although the use of sarcasm is often an effective rhetorical device.
20. Roland Barthes, *Mythologies* (New York: Noonday, 1972), 12.
21. "The mythologist is condemned to live in a theoretical sociality; for him, to be in society is, at best, to be truthful: his utmost sociality dwells in his utmost morality. His connection with the world is of the order of sarcasm" (ibid., 157).
22. Ivo Banac says, "To define the war as a tribal feud or a civil war is simply an easy way of dismissing the whole thing. The argument then is that if something has been going on forever, presumably, it will continue forever and hence nothing need be done to alleviate the situation. The best thing to do, therefore, is simply sit back and watch as this hellish situation plays itself out. . . . It all adds up to . . . intellectual laziness" ("Separating History from Myth: An Interview with Ivo Banac" in *Why Bosnia: Writings on the Balkan War*, edited by Rabia Ali and Lawrence Lifschultz [Stony Creek, Conn.: Pamphleteer's Press, 1993], 136. I would say as well that Christopher's position adds up to fatalism and sadism).
23. "There is no sane reason," Ivo Banac observes, "to believe that in this particular corner of the world there is some sort of special concentration of hate. Human beings are human beings everywhere" (Ibid., 164).
24. Goffman, *Interaction Ritual*, 31.
25. Talcott Parsons, *The Structure of Social Action* (New York: Free Press, 1968).
26. Émile Durkheim, *The Division of Labor in Society* (New York: Free Press, 1964), 2–3.

27. Saul D. Alinsky in *Rules for Radicals,* excerpted in William A. Gamson's *SIMSOC: Simulated Society: Participants Manual with Selected Reading,* 4th ed. (New York: Free Press, 1991), 69.
28. David Owen, the European Community (EC) mediator, took advantage of this situation on behalf of the Bosnian Serbs. His opportunism, however, did not succeed. The question is if the Dayton accord is any more or less opportunistic than Owen's work was, which could explain why Owen is envious of the Dayton accord.
29. On December 12, 1995, in the *New York Times* George Kenney writes, "The United States has another reason to keep the Bosnians at arm's length: their Government is rife with corruption . . . a 'Balkan Tammany Hall.'"
30. Goffman, *Interaction Ritual,* 45.
31. "What Milošević has done," Ivo Banac observes, "and with greater effectiveness than many realize, is to demonstrate that there are no real restrictions on aggressive behavior" (Ali and Litschultz, 150).
32. Parsons, *Structure of Social Action,* 56.
33. Ibid., 59.
34. Richard McKim makes an interesting argument on this matter of how to read Plato. He says that Socrates's ability to refute the sophists has nothing at all to do with reason. "If we demand a logical proof that shameful acts are harmful to their agents, instead of acknowledging, as Polus must in the end, that we feel them to be shameful because we already believe this, we lower ourselves in Plato's view to the level of sophistic debaters, refusing to admit what we really believe in order to 'win' the argument regardless of the truth" ("Shame and Truth in Plato's *Gorgias,*" in *Platonic Writings, Platonic Readings,* edited by Charles L. Griswold, Jr. [New York: Routledge, 1988], 48).
35. "The military defeat of Serbia would be good not only for everybody who was subjected to Serbian aggression, but it would be good for Serbia too" (Ali and Lifschultz, 162).
36. See Norman Cigar, *Genocide in Bosnia: The Policy of "Ethnic Cleansing"* (College Station: Texas A&M University Press, 1995).
37. See Jean Baudrillard, "No Pity for Sarajevo," in *This Time We Know: Western Responses to Genocide in Bosnia,* edited by Thomas Cushman and Stjepan G. Meštrović (New York: New York University Press, 1996).
38. Playing the devil's advocate, Socrates says, "If the enemy injures a third party, one must clearly make every effort, both in speech and action, to prevent his being brought to book and coming before the judge at all; if that is impossible one must contrive that he gets off unpunished. . . . The most desirable thing would be that he should never die, but live for ever in an immortality of crime; the next best that he should live as long as possible in that condition" (Plato, *Gorgias* [Hammondsworth, England: Penguin, 1960], 74). Socrates ironically describes how one brings the greatest harm to an individual, and it is exactly what Holbrooke is doing to Milošević.

39. Ibid., 73.
40. The concluding sentence of *Yugoslavia: Death of a Nation* reads, "Victory, in former Yugoslavia, will fall not to the just, but to the strong" (Silber and Little, 372). No matter how informed Silber and Little are, their last sentence, which serves as an epitaph not so much for former Yugoslavia, but for the Republic of Bosnia and Herzegovina, is wrongheaded. Silber and Little's resignation prevents them from going beyond a Hobbesian understanding of their subject, which moves them, however unwittingly, to echo the reasoning of the strong.
41. Miloš Vasić in Noel Malcolm, *Bosnia: A Short History* (Washington Square, N.Y.: New York University Press, 1944), 252.

CHAPTER FIVE

Labeling Theory and the Wars in Croatia and Bosnia-Herzegovina
SLAVEN LETICA

Labeling Theory
Are the conflicts, war, war crimes, and genocide that are found today in the Balkans accidental events ("conflict of coexistence") or, bluntly, unchangeable historical fate and destiny ("coexistence of conflicts"). To answer this rhetorical question I will use a rather unordinary perspective, that is, the labeling theory, which is frequently used in medical sociology.

The task that has been carried out for some years now by many people who have tried intellectually to probe into the secrets of our post-Communist societies, conflicts, and tragedies — scholars, diplomats, journalists, humanists, Nobel Laureates, UN peacekeepers, European Union observers, and many other war watchers — is in some ways an exercise in diagnosis.

This task involves the filming of signs and symptoms of "illness" (the violation of human rights, war crimes, political extremism, and so forth), the documentation of its historical development, and finally, the diagnosis of "illness." Diagnosis presupposes arriving at conclusions concerning the etiology and possibility of treating this "illness," but also the possibility of practical strategies for coping with "illness."

Many of these diagnosticians — inebriated with puppy love toward the "Yugoslav experiment," "the third way," "federalism," and "multiculturalism" or the "rebirth of history"—have simply misdiagnosed our Balkan "illness."[1]

Outline of Labeling Theory

Labeling theory is one of those classical sociological theories that is most often used to describe deviance and deviant behavior but that, in a wider context, is used in medical sociology to explain the reactions of various actors to the stigmatic effects of various labels and diagnoses.

The gist of labeling theory's contribution to medical sociology is as follows: At the moment when the physician uses a label such as "stammer," "a cold," "epilepsy," "insanity," "pneumonia," "cancer," "AIDS," or "schizophrenia," that label immediately changes the victim's perception of himself or herself, his or her behavior, and the behavior of others toward him or her (members of the family, medical professionals, the larger community).

Some labels have a minimal impact ("a cold"). Other labels have more drastic effects, ranging from compassion and wanting to help ("cancer") to stigmatization ("schizophrenia," "AIDS").

If we now apply labeling theory to the theme of the Balkans in the 1990s, we arrive at the following hypothesis: The behavior of actors involved in these conflicts as well as the behavior of the international community toward these actors depends not only on the factual roles these actors play but also on the labels that this conflict receives.

The international community's public, media, diplomats, military alliances and organizations, and humanitarian and other nongovernmental organizations will behave one way if this conflict is labeled as "Balkan quagmire," a different way if it is called a "civil war," a third way if it is conceived as a "war of aggression," and a fourth way if the dominant label is "genocide" and it is compared and contrasted with the Holocaust.

The labels "quagmire" and "civil war" suggest to the Western European or American, "Stay away, it's none of your business," while the labels "war of aggression" and "genocide" carry the cultural imperative: "Do something to stop it, now!"

It would be an enormous task to analyze empirically all labels concerning the character, location, and etiology of this war. According to the bibliographic research carried out by the European Movement in Croatia, more than 180 books and monographs have been published on this war between 1990 and 1995. The number of scholarly articles during this same time period is more than a thousand, while the number of newspaper articles, television news stories, and television programs and documentaries comes to several hundred thousand.

If we restrict our analysis to just the titles and main theses of books and significant articles on the Balkans from 1990 to 1995, we shall easily arrive at the conclusion that these writings have produced a state of terminological chaos and intellectual anomie.[2] Journalists, scholars, and other authors on this war contradict each other and fail to agree on the issues of who started this war, when, and why.

In arguing the thesis of intellectual anomie and ideational chaos concerning this Balkan War, I will analyze only the questions concerning the naming, place, causes, and time of the "Balkan" happenings. Such an analysis demonstrates immediately that because of the "labeling" at work here, a rigorous scholar as well as a weakly informed intellectual will have a difficult time addressing the most elementary journalistic questions concerning this war: what, where, why, when, and who?

WHAT?: LABELING A NATURE OR CHARACTER OF THE WAR EVENTS

There is no consensus in existing books and articles concerning basic ideas and concepts related to the war in Bosnia. Let us examine some of the labels from titles of well-known books: "remaking the Balkans," "Balkan ghosts," "ethnic nationalism," "death of Yugoslavia," "a lost Yugoslavia," "the fall of Yugoslavia," "the ending of Yugoslavia," "death of Yugoslavia," "the Yugoslav crisis," "tensions in the Balkans," "the third Balkan war," "bloody collapse," "Balkan tragedy," "catastrophe," "the tenth circle of hell," "Balkan odyssey," "disintegration of Yugoslavia," "destruction of Yugoslavia," "civil wars," "the case for intervention," "an aggression," "war crimes in Bosnia-Herzegovina," "mass raping," "slaughterhouse," "genocide," "ethnic nightmare," and so forth.[3]

One should also note the global labels: "the clash of civilizations,"[4] "the lost civilization," "bestial war,"[5] and "cultural genocide."[6] The use of the ghost-metaphor "another Vietnam" or "Vietnam quagmire" plays a large role in American politics concerning the Balkans.

If we examine these labels chronologically from 1990 to 1995 we find the following:

- 1990–91 are dominated by the labels "disintegration-destruction-fall" of Yugoslavia, "ethnic conflict," "rebel republics," "secessionist republics";
- in 1991–92 the leading labels are "ethnic conflict" and "civil war";
- after CNN in the summer of 1992 reported on the Serbian concentration (detention) camps, the labels in 1992 and 1993 more often became "aggression," "war crimes," and "genocide." Meanwhile, and parallel with these, the label of "civil war" continued to be used in Bosnia;
- 1993–95 "finally" saw the labels "Serbian aggression" and "genocide" come into regular use.

The ambivalent stance of the international community toward the victims of aggression in the Balkans was less the result of considerations based on realpolitik and national interests than the result of labeling in the media. That is, the labels "ethnic conflict-war," "tribal conflict," and especially "civil war" and/or "religious conflict-war" cause paralysis in the West. Their effect in terms of mass psychology is the same as with such labels as "cholera" and "AIDS": Consciously or unconsciously, these labels immobilize the Westerner and lead to caution, emotional and practical neutrality, even to the search for scapegoats and blaming the victims for the tragedy that has befallen them.

A different effect is caused by the labels "aggression," "war crimes," and "genocide" and by efforts to make comparisons and contrasts to the Holocaust. Refrains of "Never again!" and comparisons with the Holocaust cause ambivalence within as well as outside the Jewish community, with some rabbis and scholars, for example, making such comparisons on a qualitative basis, and others arguing that the Holocaust is a unique instance of genocide.[7]

These labels lead to discussions of responsibility and moral obligation on the part of the world community. However, these labels entered the mainstream of political and public discourse when it was already rather late: genocide, euphemistically called "ethnic cleansing" in this war, had already led to the destruction of more than 200,000 lives and to crimes unknown in Europe since 1945.

The accurate labels — (Pan or Greater) Serbian "aggression" and "genocide" — were used by leading opinion makers such as Anthony Lewis, William Safire, and Leslie H. Gelb, but their effect was offset by the persistent usage of the labels that lead to paralysis — "civil war," "ethnic hatred" — by their colleagues Rodger Cohen and David Binder.

In sum, the central problem was in timing: the labels that dominated 1990 and 1991 restrained the international community from preventing the tragedy that ensued. By the time the tragedy had occurred, the correct labels could no longer help.

WHERE?: LABELING THE LOCATION(S) OF THE WAR EVENTS

The largest number of authors localized the place of the war events in "the Balkans," "the former Yugoslavia," "ex-Yugoslavia," and "Bosnia-Herzegovina." Only the last label is accurate for the most part. Some authors refer to "Europe's backyard war,"[8] and others even bring up the possibility of a new world war.

The current Balkan War is actually a series of wars that were waged in 1991 in Slovenia, in 1991–92 in Croatia, and from 1992 to 1995 in Bosnia-Herzegovina. It is not accurate to speak of the "Balkan war(s)" or the "war(s) in the Balkans," and ethically it is incomprehensible to refer to the "war in Yugoslavia," because Slobodan Milošević's Yugoslavia has not seen even one hour of war if one excludes the organized state-sponsored terror that began in Kosovo in the 1980s.

WHY?: LABELING THE CAUSES AND AIMS OF THE WARS

What were the main cause(s) and the aims of the wars in Slovenia, Croatia, and Bosnia-Herzegovina?

Various scholars, diplomats, and opinion makers cite diverse causes and aims: "the Balkan ghosts" (Kaplan), "nationalism" (numerous politicians and opinion makers), "tribalism," "history," "historic hatred," "the quest for a Greater Serbia," "racism," "national socialism," "fascism," and so on.

Thus, labeling has led to three main hypotheses regarding the causes and aims of the war: (1) the return of history (Fukuyama), (2) nationalism (as opposed to federalism and multiculturalism), and (3) Serbian national socialism, racism, and imperialism.

In his recent book on genocide in Bosnia, Norman Cigar illustrates the typical thinking found in *Balkan Ghosts* by quoting Senator John Warner during the hearings on the Yugoslav crisis: "My own research . . . indicates that . . . these people have fought each other for not hundreds of years, but thousands of years for religious, ethnic, cultural differences . . . there is certainly a history, going back, at least into my study of the problem, as far back as the 13th century, of constant ethnic and religious fighting among and between these groups."[9]

Such fatalistic and nihilistic comprehension of history as a determining factor for this Balkan war is typically linked to the year 1389 and the Battle of Kosovo and/or World War II. Yet empirical research in ethnic relations in Croatia and Bosnia-Herzegovina carried out in 1986 and 1989 reveals that ethnic distance and prejudice in these lands were considerably less than in many other multiethnic European nations. Ethnic relations in what used to be Yugoslavia deteriorated suddenly due to the nationalistic political and war propaganda that emanated from Belgrade, Knin, and Pale.

The most striking contradiction in the labeling of the causes of the war is that the most often-used labels ("civil war," "nationalism," "ethnic hatred," "the return of history," and so forth) suggest chaos but fail to explain the glaring fact that a rationally planned Greater Serbia has emerged from the ruins of the war. As late as 1995, many commentators still fail to see that Milošević's aims have been to conquer territory cleansed of "impure" non-Serbs, and that Milošević is more than a nationalist bent on preserving power.

WHEN?: LABELING THE STARTING POINT OF THE WAR EVENTS

It is important to determine when "nameless wars" began.[10] Most authors write as if it began *in April of 1992,* when Serbian shells slammed into a Holiday Inn in Sarajevo. A relatively few authors point to *June of 1991,* when Yugoslav Army Forces attacked both Slovenia and Croatia. Branka Magaš argues that the war actually began with Serbian suppression of the Kosovars in Kosovo *in 1989*.[11]

I suggest that the war began latently in Slobodan Milošević's nationalist-socialistic movement and seizure of power in 1986 and 1987.

WHO?: LABELING THE KEY ACTORS AND ASSESSING RESPONSIBILITY

The CIA's report leaked to the *New York Times* offers the well-known "formula" 90:10 for the distribution of responsibility for crimes against humanity (genocide) and asserts that *"Serbs carried out at least 90% of the ethnic cleansing."*[12] But this finding raises the question of responsibility for the war crimes and the war overall. The report addresses political responsibility for the war crimes as well: *"More significantly the systematic nature of the Serbian actions strongly suggests that Pale and perhaps Belgrade exercised a carefully veiled role in the purposeful destruction and dispersal of non-Serb populations"*.[13]

The problem of allocating personal responsibility as well as the more controversial notion of collective responsibility will be resolved in the years and decades to come in theoretical discourse and in international war crimes tribunals. Nevertheless, up to now, many intellectuals, diplomats, and journalists use the labeling method in approaching the issues of responsibility. Thus, former U.S. secretary of state Lawrence Eagleburger some years ago labeled Slobodan Milošević, Radovan Karadžić, Ratko Mladić, and some other Serb leaders as suspected war criminals.

In a recent text, the last United States ambassador to the former Yugoslavia Warren Zimmermann[14] performs an anatomy of the conflict and concludes that it stems completely from nationalism[15] and the *personal characteristics* of the leading politicians in former Yugoslavia.

For Zimmermann, Slobodan Milošević is *"a man of extraordinary coldness"* and a man *"driven by power,"* while Franjo Tudjman is *"obsessed by nationalism."* The real bad guy and incarnation of evil is Radovan Karadžić: *"the architect of massacres . . . ethnic cleansing . . . a monster from another generation, Heinrich Himmler."*[16]

This reductionistic model of labeling is interesting because the "lost (instead of the 'last') ambassador" was the source of information that in 1990–92 formed United States foreign policy toward the lands that made up the former Yugoslavia.

Especially interesting is the honesty with which the lost ambassador rationalizes what is arguably the largest foreign policy and diplomatic mistake committed by the U.S. State Department in this century: "Eagleburger and I agreed that in my introductory calls in Belgrade and the republican capitals, I would deliver a new message: *Yugoslavia no longer enjoyed the geopolitical importance* that the United States had given it during the Cold War".[17]

The Yugoslavia to which Zimmermann refers represents less a state than a corridor, a geopolitical corridor. And this is where the error lies: Even though the fall of Communism and the creation of democratic and free-market institutions were the most important strategic interests of the United States and all of Western civilization, at the moment of the possible "democratic revolution" in the Balkans, Zimmermann openly proclaimed that this corridor no longer had any geopolitical interest for the United States. In terms of the power relations in the former Yugoslavia, Slobodan Milošević and the leadership of the Yugoslav People's Army (JNA) understood this message in only one way: You can do whatever you want!

Zimmermann is by no means the only one to evaluate and label the key individual and collective players in the wars in Croatia and Bosnia. The labels attached to them by journalists, diplomats, UN officials, researchers, and so on have often changed over the long duration of the wars according to changes in the situation, diverse interests of those doing the labeling, and changes in the behavior of such individuals and groups.

The importance of the labels depends on the importance and influence of the individual or organization applying them. For example, when the chief prosecutor of the War Crimes Tribunal in The Hague describes an individual as a war criminal, it seems rather different from when an obscure writer uses the same label.

The labels applied to the key individuals—Milošević, Karadžić, Mladić, Tudjman, Alija Izetbegović—have sometimes depended on the situation, on the battle lines, and on the intentions of the international community to direct the conflict. Brief attempts to create the myth or fiction of the "reasonable Karadžić" (as in the United States during the Carter peace mission) or the "good Milošević" or "Milošević the peacemaker" must be viewed in that context.

Another phenomenon connected with individual and collective labeling is *fascination with evil* or *obsession with victors*. Western culture in general and American culture in particular adore victors and have an ambivalent attitude toward evil and its protagonists. Sometimes even murder suspects (the O. J. Simpson and Charles Manson cases are good illustrations) can become television stars and hence the objects of ambivalent feelings of love and hate, contempt and admiration, of a need to destroy and a need to protect (in the name of "Christian" charity).

Perhaps the best example of fascination with evil and ambivalent attitudes toward it is an article on Ratko Mladić by *New York Times* journalist David Binder entitled "Pariah as Patriot."[18] The article begins thus: "He is a child of war and now a man of war. His eyes are a piercing light blue, his hair close cropped and steel grey, his face as wide as a shovel. Slated at a conference table, Gen. Ratko Mladić talks in a husky baritone about the war in Bosnia and Herzegovina that has left several hundred thousand dead or missing and driven a million people from their homes."[19]

Whoever reads such *poetic lines* will conclude that the journalist wants to present his readers with some kind of film star rather than a notorious war criminal and a key perpetrator of the second largest act of genocide in Europe (that in Croatia and Bosnia). The entire article is imbued with such dualism and the ambivalent attitude of the journalist toward someone who on one side personifies evil and crime but on the other personifies military strength and victory.

This account is an almost ideal example of American "civil religion" and its ambivalent attitude toward the Billy-the-Kid–type Bosnian-Balkan hero-bandits such as Radovan Karadžić, Ratko Mladić, Željko "Arkan" Ražnjatović, and Slobodan Milošević.

The stories about them, as well as the photographs and caricatures that are offered to the American public, regularly repeat the stereotypic and culturally ambivalent dichotomies: *criminal and hero, mountain bandit and mythical avenger, the rebel barbarian who "romantically" rejects European and Western values, customs, and rules of behavior and the military victor and commander who shares the risks and cares of each and every one of his soldiers.*

All in all, the *mass perception* of such criminals often approaches the stereotype of the Spanish commander in the last scene of the legendary film *The Alamo,* who — after breaking down all the defenses with overwhelming force and killing every one of the defenders — in a "gentlemanly" manner allows a woman and child to leave the scene of the battle.

Such a stereotype is often carried over, consciously or unconsciously, into illustrations. An illustration in *Time,* depicting Ratko Mladić manneristically inserted into the tableau of Picasso's "Quernica," is typical in this respect. For the majority of readers, the composition of the illustration itself, linking Ratko Mladić with the victim town and with the cultural and artistic symbol of suffering and artistic dignity (Pablo Picasso), transfers part of the positive image onto Ratko Mladić.

The notion that the "Prince of Darkness" is nothing but a fallen angel is deeply woven into the very foundations of Western civilization. The idea that every person and the whole world is an arena for the constant conflict between Satan and God is reinforced by the general ambivalence of every person toward the "Princes of Darkness."

Also in that fact is a paradox: if we compare the labels applied to the leaders of the victims (Tudjman and Izetbegović) with those of the leaders of the aggression (Milošević, Mladić, Karadžić, Milan Martić, Arkan, and so forth), that ambivalence becomes even more visible.

We present some of the main labels arranged into four groups according to the criteria of their *likely reception in Western political culture:* positive, neutral, negative, and criminalizing (demonic); and arrive at table 1.

TABLE 1.
Typical labels applied to key players in the conflicts in Croatia and Bosnia and Herzegovina

Player	Positive	Neutral	Negative	Demonic
Franjo Tudjman	Anti-Fascist Political prisoner, Dissident, Rational president, Strongman	Croatian president, Tito's general, Former Communist	Nationalist, Croatian nationalist, Hard-liner, Nationalist leader, Populist leader	Anti-Semite, Anti-Zionist, Dictator, Butcher's apprentice, Despot
Slobodan Milošević	Cunning statesman, Strongman of the Balkans, Serbian czar, Peacemaker, Capable politician	Serbian leader, Serbian president, Former Communist, Communist bureaucrat, Cynic, Man of extreme reserve	Dictator, Nationalist	Butcher of the Balkans, War criminal, Nazi, Nazi-like leader, Balkan Hitler
Radovan Karadžić	Leader of Bosnian Serbs, Serb leader, Poet, Doctor, Psychiatrist, Politician	Psychiatrist in asylum, Self-styled leader	Barbarian, Nationalist	War criminal, Butcher of the Balkans, Monster, Bosnian butcher, Happy Bosnian cutthroat

TABLE I. CONT.

Player	Positive	Neutral	Negative	Demonic
Ratko Mladić	Serbian Napoleon, Victorious general, Gentleman officer, Strategic genius, War commander, Military genius	Serbian general, Leader of Serbian army, Mountain warrior	Nationalist general	War criminal, Commander of ethnic cleansing, Murderer of Sarajevo
Alija Izetbegović	Calm president	Bosnian president, Bosnian leader	Opponent of peace	Muslim fundamentalist, Warmonger, Leader of Jihad, Mujahadin

Although it is difficult to draw up any kind of hierarchy of negative or demonic labels and measure their influence on the attitudes of the various people with political and diplomatic power in Western countries and the international community, it is beyond doubt that the *labels of potential war criminals* (as applied to Radovan Karadžić, Ratko Mladić, Željko "Arkan" Ražnjatović, and others) are the *most serious.* However, the label *anti-Semite* (*anti-Zionist*), for which the Croatian president is unique, is no less serious.

It could be easily shown that such demonic labels have cost the Croatian people and state much, since in Western media and diplomatic circles they have often neutralized the horrific crimes committed by Serbs in Croatia and Bosnia.

The labels attached to collective players — Croats, Bosnian Muslims, and Serbs — also follow the logic of the CIA "formula." The responsibility and guilt of the "Chetniks" (Serbs), "Ustashe" (Croats), and "Mujahadin" (Bosnian Muslims) is based on the following logic: the Croats are responsible for what happened during World War II and for some of the crimes in Bosnia; the Bosnians could be responsible for establishing a theocratic state and culture; the Serbs are responsible for what has happened in the last four to five years.

AN APPROPRIATE LABELING MODEL

An appropriate labeling model for use by theoretical and international-legal "diagnosticians" of the causes, origins, character, and other elements of the post-Communist wars in Slovenia, Croatia, and Bosnia-Herzegovina must take into account the full range of "symptoms" and "signs" of illness, even historical, contextual, and cultural factors.

There is no village, city, or land in which ethnic relations among various races, religious, linguistic, and cultural groups are ideal, harmonious, or without conflict. For this reason it must be said that even in the Balkans it is not a question of either "conflict of coexistence" or "coexistence of conflicts."

The conflicts and wars in the Balkans did not occur because of any "ghosts" or inherent weakness in the peoples who live there but because of global and/or totalitarian ideologies and movements that contaminated their thinking and passions: colonialism and its ending (the fall of the Ottoman and Austro-Hungarian Empires), Fascism and its ending (genocidal crimes committed by Croats as well as Serbs during World War II), Communism and its fall (today's wars and war crimes).

Post-Communist conflicts and wars have emerged in a completely concrete historical context and owing to completely concrete factors: the fall of Communism, the creation of a nationalist-socialist movement in Serbia, the yearning of nations for self-determination and freedom,[20] and the characteristics of people who had and continue to hold leading roles in the conflicts (the main ones being Milan Kucan in Slovenia, Franjo Tudjman in Croatia, Alija Izetbegović in Bosnia-Herzegovina, Slobodan Milošević and Radovan Karadžić in Serbia, and Kiro Gligorov in Macedonia).

Of course history, religion, and culture play roles in these conflicts, but they are secondary to the roles played by ideologies and movements that brought forth a cycle of evil.

All in all, it can be shown that in the *Western part of the former Yugoslavia* in the period from 1990 to 1995 there have been *three wars,* which to a certain extent differ according to their structural characteristics, aims, and durations. Following the logic of the labeling theory, the basic characteristics of the three wars are shown in table 2.

TABLE 2.

Label	Slovenian war	Croatian war	Bosnian war
"Civil War"	5%	10%	20%
"Serbian aggression"	95%	80%	40%
"Genocide"*	0%	10%	40%**

*so-called ethnic cleansing
**90% of the crimes have been committed by Serbs and 10% by Croats and Bosnians

In our labeling of the basic characteristics of the wars in Slovenia, Croatia, and Bosnia-Herzegovina we have taken into account the following definitions of "genocide" and "crimes against humanity":

> ... genocide means any of the following acts commited with intent to destroy, *in whole or in part,* a national, ethnic, racial, or religious group, as such: (a) Killing members of the group; (b) Causing serious bodily or mental harm to member of the group; (c) Deliberately inflicting on the group conditions of life calculated to bring about its physical destruction in whole or in part; (d) Imposing measures intended to prevent births within the group; (e) Forcible transfering children of the group to another group. (Source: Article II, The United Nations Convention of Prevention and Punishment of the Crime of Genocide [Resolution 260A, III, December 9, 1948])

> There are many different types of abuses which qualify as crimes against humanity. The following acts are defined as crimes against humanity: (1) murder and extermination; (2) enslavement and forced labor; (3) deportation outside of the country; (4) imprisonment without due process of law; (5) torture; (6) rape; (7) "inhu-

man acts," including: a) medical experimentation; b) mutilation; c) food deprivation; d) sterilization; e) violation of cadavers; f) other serious mental or physical harm; (8) persecution, including: a) removal of children from school; b) forced wearing of distinctive clothing; c) closure of religious institutions; d) banning of religious leaders; (9) property crimes, including: a) destruction and plunder of private property (e.g., homes, cars); b) destruction and plunder of cultural property (e.g., mosques, holy books) (source: Crimes Against Humanity: http://www.pactok.net.au/docs/dccam/hcrimes.htm)

Notes

1. Many authors of books on the breakup of Yugoslavia were enamored with the former Yugoslavia and its politics, as were many diplomats (for example, James Baker, Lawrence Eagleburger, and Warren Zimmermann) who believed in Yugo-State formula.
2. I derive the notion of intellectual anomie from Émile Durkheim's writings on anomie applied to intellectuals. Thus, in *Division of Labor in Society* (New York: The Free Press, 1893), p. 304, Durkheim writes: "There are hardly any disciplines that harmonize the efforts of different sciences toward a common goal. This is especially true of the moral and social sciences, for the mathematical, physical, chemical and even biological sciences do not seem to such an extent foreign to one another. But the jurist, the psychologist, the anthropologist, the economist, the statistician, the linguist, the historian — all these go about their investigations as if the various orders of facts that they are studying formed so many independent worlds . . . They afford the spectacle of an aggregate of disconnected parts that fail to co-operate with one another . . . It is because they are in a state of anomie." Durkheim's description readily applies to the investigations of various war watchers in the Balkans.
3. Christopher Bennett, *Yugoslavia's Bloody Collapse: Causes, Course and Consequences* (New York: New York University Press, 1994); Norman Cigar, *Genocide in Bosnia: The Policy of "Ethnic Cleansing"* (College Station: Texas A&M University Press, 1995); Thomas Cushman and Stjepan G. Meštrović, eds., *This Time We Knew* (New York: New York University Press, 1996); Misha Glenny, *Fall of Yugoslavia: The Third Balkan War* (New York: Penguin, 1994); Paul Garde, *Vie et mort de la Yugoslavie* (Paris: Librairie Artheme Fayard, 1992); Roy Gutman, *Witness to Genocide* (New York: Macmillan, 1993); Režac Hukanovič, *The Tenth Circle of Hell* (New York: Basic Books, 1996); Robert Kaplan, *Balkan Ghosts: A Journey Through History* (New York: St. Martin's Press, 1993); Branka Magaš, *The Destruction of Yugoslavia: Tracing the Break-up, 1980–92* (London: Verso, 1993); Stjepan Meštrović, ed., *Genocide After Emotions* (London: Routledge, 1996); David Owen, *Balkan Odyssey*

(New York: Brothers Jovanović, 1995); David Rieff, *Slaughterhouse: Bosnia and the Failure of the West* (New York: Simon and Schuster, 1995); Michael A. Sells, *The Bridge Betrayed: Religion and Genocide in Bosnia* (Berkeley: University of California Press, 1996); George Stamkoski and Ben Cohen, eds., *With No Peace To Keep — United Nations Peacekeeping and the War in the Former Yugoslavia* (London: Grainpress, 1995); Laura Silber and Allan Little, eds., *Yugoslavia: Death of a Nation* (New York: TV Books, 1995); Alexandra Stiglmayer, ed., *Mass Rape: The War against Women in Bosnia-Herzegovina* (Lincoln: University of Nebraska Press, 1994); Mark Thomson, *A Paper House: The Ending of Yugoslavia* (New York: Pantheon Books, 1992); Jasminka Udovački and James Ridgeway, *Yugoslavia's Ethnic Nightmare: The Inside Story of Europe's Unfolding Ordeal* (New York: Lawrence Hill Books, 1995); Edward Vulliamy, *Seasons in Hell: Understanding Bosnia's War* (New York: St. Martin's Press, 1994); Susanne Woodward, *Balkan Tragedy: Chaos and Dissolution after the Cold War* (Washington, D.C.: Brookings Institution, 1995); Warren Zimmermann, *Origins of a Catastrophe: Yugoslavia and Its Destroyers — America's Last Ambassador Tells What Happened and Why* (New York: Times Books & Random House, 1996).

4. Samuel Huntington, "The Clash of Civilizations?" *Foreign Affairs* 72 (1993): 21–49.
5. *New York Times,* May 25, 1993.
6. *New York Times,* September 29, 1992.
7. Irving L. Horowitz, *Taking Lives: Genocide and State Power* (New Brunswick, N.J.: Transaction Publishers, 1997).
8. Mark Almond, *Europe's Backyard War: The Wars in the Balkans* (London: Heinmann, 1994).
9. Cigar, *Genocide in Bosnia.*
10. Meštrović, ed., *Genocide After Emotions.*
11. Magaš, *The Destruction of Yugoslavia.*
12. *New York Times,* Mar. 9, 1995, p. A1.
13. *Wall Street Journal,* Mar. 13, 1995.
14. Warren Zimmermann, "The Last Ambassador: A Memoir of the Collapse of Yugoslavia," *Foreign Affairs* 74 (March–April, 1995): 2–20.
15. "Nationalism is by nature uncivil, antidemocratic and separatist because it empowers one ethnic group over all others." Ibid., 7.
16. Ibid., 18.
17. Ibid., 2.
18. The term "pariah" comes from India and means renegade, outcast, one who does not belong to any of the castes.
19. *New York Times Magazine,* Sept. 4, 1994, p. 26.
20. Daniel P. Moynihan, *Pandaemonium: Ethnicity in International Politics* (Oxford: Oxford University Press, 1993).

CHAPTER SIX

Idle Curiosity and the Production of Useless Knowledge:
Academic Responses to Genocide
BRAD K. BLITZ

In the introduction to this book, Stjepan Meštrović asks how Westerners, "steeped in a tradition derived from the Enlightenment, [can] make sense of the West's responses" to genocide in Bosnia. This chapter addresses this question by examining how the American university, the most visible descendent of the Enlightenment, and its intellectual cousins off campus reacted to this challenge. Developing Thorstein Veblen's notions of leisure and idle curiosity, I consider the ambivalent role of the university as a source of ideas, struggling to maintain its autonomy, and as an institution corrupted by encroaching capitalist values. Contrary to Veblen's ideal, I argue that in the face of an all-pervasive market capitalism, the academy can no longer present itself as a source of learning divorced from the "real" world. Yet, rather than reassert a connection between these two spheres, the forces of market capitalism are actually encouraging a powerful drive away from the ideal, toward what sociologist David Riesman terms "other-directedness."

This phenomenon describes a situation in which the academy is increasingly unsure of its values and the university in particular produces and disseminates knowledge uncritically. It is at odds with Veblen's demands for academic "disinterest" since genuine objectivity assumes a sense of openness and pluralism as opposed to retreat and deflection. Focusing on illustrations taken from the media and a study of the academic practices at select universities, I argue that the conflict between the ideal of objectivity and the trend toward disengagement is already taking its toll on the nature of scientific inquiry. In this setting, the organization of knowledge — especially in the social sciences — is often far from systematic. Nowhere is this more evident than in the academic record on contemporary moral and political issues such as genocide. In this context, Veblen's discussion of the university, the intellectual leisure class, and his notion of "idle curiosity" therefore takes on new significance.

Veblen and the Production of Useless Knowledge

In 1916, Thorstein Veblen published *The Higher Learning in America*. This study developed his earlier thoughts on leisure, defined as the abstention from productive work, and juxtaposed two analytical concepts that would have significant bearing on the late–twentieth-century academy: "idle curiosity" and the "instinct of workmanship." Idleness or nonproductivity distinguished academic learning from "real work," which was measured in economic terms. The university in particular had a unique status in Veblen's order. It was outside the economic sphere and hence was considered to be the most protected site of knowledge production. This protection ensured that the university operated on the basis of "idle curiosity," which he described as a "disinterested proclivity to gain a knowledge of things and to reduce this knowledge to a comprehensible system."[1]

In the barbarian cultures that Veblen discussed, in which war and ritual were considered honorable characteristics, labor became "irksome." Leisure or idleness gained a sense of prestige, as it was removed from industrial work. Yet, even if it was truly divorced from labor, in order for idleness to carry any sense of esteem, it had to be put on display. Ostentation was thus a key function of leisure; and the classes that engaged in idle pursuits, such as academics, therefore had to be "conspicuously exempt" from all useful employment.[2]

The form whereby Veblen contrasts intellectual inquiry and productive work reflects a common and ambiguous theme in Veblen's order. Just as Veblen opposed industry with intellect, work with leisure, his writings on bankers, brokers, and lawyers whose pecuniary habits he disliked also suggest a particularly idiosyncratic dualism. In essence, Veblen's critique rests on the existence of many competing worlds, each one defined by a single mission. In Veblen's order, universities should limit their mission to conducting research while businesses should only make money.[3]

Veblen and the Market-Driven University

Although Veblen's studies might be dismissed as simple satire,[4] and with the exception of David Riesman and C. Wright Mills, few contemporary social theorists have paid much attention to his writings, his concerns are nonetheless grounded. In particular, his discussion of the production of knowledge, academic exemption, and the relationship between intellectual centers and the external world could not be more relevant today. In an age of "live genocide" and nightly news from Grozny, the American academy is confronted with a major challenge as it faces Veblen's concerns. These are notably the attempt to separate the intellectual realm from the "real world" and the demands that academia should be a "disinterested" party in the collection of knowledge as well as a systematic organizer of its findings.

In Veblen's account, the university was the true ivory tower. It was a source of ideas and a font from which knowledge was produced. At the time of his writing, his fear that the university would be corrupted by external influences was, however, limited to the question of direct ownership. Veblen was largely concerned about the influence and conditions that the Rockefellers, Carnegies, Mellons, and Vanderbilts brought to their universities. The situation today is far more complex. The American academy in the late twentieth century no longer exits independently in a separate sphere. Rather, the ivory tower coexists with the market.

In his book, *Higher Learning,* former Harvard University president Derek Bok explicitly argues that the university relies on the marketplace and bears all the traits of a contaminated institution — a fallen ivory tower. He cites the university's emphasis on competition and the influence of groups of constituents and notes the contradiction in values, while still opting for the market-driven system.

> The very terms seem to clash with cherished notions of learning and discovery. Whatever the language used, however, the characteristics themselves have much to recommend them as sources of motivation for those who staff educational institutions. Scientists, scholars, and university presidents are all undoubtedly animated by a desire to help their students and to contribute to learning. Still, competition provides a powerful supplement that pushes professors and administrators to perform better in the eyes of those whose opinions matter, be they students, faculty, alumni, scientific review panels or other peer groups that evaluate scholarly quality, At the very least, these influences make a university administration continuously responsive to the needs of the groups it serves.[5]

In fairness, Bok's recommendation is the result of a realization that American universities simply must "react to outside pressures if they are to compete for faculty, students, and funding."[6] These are survival tactics.

Today, however, tracing the overlap, defining points of contact and differentiation within this market-driven system is an extremely difficult task. The emulation of market practices within the university—for example, the introduction of "user fees," the institution of achievement based criteria, and the elevation of production in the form of public research over teaching that is relegated to the level of "internal consumption"—makes it particularly challenging to identify the specific values that once defined the ivory tower. Within the university, the forces of marketization are easier to detect. The rise in tuition fees; the use of approved academic "credit" as a means of determining if intellectual prerequisites have been met; the fragmentation of university services, including membership to unions and associations that now operate on a pay-to-use basis, are just some of the most obvious examples. Research by Zemsky, Massy, and Wilger on the "academic ratchet effect" further illustrates this trend: the gulf between research and teaching expands as faculty are encouraged to take on more profitable jobs in their nonteaching hours.[7]

Not only does the ratcht effect practice further elevate research over teaching, but, as Massy, Wilger, and Zemsky argue, it actually drives the forces of marketization within the university since it also grants them greater status. The value of "profit" is therefore privileged over the value of "pure learning," making the ideal of the ivory tower even more remote.

Yet, while the academy is undeniably touched by the economic sphere, its "idle" influence now extends well beyond its borders. Once obscure subjects such as the themes of multiculturalism and identity politics, the schools of poststructuralism, and in particular the deconstructionist writings of Michel Foucault and Jacques Derrida are now regularly discussed outside the ivory tower. Academic journals, which are considered to be the entry point for young scholars into this intellectual community, now include much journalistic research and commentary in addition to traditional university-based studies.

The role of the university in the late twentieth century is therefore profoundly ambivalent. It straddles the economic world that Veblen described, carving out a role as a producer, while still militating for its own identity as an intellectual center and source of ideas. The influence of the market is pervasive, yet there is a degree of cultural spillover from the university sector. What unites the "idle-university" and the "market-university" is more notable. Within the corrupted academic sphere, the values associated with the world of production have gained entry into both the university's cultural and material identities. Within one site, the drive to maximize profit, as illustrated in new funding mechanisms such as user fees and the kind of management practices that enable large research universities to be compared with Fortune 500 firms, coincides with another example of a radical change in the university's identity. This is nothing less than a new ethic of academic retreat. While one can cite external sources that may have influenced this trend, the evolution toward academic retreat or what Riesman describes as other-directedness, stands in sharp contrast to Veblen's requirement that scientific inquiry should promote a sense of curiosity and open the way to the acquisition of knowledge.

Disinterest and the Pretense of Objectivity

In *The Lonely Crowd*,[8] David Riesman argues that there are three types of character and society. These are "traditional-directedness," "inner-directedness," and "other-directedness." The first category describes holistic societies while the second refers to early Protestant communities in which the individual is considered the primary value. The notion of other-directedness, however, is exclusively modern and is an end product of mass industrialization. The other-directed person relies on forces outside for validation and is less discriminating in his/her moral judgments. In the context of the academy, intellectual other-directedness, which may be defined by the university's reliance on the external world as both sponsor and sanctioner, is at odds with Veblen's prescription. For Veblen, the university's foundation is built on strong defining values.

In Veblen's model, disinterest was supposed to protect the university, within its own sphere. It was a positive value. In the context of the modern university, Veblen's notion of detachment, though no longer applicable, is still prescribed in the social sciences under the banner of objectivity. Yet, objectivity brings with it other requirements—not least the demand for correspondence as a basis for truth and evaluation. This presents a number of problems.

First, the contamination of the university's sphere of influence introduces a new twist, undermining Veblen's logic. If the larger academic environment must coexist within a market system and with its conflicting values, then the idea of detachment no longer stands. In contrast to Veblen's ivory tower, the American university and the academy in general is part of the world it observes. As postmodernists insist, the demand for objectivity immediately solicits a response or recognition from the point of the observer.

Although this fact is recorded in the proliferation of new journals on postmodernism, cultural studies, and undergraduate courses that attempt to reflect the student populace (for example, ethnic studies, multiculturalism, women's studies), as Allan Bloom argues, the bigger picture is often missed inside the academic arena. He maintains that the sense of connection rooting the scientific observer, professor, or student to the world on observation is frequently twisted as "objective" knowledge is sought within a context of cultural relativism. In effect, the goal of objectivity is eliminated and replaced by a simplistic idea of personal interpretation. "Openness used to be the virtue that permitted us to seek the good by using reason. It now means accepting everything and denying reason's power. The unrestrained and thoughtless pursuit of openness, without recognizing the political, social or cultural problem of openness as the goal of nature, has rendered openness meaningless. Cultural relativism destroys both one's own and the good."[9]

Yet, there is another side to this that is not limited to the university sector but applies to academic inquiry as a whole. In the larger context, one may talk about a pervasive mood of "academic other-directedness." By academic other-directedness, I am suggesting that on matters relating to the social sciences, the academy has become increasingly self-referential and, in short, less curious. The notion of correspondence, so essential to the ideal of objective investigation, is frequently discarded. The search for "truth" becomes not only a subjective act but an extremely selective one. Hence, rather than foster a sincere pluralism that encourages multiplicity and exploration, in a number of cases the current academic mood is taking us down a different path. Let me offer some examples.

In a recent issue of the journal *Political Theory*, Jeffrey C. Isaac, a professor at the University of Indiana at Bloomington, argued that his fellow academics had ignored the significance of the collapse of Communism.[10] Having surveyed *Political Theory, Polity,* the *American Political Science Review, Philosophy and Public Affairs,* and *Ethics,* Isaac found that "in the four years following the revolutions of 1989, political theorists published a total of 384 articles, of which a mere 2—roughly one-half of one percent—dealt with the dramatic current events of earth shattering importance."[11] Isaac recognized that political scientists, especially comparativists, had written on these issues but insisted that "the principal journals in the field, the main origins of scholarship and intellectual exchange, have been silent. When academic political theorists have written scholarly papers or made presentations at scholarly conferences, they have consistently avoided dealing with the revolutions of 1989 and their implications."[12] He then exposed his colleagues. "This avoidance strikes me as a shocking indictment of academic political theory. How can it be? How can an inquiry that claims to be the heir of Plato, Machiavelli, Tocqueville, and Marx, thinkers profoundly caught up in the events of their day, be so oblivious to what is going on around it?"[13]

These questions later prompted a response. *Political Theory* invited a number of academics to respond to Isaac's accusations that "political theory fiddles while the fire of freedom spreads and perhaps the world burns."[14] In Veblen's terms, the issues raised by Isaac were particularly important. He acknowledged that this corner of academia remained productive — articles were being written, conferences were taking place, "knowledge" was being produced — but there was a demonstrated lack of curiosity concerning the larger world outside.

In the introduction to his book, *The Balkanization of the West*, Stjepan Meštrović launched a similar accusation against his colleagues in the American Sociological Association. Meštrović published the response he received from the president-elect of the American Sociological Association regarding his suggestion to hold a session on the war in the Balkans and its significance for social scientists. "Thank you for your January 23 letter suggesting a session on Sociological Perspectives on the Balkan War of 1991–93 for the American Soc. Assoc. meetings in Los Angeles, August 5–9, 1994. The Program Committee has planned several thematic sessions which, while they do not focus exclusively on the Balkan War, take up issues which are highlighted by it. You may want to consider submitting a paper to these sessions."[15] The response that Meštrović received was significant in that it confirmed that sociologists were equally indifferent to the Balkans as political theorists were to the changes in Eastern Europe and the former Soviet Union.

Isaac's research was later picked up by Russell Jacoby, writing in the *Chronicle of Higher Education*. In an article entitled "America's Professoriate: Politicized, Yet Apolitical," Jacoby maintained that the sort of political engagement that once attracted members of the academy to study social and international affairs had been killed off. He cited specifically moral cases such as the struggle against fascism. Jacoby concluded that this disenfranchisement was the result of major ideological shifts: the traditional area of politics had grown to such an extent that everything could be classed as "political." This trend of inclusiveness makes discriminatory inquiry impossible, Jacoby insisted. "The difficulty is that when everything is political, nothing is; when everything is political nothing assumes more significance than anything else." The situation that Jacoby discusses — the removal of traditional boundaries once considered as absolute — mirrors Bloom's discussion of the student body. Both of these accounts present an indictment of the university system and intellectual milieu in general.

In effect, many of the great challenges to international security that were recorded in daily news reports were simply ignored by the academy and the intellectual scene off campus. Writing in the *Nation* in December, 1995, Susan Sontag made this point explicitly. American intellectuals were ostensibly disinterested in the fate of Bosnia and its people. Four months later, she would say the same thing publicly of Chechnya. Charles Maynes, editor of *Foreign Policy*, offered his own assessment for intellectual disinterest. "In any age intellectuals may perform one of two functions. They may work to open people's eyes to the way things ought to be, or they may push people to understand things the way they are. The former tend to present themselves as philosophers and visionaries. The latter often assume the role of sociologists or political scientists. The former have a bias toward acceptance."[16]

Social scientists for Maynes are therefore conservative creatures who are able to observe, interpret, and describe the world as it is. Nonvisionary intellectuals—sociologists and political scientists—are thus privileged. They can see the world while the others can only create visions of it. Reality is theirs.

Does Maynes's characterization explain the deep-seated indifference, recorded by Sontag? Does it explain the desire to bracket off certain real world events and exclude them from investigation, as witnessed by Isaac and Meštrović? Robert Lieber, professor of government at Georgetown University, maintains that among a major group of social scientists—the hard-line realists—it does. He argues that realists have a worldview that forces them to look beyond these transformations. "In essence, neither the passing of the Cold War, as momentous a development as that has been, nor the strengths or weaknesses of specific variants of realism . . . should distract attention from the essential characteristics of international relations and the realist appreciation to which these give rise."[17]

Lieber's statement has powerful implications. It takes the form of a prescriptive rule: realists should overlook the passing of the Cold War era. The new political alignments outside the former bipolar system are in some way "inessential" to understanding the nature of international relations. And yet, when one asks how realists account for these alterations in the international power system, by citing the failure to stop the genocides in Bosnia, Rwanda, and Burundi, the responses are far from uniform. It is here that objectivity and the presentation of scientific knowledge takes a beating.

The Attack on Scientific Presentation

Since the Gulf War of 1991, there has been little serious attempt to assemble a coherent theory of international relations that takes account of the major transformations in world power. Francis Fukuyama and Samuel Huntington offered two theses: the first placed great emphasis on the unstoppable role of capitalism; the second focused on culture and "civilization" as a source of conflict. While Fukuyama's essay was premature and failed to recognize the possibility of state resistance, as we witness in the rebirth of Communism and chauvinism in Poland, Slovakia, and Russia, for example, Huntington's was speculative and short on evidence. Huntington's discussion of "civilizations" and "cultural fault lines" introduced an essentialist logic that challenged many of the premises of a multiethnic order and, in so doing, converted the sociological construct of "tribalism" into an analytical tool of conflict resolution, or rather nonresolution.

While Fukuyama and Huntington offered theses of their own, several scholars writing on the international system after the Cold War struggled with the basic skills required for sociological analysis. Studies on the Bosnian war published in journals, newspapers, and textbooks suggested that, in fact, the mood of academic other-directedness and conceit was an accurate description of the intellectual situation both on and off campus. Sound analysis that would require a moral response was frequently neglected. Even staunch realists such as University of Chicago professor John Mearsheimer, who would advocate ethnic partition and offer their own rationalizations for the conflict as a war ignited by ethnic hatreds rather than political demagoguery, would admit that there was a moral dimension to the war and that human rights abuses should occupy some part of the political discussion, however ancillary that might be.[18] Instead, we found weak substitutions that challenged the very principles of academic inquiry.

An excellent illustration of this retreat from scientific inquiry is found in Maynes's article in *Foreign Policy,* cited above. Maynes's essay is full of the traits that disinterested academics use to undermine a moral response. These include argument from false premises, historical revisionism, and moral equivalence. Maynes chose a maximalist definition of the term "ethnic cleansing" to describe what he saw in Bosnia. The debate was reset, though his premises remained highly questionable. He began by denying the essential characteristics of the genocide and the fact that Bosnia was the site of the most serious war crimes since World War II. For Maynes, the "ethnic cleansing" amounted to little more than terrorism and population transfer. "Moreover, it is regrettably not true that, as often stated, the crimes committed in the former Yugoslavia are the first example since World War II of ethnic cleansing in Europe."[19]

There is also a problem of proportionality implicit in his analysis: one bombing attack in Istanbul is compared with the hundreds of thousands of shells launched against the people of Bosnia in dozens of cities. "In the mid-1950s, Turkish authorities allowed mobs incited by a bombing attack on the Turkish consulate in Thessaloniki to drive more than 100,000 Greeks from Istanbul."[20]

Elsewhere, established prejudices indicated in a refusal to treat Bosnia as an objective case of a victim state were concealed behind well-developed rationalizations in public academic statements. These rationalizations took the form of factual inaccuracy and revisionism. In 1993, for example forty-three Stanford faculty signed a petition against the calls to strike Serbian weapons sites and the lifting of the arms embargo against the Sarajevo government. The advertisement was placed by the "Balkan Peace Committee" and was addressed to President Bill Clinton. At the time, even though it was well known that Bosnia was 70 percent occupied by Serb troops and subject to an international arms embargo, the protesting academics argued that no side had "a monopoly on either atrocities or suffering in the war." Three years later, Maynes would use such an argument of moral equivalence to explain his position. "The end of the Cold War has lifted the blanket that was smothering some ethnic conflicts," he suggests. Who or what was lifting the blanket was actually much harder to point to. Instead, he uses questionable data to make his case. "But we have not seen the kind of sustained carnage in recent years that our grandparents and parents did, press hyperbole not withstanding. The war in Bosnia is a terrible tragedy, but many casualties appear to be lower than the civil wars in Central America or Lebanon. More than 100,000 died in these wars. It is estimated that roughly 20,000 to 50,000 have died in Bosnia."

From his line of reasoning, the destruction of Bosnia was inevitable but less destructive than actually reported. He maintains that information circulated by the press was exaggerated. Maynes fails to cite reliable sources for the estimated death toll cited and continues with a line of reasoning that amplifies his indifference. As he tries to explain away Western ambivalence, belittling the actual destruction of Bosnia, he implies that what happened to the citizens of Bosnia was no different from previous tragedies. "Contrary to accusations of Muslim countries, in other words, it is not true that the Western states are permitting Muslims in Bosnia to suffer in a manner the West would never tolerate if all Bosnian citizens were Christians. Twice since World War II the West has permitted Orthodox Christians to suffer in a similar manner at the hands of Muslims."[21]

There is no evidence to suggest that Orthodox Christians were sent by rail and tortured in concentration camps, subjected to mass rape, constant shelling, and sniping or mass slaughter as the Bosnians were. Yet, Maynes felt free to publish his opinions. Not only was he factually incorrect, he seemed to excuse the practice of "ethnic cleansing" as an ordinary event. It was sad but tolerable.

On the university campus, similar examples of analytical disarray could be found in an equally moralizing environment. John Mearsheimer, whose advice on American foreign policy would appear on the pages of the *New Republic* and *Christian Science Monitor*, argued that ethnic-based partition was the only solution—even when the Bosnian army was gaining ground and in a position to liberate much of Serb-occupied territory. From 1993 on, Mearsheimer would insist that "partition was inevitable and we should have seen it coming."[22]

The notion of "inevitability" permeated Mearsheimer's logic, and he consistently exhibited an underlying bias to view the world in ethnic categories. In December, 1995, in a *New Republic* article, he would write about the "intractability of nationalism" as the root evil. Commenting on the Dayton Peace Accord, Mearsheimer, writing with M.I.T. professor Stephen Van Evera, revealed that Maynes's "blanket smothering ethnic conflicts in the Cold War" was nothing other than his own disbelief in the possibility of multiethnicity and peaceful coexistence in Bosnia. Unlike Ernest Gellner, who argued that nationalism was a theory of political legitimation, imposed to create a base of ideological homogeneity, Mearsheimer and Van Evera took the issues of agency and political leadership out of the equation and reduced the Bosnian conflict to a competition between incompatible peoples. In this account, America cherished multiethnicity, but in reality the peoples of Bosnia were incapable of it. Writing on the Dayton Peace Accord, the authors argued, "This error reflects a general American tendency to underestimate the power and intractability of nationalism; it reflects, too, a dogmatic American faith that other multiethnic societies can harmonize themselves, that ethnic groups elsewhere can learn to live together as America's immigrants have done."[23]

Yet, if America has a "dogmatic faith" in multiethnicity, the above mentioned academics had a certain dogma of their own in their evaluation of the war as a conflict between ethnic groups. That the Bosnians had a longer history of multiethnicity, which began well before the first Puritan settlers arrived in the New World, was simply ignored. Did the authors want to see ethnic contest? It appears that Mersheimer and Van Evera did. "The U.S. should also accept the need to organize some further transfer of populations," they recommended.[24] Obviously, multiethnicity was a privilege only available to certain societies. Even if Mearsheimer could not be compared to the ultranationalists who insisted on ethnic purity as a right, his early support for the establishment of a de facto state for Serbs, another one for Croats, and another one for Muslims laid bare much of his own commitment to multiethnicity and objective political analysis.

Interestingly, even academics sympathetic to the plight of the Bosnians and who were genuinely outraged at the Serb-sponsored genocide would reveal similar prejudices with regard to the principles of multiethnicity and multiculturalism. For Todd Gitlin, professor at New York University, there was a peculiarly American bias. With much passion, Gitlin wrote in the *Los Angeles Times* of the failure of left-wing intellectuals to engage against contemporary evils as they had done in the Spanish Civil War and the struggle against Fascism in the 1930s.[25] Citing Bosnia as his primary example, Gitlin noted the discrepancies among his friends on the left. Some believed that the Serbian aggressors should be bombed; others thought that the United States had no interest in this issue. For the left, Bosnia was a difficult case and there was no guiding script, he maintained. "Because you were on the left — believed in equality — it did not follow that your position on a given foreign policy issue would be X, Y or Z."[26]

Gitlin's assumption that foreign policy considerations could not also be made in accordance with the principles of equality exposed a genuine shortcoming in the logic of left-wing intellectuals — especially those who once flouted the language of internationalism. Equality was central to Bosnia's struggle as a multinational and multiethnic state. It was the language in which difference was mediated and protected. As communitarian philosophers argued elsewhere,[27] the principle of equality is essential to the concept of an inclusive multiculturalism. As the Serb-sponsored genocide gathered steam and thousands of victims and later as Herzegovinian terror would also threaten citizens in central Bosnia and westward, the ideal of a state where ethnic groups could live intermingled and the reality of an army in which its citizens fought together as *Bosnians* affirmed a basic belief in equality. For Americans, questioning their country's foreign policy in the Balkans, how could this have slipped their minds? In its darkest hour, Bosnia's struggle for survival was expressly about equality and the preservation of its identity as a multiethnic state based on communal existence.

Yet, this reluctance to understand that equality was an ideal that one could advocate for both in a domestic and international context, was lost by many academics who self-identified with the left. In essence, recognition of Bosnia's multiethnic character was at odds with their understanding of a conflict that could not be cast in the language of the Cold War. One example of this bias was produced by Secretary of State William Perry's close colleague and codirector of the Stanford Center for Arms Control, Dr. Robert Hamerton-Kelly. Although Hamerton-Kelly would later teach a course on just wars, his public statements on the issue of Bosnia in 1993 suggested he too was confused about the application of his ethical code and the form of academic inquiry in the social sciences.

Hamerton-Kelly's confusion is illustrated in a letter entitled

"Religion of Victims in Bosnia is Not the Only Reason for Persecution" sent to the *Stanford Daily* in response to a forum on Bosnia organized by Stanford Hillel (May 27, 1993). In it he compared Bosnia to the Sudan and suggested that religion was only one reason for the persecution against Bosnians and that Islam itself was not the only cause. The forum in which Serbian aggression was condemned Hamerton-Kelly dismissed as a "propaganda exercise," which he considered to be "unbalanced." Having recorded this prejudice in print, Hamerton-Kelly admitted that he did not attend the event. Nonetheless, he offered an opinion: "The whole meeting in question causes me concern because it seems to have been a propaganda exercise. I did not attend for that reason. The diplomatic and security issues are complicated, and one would surely have valued a balanced consideration. We surely have enough indignation and horror, what we need now is clear thinking and resolute action."[28] He accused the Jewish students of hypocrisy, noting that Hillel Foundation frequently questioned "one-sided" meetings where only Palestinian speakers were invited. Finally, he suggested that the memory of the Holocaust might have "pushed them from morality to moralizing." He then ended with a quote from Joseph Nye's *Nuclear Ethics:* "Moral virtue would consist in the care, the quality of moral reasoning, and the procedures that went into weighing such choices, rather than an arbitrary assignment into one or other philosophical tradition."[29]

This letter is a valuable source of information. Hamerton-Kelly's assimilation of the conflict in the Sudan to the war in Bosnia is evidence that he misunderstood the ideological basis for the aggression in the Balkans. Confusing the terms "objectivity" and "balance" he failed to distinguish legitimate territorial claims, such as those made by Jewish and Palestinian groups with respect to Israel/Palestine, from illegitimate ones. In fact, he offered no grounds whatsoever on which one could discuss the legitimacy or illegitimacy of the demands made by the groups he cited. While only the most hardened extremist would deny that either Palestinians or Jews have a rightful claim to the region called Israel/Palestine, the tone of Hamerton-Kelly's letter went beyond this. He seemed to be making a case for the Serb nationalists who were shelling Sarajevo and who could not boast of an exclusive claim as a result of history, culture, or religion to the territories around the city. Who else but Bosnia's destroyers and their apologetic friends would "balance out" the "pro-Bosnian" point of view he criticized? These analytical distinctions were overlooked, and instead Hamerton-Kelly attacked the Jewish students.

With his reference to the Holocaust and his citation from Nye, Hamerton-Kelly further displayed his own prejudices. He not only revealed that he was suspicious of the Jewish students' motivation to host a forum on Bosnia but also dismissed it as an "arbitrary assignment" insufficiently reasoned. In effect, Hamerton-Kelly rejected the students' appeal on no other basis than their Jewishness. The idea that there may have been some corresponding truth between their statements and the world outside was excluded on the grounds that it was just too complicated. That the students may have had universal reasons for condemning the genocide irrespective of their collective history and association with the Holocaust and that these reasons may have been voiced in a universal language, accessible to all, was also ignored. Rather, Hamerton-Kelly proceeded to argue from a statement of fact (the organizers were Jewish) to a statement of value (they were moralizing and were influenced by the Holocaust). These students were mistaken and that is why he did not support their forum. By his own logic, he too was condemned to the heresy of moralizing.

While Hamerton-Kelly may not have been aware of his hypocritical response, there was an interesting epilogue to this incident. In 1993, when Hamerton-Kelly was writing, Joseph Nye—whose quote Hamerton-Kelly used to assert his own position of moral and intellectual superiority—was still chairman of the CIA's National Intelligence Council. Nye was in charge of the federal advisory group that established overall U.S. intelligence policy. Hamerton-Kelly's source of moral authority was actually a participant in the genocide, a voyeur whose policy recommendations ensured that considerable evidence of war crimes would sit in the beltway. This source of moral authority would not release the CIA's evidence to the International War Crimes Tribunal in The Hague, and instead, the task of proving that Serbia launched a genocide against the people of Bosnia would fall to lawyers, journalists, human rights workers, and researchers. Not only Hamerton-Kelly's line of argument but his presumption of morality was infected.

It is interesting to note to what extent dissident voices were attacked within the intellectual and academic scene. It was not only Jewish students who were brushed aside by critics with competing ideological opinions. For example, authors Rabia Ali and Lawrence Lifschultz were charged with prescribing "counter-genocide."[30] Susan Sontag's accusations against her colleagues were later thrown back at her by angry columnists. Ironically, they actually reinforced the points that she was making. Sontag's claim that "actually we are already living in the twenty-first century, in which such twentieth century certainties as the identification of fascism, or imperialism, or Bolshevik-style dictatorships as the principal 'enemy' no longer offer a framework for thought and action"[31] proved significant, when tested against the backlash launched against her. Just as Flaherty ignored the essential characteristics of a war of transborder aggression in his attack on Ali and Lifschultz, Sontag's antagonist lacked the skills required to respond in kind.

Writing in the *Village Voice,* James Ledbetter unleashed a vicious personal attack against Sontag, arguing that she was trafficking in "morality myths."[32] He denied her charges of intellectual indifference and, like Maynes, sought to downplay the actual devastation of Bosnia. Again, however, the tools used to make his case were deficient. He argued that U.S. newspapers had published much on Bosnia and that that suggested ample evidence of a sincere interest. "The *New York Review of Books*—arguably America's premier intellectual publication—has practically established a Sarajevo bureau, publishing tens of thousands of words by Michael Ignatieff, Misha Glenny, Warren Zimmerman, George Soros, Timothy Garton Ash—and Susan Sontag."[33]

What Ledbetter did not recognize was that there were serious ideological differences among the authors he mentioned. What is more, not all of them were intellectuals—the subject of Sontag's criticism. While Michael Ignatieff would offer a voice of caution, Misha Glenny could not be considered part of a "Sarajevo bureau." Glenny consistently appeased the Serbs by appealing against air strikes in a most public manner—with prescriptive headlines on the pages of the *International Herald Tribune, New York Times,* and *London Times* — and was remembered for articles such as "How the West Can Help? Not by Dropping Bombs."[34] While Sontag called for intervention, Glenny forewarned of apocalypse: "If the world accepted the advice of Senator Bob Dole and former Prime Minister Margaret Thatcher, these consequences would be likely to close in on us like a garrote."[35]

As the air strikes launched against Serbian positions in late 1995 would prove, Glenny's assessment was grossly exaggerated. Appealing on the grounds of his own authority, Glenny was later discredited by his own words: "It may be satisfying from inside the Beltway to demand a quick fix by bombers. For those of us who live and work in the Balkans, things look a little different. We know that a bombing of the Serbians will let loose a sea of blood in which southeastern Europe will drown."[36]

Of all those listed by Ledbetter, besides Sontag, only Soros was a consistently true friend of Bosnia. There was no Sarajevo bureau, and informed readers would detect the ridicule and hyperbole in Ledbetter's writing. As he mocked Sontag's solidarity with the people of Sarajevo — "Nor do I recall the good citizens of Kigali being treated to a Sontag-sponsored Beckett production" — Ledbetter again failed to offer any analysis of the two genocides. Instead he relied on invective and name calling. Did someone need to explain to him that Sarajevo was besieged while Kigali was overrun? That there was no time for physical demonstrations of solidarity with the "good citizens of Kigali" who were murdered in a matter of weeks while the Sarajevans were held hostage and victimized over three years? Instead of recognizing these essential facts, Ledbetter accused Sontag of "holiday parties" and "romanticism."

Back on campus, some of the cases that so irked Sontag were granted no significance whatsoever. At Stanford, a "peace studies" course offered during the academic year 1992–93 omitted any discussion of genocide. The fate of Bosnia and its people assumed no significance. Instead, the course focused on theories of pacifism and justice. In the following year, the president of the university refused to meet with the Bosnian ambassador on two occasions. His assistant, Dean Jean Fetter, put it down to the tremendous demands placed on him and insisted that there were many other "noble causes." In private, President Gerhard Casper offered an essentially liberal argument and admitted that he did not believe he could address the issue of genocide without politicizing the campus and undermining the university's provision of "pluralism" to all.[37] He had to remain neutral and therefore elected silence. In 1993, a workbook published by the Stanford Program in Inter-Cultural Education for Secondary Schools on "the Collapse of Yugoslavia" concentrated on the idea of nationalism and only devoted a couple of concluding sentences to the actual war in Bosnia. The violence used to destroy the country and kill off its people was edited out of the textbook that was prepared for California children under a grant from the U.S. Institute for Peace. There were many such examples, and this was only one university.

Conclusion

The American university of the 1990s is a distant relation to Veblen's model. Having adopted many of the practices of market-driven institutions, it is difficult to describe the university as Veblen's protected site of knowledge production. The mechanistic and instrumental world that Veblen studied and attempted to bracket off from the intellectual realm, however, has found its entry in the university's sphere. Riesman's notion of other-directedness offers some analytical value to explain this phenomenon. In essence, the academics mentioned above were unsure of their positions and deferred to others outside while still going through the motions expected of knowledge producers. In practice, in spite of their articles, conferences, and scholarly publications, the majority of academics remained detached and refused to consider the relevance of the changing world outside. Few were prepared to grapple with the major moral and political challenges of the post–Cold War era and in particular reflect on the implications posed by the use of genocide and the perpetuation of massive human rights violations against civilians. In Isaac's language, this amounts to nothing less than "ethical abdication."[38]

Most academics and intellectuals were not deliberate agents of confusion and disinterest. That they retreated and refused to recognize that genocide really was taking place while some of their colleagues crafted rationalizations for inaction is beyond dispute. Perhaps it would be more accurate to describe them as Susan Sontag did, as "conformist, as willing to support prosecution of unjust wars, as most other people exercising educated professions."[39] Professors Hamerton-Kelly, Mearsheimer and Van Evera were operating from a basis of principle. Even if their recommendations were morally suspect in that they tolerated genocide, it would be difficult to make a case of deliberate malicious intent. Their actions were not morally improper, but their thinking was confused. Where they fell down was on method, argument, and self-certainty. One must question the extent to which their prejudices and their inability to establish sound critiques prevented them, as academics, from adhering to the academic ideal. During the most intensive period of the conflict, they misunderstood the war in Bosnia and failed to demonstrate the sort of intellectual rigor once expected of tenured professors in the social sciences.

In Veblen's order, they would have clearly betrayed the ideals of academic investigation. One could also make a case for ostentation: John Mearsheimer especially was a highly visible figure in the press and in academic journals. The accusations of "idleness" and of producing "useless knowledge" reflect not only a statement of fact in Veblen's terms, since these academics really were divorced from the world they claimed to observe, but also a judgment in terms of the expectations of academic inquiry. Few academics recognized this expectation and pleaded as Isaac did: "It is thus incumbent upon us to acknowledge this world as a source of intellectual and practical problems, to engage in it in all of its empirical and historical messiness, to demonstrate that our categories help to illuminate this political reality and even, dare I say, to improve it."[40]

In the era of televised slaughter, the rationalizations sought by members of the academic and intellectual community, in addition to the silence and lack of curiosity exhibited by so many others in the face of genocide, challenge the place of the intellectual and the established view of the university as a useful institution in the late twentieth century. Overwhelmingly, it would be fair to say that American academics and their intellectual cousins off campus failed not only on Veblen's terms but also on their own. In sum, they missed the point and couldn't make theirs in their own language of academic rigor.

Notes

1. Thorstein Veblen, *Higher Learning in America: A Memorandum on the Conduct of Universities by Business Men* (Stanford, Calif.: Academic Reprints, 1954), 8.
2. Thorstein Veblen, *Theory of the Leisure Class: An Economic Study of Institutions* (1912; new edition, New York: Viking, 1931), 40.
3. And yet, many commentators are still confused by the ambiguities in Veblen's writings. If he favored the market over the university, or if he sincerely believed that the academic world could exist independently, it is far from clear where Veblen actually stood.
4. See David Riesman's introduction, entitled "Veblen and the Higher Learning," in Veblen, *Higher Learning in America*.
5. Derek Bok, *Higher Learning* (Cambridge, Mass.: Harvard University Press, 1986), 20.
6. Ibid., 21.
7. "The Academic Ratchet: A term to describe the steady, irreversible shift of faculty allegiance away from the goals of a given institution, toward those of an academic specialty. The ratchet denotes the advance of an independent, entrepreneurial spirit among faculty nation-wide, leading to increased emphasis on research and publication and on teaching one's specialty in favor of general introduction courses, often at the expense of coherence in an academic curriculum. Institutions seeking to enhance their own prestige may contribute to the ratchet effect by reducing faculty teaching and advising responsibilities across the board, thus enabling faculty to pursue their individual research and publication with fewer distractions. The academic ratchet raises an institution's costs, and it results in undergraduates paying more to attend institutions in which they receive less faculty attention than in previous decades." This is Robert Zemsky and William F. Massy's definition, recorded in "Cost Containment: Committing to a New Economic Reality" in *Change* 22 (Nov./Dec., 1990): 16–22. See also Massy and Andrea K. Wilger, "Productivity in Postsecondary Education: A New Approach," *Educational Evaluation and Policy Analysis* 14, no. 4 (Winter, 1992): 361–76.
8. David Riesman, *The Lonely Crowd* (New Haven, Conn.: Yale University Press, 1961).
9. Allan Bloom, *The Closing of the American Mind* (New York: Simon and Schuster, 1987), 38.

10. "The Strange Silence of Political Theory," *Political Theory* 23, no. 4 (1995): 636–88.
11. Ibid., 637.
12. Ibid.
13. Ibid.
14. Isaac, "The Strange Silence of Political Theory," 649.
15. Stjepan Meštrović, *The Balkanization of the West: The Confluence of Postmodernism and Post-Communism* (London: Routledge, 1994), xiv.
16. See Charles William Maynes, "The New Pessimism," *Foreign Policy* 100 (Fall, 1995): 33–49.
17. Robert Lieber, "Existential Realism," *Washington Quarterly* 16, no. 1 (1993).
18. Peter Grier, "Should U.S. Fight War in Bosnia? Question Opens Age Old Debate," *Christian Science Monitor*, Sept. 14, 1992.
19. See Maynes, "New Pessimism."
20. Ibid.
21. Ibid.
22. John J. Mearsheimer, "U.S. Quietly Concedes Bosnia Focuses on Limiting Conflict," *Christian Science Monitor*, June 23, 1993.
23. See John J. Mearsheimer and Stephen Van Evera, "When Peace Means War: The Partition that Dare Not Speak Its Name," *New Republic*, Dec. 18, 1995, p. 25.
24. See ibid., 21.
25. See Gitlin's "The Culture Wars Lost Cause: Why Intellectuals of the Left Miss Communism," *Los Angeles Times*, Jan. 14, 1996.
26. Ibid.
27. See for example Amy Gutmann's *Multiculturalism Examining the Politics of Recognition* (Princeton: Princeton University Press, 1984).
28. See Hamerton-Kelly's letter "Religion of Victims in Bosnia Is Not the Only Reason for Persecution" in the *Stanford Daily*, May 27, 1993.
29. See ibid.
30. Patrick Flaherty, "The Balkan Wars and Ethnic Cleaning: Solution Recommendation Includes Historical and Sociological Analysis," *Monthly Review*, Oct., 1994, p. 32.
31. See Sontag's "Lament for Bosnia," *Nation*, Dec. 25, 1995, pp. 818–20.
32. See Ledbetter's "Press Clips: Bosnia as Metaphor," *Village Voice*, Dec. 26, 1995.
33. Ibid.
34. *International Herald Tribune*, Dec. 8, 1994.
35. Ibid.
36. See Glenny's article in the *New York Times*, Apr. 23, 1993.
37. See Brad K. Blitz, "Bosnian Genocide Is Affront to University's Value-System," *Stanford Daily*, Jan. 28, 1994.
38. Isaac insisted that the social sciences could still have a positive role and that

critical examination of current events presented "serious choices regarding moral responsibility, political membership, and constitutional foundations." These were choices that academic inquiry might help to illuminate and even improve. Isaac, "Strange Silence," 649.

39. Sontag, "Lament."
40. Isaac, "Strange Silence," 646.

CHAPTER SEVEN

Serbia and Russia:
U.S. Appeasement and the Resurrection of Fascism

RICHARD JOHNSON

We have direct strategic concerns. The continuing destruction of a new UN member state challenges the principle that internationally recognized borders should not be altered by force . . . Bold tyrants and fearful minorities are watching to see whether 'ethnic cleansing' is a policy the world will tolerate. If we hope to promote the spread of freedom or if we hope to encourage the emergence of peaceful multiethnic democracies, our answer must be a resounding no.

— Secretary of State
Warren Christopher on Bosnia,
February 10, 1993

The relationship between the United States and Russia has entered a new stage of mature strategic partnership based on equality, mutual advantage, and recognition of each other's national interests.

— U.S.-Russian Summit Declaration,
Moscow, January 14, 1994

> *'What is taking place between Washington and Moscow is a sophisticated, diplomatically sanctioned carve-up of Bosnia,' said a senior UN official.*
>
> — Financial Times,
> March 17, 1994

> *There's no question that Russia and the Russian military [were] very instrumental in stabilizing Mr. Shevarnadze's position in Georgia.*
>
> — President Bill Clinton,
> Moscow, January 14, 1994

> *Ukraine now stands on the brink of a Bosnia-type cataclysm.*
>
> — Janusz Bugayski,
> Washington Times,
> March 15, 1994

The Vicious Circle

A specter is haunting Europe. It is the specter of that virulent nationalism whose ultimate form is fascism — national socialism, aggression, genocide.

In Western Europe, fascism is an unsettling undercurrent, manifested in a surge of xenophobia, racism, and right-wing parties. It must compete for influence in established democratic political cultures. It can be defeated by political means, if democratic forces rally to defend their principles and values.

In Eastern Europe, democratic forces thin out and societies are more vulnerable to fascism. In most of Eastern Europe, fascism can still be defeated by political means.

In Southeast Europe, however, fascism has already ruled and ravaged for three years in Serbia and the lands it has seized and purged in Croatia and Bosnia. Serb Fascism is the fully developed form. It does not aim to conquer Europe. But it does aim to redefine the post–Cold War order in Europe to one that accepts aggression and genocide. It is succeeding. Serb Fascism can only be defeated militarily.

Democratic forces thin out still more further east, in the former

Soviet Union. And fascism reaches for power in Russia today. Russian Fascism is still in protofascist form. Its consolidation would gravely threaten U.S. national security. This outcome has already become more likely than a democratic Russia — even as Serb Fascism has demonstrated that the West, including the United States, will not defend its principles, values, interests, and security. Russian Fascism may still be defeatable by political means. But it will not remain so unless there is a fundamental change in U.S. policy.

There is a reinforcing causal nexus between Serb Fascism, U.S. appeasement, and Russian Fascism. These three phenomena are linked by three vicious circles, and form one overarching vicious circle in the pattern illustrated:

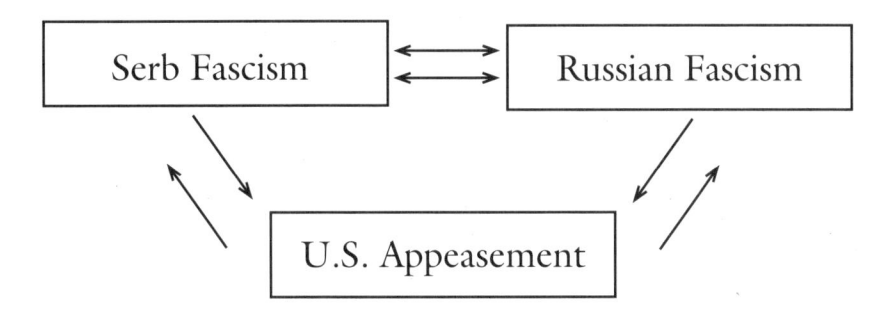

```
┌──────────────────┐  ⇄  ┌──────────────────┐
│   Serb Fascism   │     │  Russian Fascism │
└──────────────────┘     └──────────────────┘
         ↖   ↘             ↙   ↗
              ┌──────────────────┐
              │  U.S. Appeasement │
              └──────────────────┘
```

In focusing on this pattern, I do not imply that these phenomena do not have separate, internal causes. They do. But I do argue that Serb Fascism, U.S. appeasement, and Russian Fascism are mutually reinforcing, in a way that helps explain the very rapid and unexpected darkening of the world *zeitgeist* since the end of the Cold War.

In examining this thesis we must first compare Serbia and Russia, to highlight reasons to expect parallel and mutually reinforcing developments toward Fascism in the two cases. Second, we will outline U.S. appeasement of Serb and Russian Fascism and proto-Fascism in terms of the practice and pathology of U.S. policy. Third, we will address the transmission belts between Serb Fascism, U.S. appeasement, and Russian Fascism.

The vicious circle involving Serb Fascism, U.S. appeasement, and Russian Fascism is increasingly hard to escape. It puts the transatlantic community in a prewar, rather than postwar, situation.

Serbia and Russia

The rule of Fascism in Serbia and its rise to power in Russia underscore that the fall of Communism was not enough for a "Europe whole and free." It was also necessary that Serbia and Russia, the "core nations" within the former Yugoslavia and Soviet Union, accept the breakup of their respective Balkan and Eurasian supranational states. Neither Serbia nor Russia have ever been normal European states. Whether they would become ones after the fall of Communism was more an open question for them than for other old and new states in Eastern Europe. Many of the reasons behind Serbia's "no" are also present in Russia.

The Serbia/Yugoslavia and Russia/Soviet Union structures were unique in East Europe, and not just because they were the only multinational federations of their kind. They were also unique and alike in the ways outlined below.

Both Yugoslavia and the Soviet Union were created by wartime revolutions that were indigenous rather than imposed, and that projected a supranational sense of identity based on Communism. As a result, both Serbia and Russia had senses of national and state identity that were ill-defined between Serb and Yugoslav and Russian and Soviet.

Both Serbia and Russia treated their federations as lands they had the right to control. At the same time, both nourished grievances. The Serb grievance was that for Marshal Tito, a strong Yugoslavia required a weak Serbia, that more advanced Slovenia and Croatia exploited Serbia, and that while all Yugoslav republics except Slovenia were nationally mixed, only Serbia was internally divided by autonomy for Kosovo and Vojvodina. The Russian grievance was similar: the sense of having paid the "civilizer's burden" to develop the non-Russian republics, of being exploited by the Balts, and of having less "national" stature then the other republics.

Both Yugoslavia and the Soviet Union were multinational states whose non-Serb and non-Russian republics enjoyed the formal right of secession—but were home to Serb and Russian diasporas that would be "separated" by a breakup. Both Serbia and Russia, even as they set out to reverse that separation in the aftermath of breakup, also face separatist pressure from their own large non-Serb and non-Russian populations.

There are nuances. There is no equivalent in Russia to Serb memories of Ustashe Croat genocide against Serbs in Croatia and Bosnia during World War II, nor to the Serb perception that Albanians usurp "sacred" Serb lands in Kosovo. These factors were massively exploited by Serb dictator Slobodan Milošević in his mobilization of Serbs for a Fascist Greater Serbia. The absence of equivalent factors in Russia suggests a weaker basis for fascism there. However, there is more grassroots "Great Russian" sentiment among the Russian diaspora, and less integration with its new state hosts, than there was for the Serb diaspora. Russians have a much longer and deeper history of hegemony over other nations than do Serbs. These factors suggest more pressure for virulent nationalism from below (as opposed to mobilized from above) in the Russian case.[1]

Both Serbia and Russia were the largest Orthodox nations in their respective multinational/multireligious entities, and show susceptibility to racist and religious intolerance of Muslims.

Both Serbs and Russians dominated the officer corps of the Yugoslav and Soviet militaries, whose futures were threatened by Yugoslav and Soviet disintegration but who now play key roles in the Serb and Russian regimes. An important distinction is the absence (thus far) of nuclear weapons in the former Yugoslavia and their presence in several former Soviet republics. The latter can be viewed as a deterrent to aggression by Russia against, say, Ukraine, or as an added local and global danger if such aggression occurs. What is clear is the high U.S. stake in seeing those nuclear arsenals not only reduced in size but, above all, controlled by peaceful, democratic states.

Finally, and most important, for both Serbia and Russia there was an inescapable connection between the internal and external courses they would chart in the breakup of Yugoslavia and the Soviet Union: *Serbia and Russia could be empires or democracies, but they could not be both.* This is understood by the Serb and Russian political elites and by Western experts on Eastern European nationalities issues, if not by U.S. policymakers.[2]

The similarities outlined above were initially obscured by the different circumstances under which Yugoslavia and the Soviet Union broke up. U.S. policy in 1990–91 did see some similarity between Yugoslavia and the Soviet Union, insofar as the United States sought to avert or slow the breakup of Yugoslavia to avoid precipitating a breakup of the Soviet Union. Secretary of State James Baker alluded to the similarity with his late 1991 warning that the Soviet Union could become a "Yugoslavia with nukes." The Bush administration nevertheless opted to let the Yugoslav model proceed unchecked. Since then, the American foreign policy establishment has given the Serbia-Russia parallel little thought.

Serb Fascism preceded, precipitated, and then exploited the breakup of Yugoslavia. Serbia under Milošević never intended to accept the end of hegemony. On the contrary. Milošević first destroyed Yugoslavia between 1987 and 1991 precisely because its Titoist structures and Westernizing trends were obstacles and threats to his power, then in 1991–94 began to carve out a Greater Serbia fit for dictatorial rule and capable, if consolidated, of dominating the Balkans.

The ideology of Milošević's Greater Serbia is an atavistic, anti-Western variant of Serb nationalism. It reflects legitimate Serb interests no more than Nazism reflected German interests. Before 1990, this ideology dominated the mindsets of a minority of Serbs and colored the attitudes of most Serbs. In the run-up to and course of war, Milošević has made it dominant in Serb political discourse. It is summed up in the concept that all Serbs must live in one state, and that state is for Serbs only.

Unlike Communism, this concept can have no supranational attraction for any non-Serb. *Its implementation can only be initiated by aggression and completed by genocide.* This is a crucial reason that the post-Communist drive for a Greater Serbia was proto-Fascist from the start. The same applies to any drive for a Greater Russia.

The core forces for Serb Fascism were mobilized from elements of the intellectual elite, the Serb officer corps and internal security forces, the "apparat" of the socialist economy, urban "lumpenproletariat" strata, and rural primitives. Its strategy and tactics have much in common with Nazism, including aggression masked as "protecting ethnic brethren" and genocide to arrive at "final solutions." The biggest differences with Nazism are that Serbia is small and in economic collapse, that regime-connected "mafia" control most of what economic activity exists, and that senior Serb leaders call themselves not Fascists but simply patriots. This is an anachronistic fascism that has nothing to offer except blood and land. It is ready to wage genocide, but not to reveal its true name.

Similar ideologies, forces, and circumstance are now on hand in Russia. Serb Fascism has blazed their trail.

The Russian case was different at the outset. In 1991, Gorbachev sought to preserve and reform the Soviet Union. Progressives defeated the reactionary coup against Gorbachev and accepted the dissolution of the Soviet Union. Russia under Boris Yeltsin set out to give up empire and forge a peaceful, democratic Russia—although this simplification must be qualified: Russia was taken by surprise by the breakup of the Soviet Union, Russians differed on whether this was in fact acceptable, and Yeltsin himself was ambivalent from the start.[3]

Through April, 1994, there remained important differences between Serbia and Russia. In the latter, there have been free elections. There are pluralist media. The national-Communists and the overt Fascists remain formally in opposition. Russia still lacks a Führer.

However, by April, 1994, there is little momentum left in the hopeful Russian course charted in 1991. Despite reassurances from the executive branch, the increasingly common assessment in the U.S. Congress and media and among independent analysts is that (1) momentum in Russia has shifted to communist-nationalists who want Russia on a reactionary, aggressive course, (2) those reformers who are still in power are increasingly behaving like the communist-nationalists, and (3) the latter already have extensive control over Russia's domestic and foreign policies. The trend toward an ideology based on the concept that all ethnic Russians must live in one state—or at least under the military protection of a Russian state— is clear as well.

Russia now looks like Serbia did before its assault on Croatia in 1991, in terms of the dominant mood of the Russian political class, the priority it gives to the Russian diaspora and to Russian hegemony over the lands of the former Soviet Union, and the willingness of Moscow to use force to pursue these causes.[4]

Moscow's relations with Serbia have also evolved. In 1991 Russia paid little attention to the Balkans, and Milošević's support for the 1991 Moscow coup made him Yeltsin's enemy. In May, 1992, Russia was a cooperative player in Western political and economic measures against Serb aggression in Bosnia. In April, 1994, in the absence of any countervailing pressure from the West, Russia behaves like a political ally and military protector of Fascist Serbia.

U.S. Appeasement of Serbia and Russia

THE PRACTICE: "A GREATER SERBIA IS A STABLE BALKANS"

Just as there are no avowed Fascists at the helm in Belgrade, there are no avowed appeasers in charge in Washington. Yet, since 1990, U.S. policy in the Balkans has had two essential constants: (1) aversion to military confrontation of Serb aggression, whether with U.S. forces, military aid to Serbia's victims, or even allowing the latter to exercise the right of self-defense; and (2) the search for conciliation by yielding, and pressing the victims to yield, to Serb belligerence, at the expense of justice and other principles.

That is appeasement — although by 1994, and insofar as appeasement is a strategy to avert rather than reward war, it might better be called capitulation. It has been applied in the following ways to Milošević's march toward a Greater Serbia.

In 1990–91, Milošević used the threat of force and an initial limited use of force (massive repression in Kosovo, a Serb "uprising" — organized from Belgrade — in the Knin area of Croatia, and Yugoslav Army seizure of local weapons stocks in non-Serb republics) to press the non-Serb republics either to accept a Milošević dictatorship in a Serb-dominated anti-Western Yugoslavia or to cede any lands claimed by Serbia as a condition for independence. The U.S. government assessment was that Milošević was making Yugoslavia unlivable for the non-Serb republics, usurping central Yugoslav institutions, was fomenting nationalist conflict, and was irreconcilably opposed to any fair compromise between Serbia and the other republics. Nonetheless, U.S. policy supported the unity of Yugoslavia and opposed independence for non-Serb republics absent Milošević's consent.

In June, 1991–April, 1992, Milošević waged war against Croatia with the minimum objective of seizing Serb-majority areas for a Greater Serbia, and a maximum objective of seizing much of the Adriatic coast and eastern Croatia as well. Such was the U.S. government assessment, as enunciated by Secretary Baker to the UN in September, 1991. Nonetheless, U.S. policy continued to deny recognition of Croatian independence absent Milošević's consent, denied Croatia access to weapons, insisted that Croatia negotiate with rather than resist Milošević, supported the "Vance Plan" for a UN cease-fire that left Serbia in control of some 25 percent of Croatia, and took no action to punish Serbia for its aggression and extensive war crimes in Croatia.

From April, 1992, to the present, Milošević has waged genocidal war against Bosnia (while consolidating his gains behind UN protection in Croatia), with the objective of seizing as much of Bosnia as possible, and exterminating enough Bosnian Muslims and Croats (more than 200,000 thus far) to make that seizure irreversible. U.S. government assessments have varied widely, often within hours. The war in Bosnia was either a blatant case of Serb aggression that was "tantamount to" genocide or a spontaneous outburst of ancient ethnic feuds in a civil war for which all sides were to blame. The latter "big lie" has been the dominant U.S. line since late spring, 1993. U.S. policy supported recognition and UN membership for Bosnia in April, 1992, and led the way on UN economic sanctions to punish Serb aggression in May, 1992. However, U.S. policy continued to oppose Bosnian access to weapons (until May, 1993, when U.S. policy shifted to occasional rhetorical support for lifting the UN arms embargo from Bosnia) and to insist that Bosnia "compromise" with Serbia.

To the extent that U.S. policy has threatened or used force in Bosnia, its threats have targeted "all parties" and its use of force has been "neutral." Since August, 1993, the threat and use of U.S. force has also been linked to (1) U.S. pressure on the Bosnian government to accept the formal partition of Bosnia, and (2) the notion of lifting UN economic sanctions from Serbia-Montenegro after such a partition. By mid-April, 1994, President Bill Clinton was stressing, after feeble North Atlantic Treaty Organization (NATO) air strikes around Goražde, that the U.S. "had no interest in using NATO airpower to affect the outcome of the war," but only to comply with UN requests and encourage further "negotiation." In short, UN sanctions initially imposed to reverse aggression will be lifted when the results of aggression have been ratified. U.S./NATO military power is applied not to reverse aggression but to advance "negotiations" to ratify aggression.

THE PRACTICE: "A GREATER RUSSIA IS A STABLE EURASIA"

U.S. policy appeases Russian aggressivity in four areas: Russia's relations with its neighbors, Russia's specific relations with Ukraine, Russia's relations with Eastern Europe, and Russia's specific role regarding Bosnia.

As of April, 1994, Russia has used force to violate the independence, sovereignty, and territorial integrity of Tajikistan, Georgia, and Moldova. It has rendered active support to Armenian use of force against Azerbaijan and to internal insurgency within Azerbaijan. It has imposed conditions on its military withdrawal from Latvia and Estonia that violate the UN Charter and Helsinki Final Act. Russian military activities in Ukraine are increasingly assertive and inconsistent with the sovereignty of Ukraine.

U.S. policy has not opposed these applications of Russian force. On January 25, 1994, Deputy Secretary Strobe Talbott did tell Congress that "Russian conduct in several of the neighboring states, particularly the Transcausasus, has been troublesome, and has occasioned some blunt exchanges in our diplomatic exchanges with Moscow." The U.S. side of these "blunt exchanges" cannot have been forceful. U.S. ambassador to Russia Thomas Pickering denied any danger of Russian imperialism, in a February 10 speech to the Council on Foreign Relations. President Clinton signaled U.S. acquiescence to Russian military interventions, in his public remarks in Moscow on January 10. Here, the president: (1) tacitly accepted the notion that common ethnicity was a valid grounds for external military action; (2) praised the Russian military for "stabilizing" Georgia, while ignoring its initial destabilization of Georgia and the quid pre quo demanded by Russia for "restabilization," that is, Georgia joining the Moscow-dominated Commonwealth of Independent States; and (3) legitimized future Russian military interventions against neighboring states by predicting they would occur and likening them in advance to past U.S. actions in Panama and Granada.[5]

With regard to Ukraine, and under the overall U.S. "Russia First" policy, the United States shares Russia's preference for a denuclearized Ukraine. There are telling nonproliferation arguments for such a stance, but there are also telling arguments that a nuclear Ukraine may be a more stable option.[6] In practice, U.S. policy favors Russia's interest in a non-nuclear Ukraine over Ukraine's interest and guarantees against Russian aggression. In the talks for the January, 1994, U.S./Russian/Ukrainian statement on removing nuclear weapons from Ukraine, Ukraine pressed for strong assurance that the Ukraine/Russia border was inviolable and permanent. Russia wanted no references to the matter. The U.S. supported a compromise that gives Ukraine only a weak assurance: a Russian promise to observe Conference on Security and Cooperation in Europe (CSCE) principles. This requires that any change to the Russia/Ukraine border be by "mutual consent."[7] The elasticity of this requirement in 1994 is being demonstrated in the U.S.-led talks on the forced partition of Bosnia.

With regard to Eastern Europe, and in response to Russian demands, U.S. policy in late 1993 rejected Eastern European states' bid for a mechanism and timetable for NATO membership, and offered instead to all states in Eastern Europe and the former Soviet Union the vague "Partnership For Peace." To Warsaw, Prague, and Budapest, the United States implied that "Partnership For Peace" meant their entry into NATO was a question of when, not if. To Moscow, the United States implied that NATO membership for Eastern European states had been indefinitely postponed.

With regard to Bosnia, U.S. policy has (1) invited Russia into the UN/European Union (EU) "mediation" process in early 1993, thus exposing ambivalent Russian leaders to direct Serb pressures and manipulation; (2) given Russia heavy influence over Western strategy since the May, 1993, "Action Program," including the emphasis on "neutrality" and the maintenance of the UN arms embargo on Bosnia; (3) welcomed the February, 1994, Russian troop deployment of Sarajevo as UN peacekeepers—which was imposed on the Bosnian government and the UN, and serves as a trip-wire against NATO air strikes around Sarajevo and against any Bosnian government attempt to break the siege of Sarajevo by force; and (4) allowed Russia to restrict the scale and rules of engagement for the U.S./NATO response to the Serb assault on Goražde.

THE PATHOLOGY:
APPEASEMENT AS A "STEALTH STRATEGY"

The heart of appeasement, today as in the 1930s, is (1) the lack of moral and strategic vision, leadership, backbone, and empathy for human suffering; and (2) the tendency of a stronger power to make concessions to a weaker but aggressive power, who thereby gains in strength and becomes a deadly threat. These traits are embarrassing and hard to admit for the U.S. foreign policy establishment and particularly U.S. policymakers. But they are fundamental.

The pathology of U.S. appeasement in the 1990s includes the following symptoms:

(1) Projection, or the tendency to ascribe to others feelings, thoughts, or attitudes present in oneself. U.S. leaders assume that because they want to see a peaceful, integrated Europe, this vision is also attractive to Serb and Russian hard-liners, and can be used as leverage. A related fallacy is economic determinism, or the notion—powerfully disproved by twentieth-century nationalism—that economics determine political outcomes. A third is the sense that because American leaders are tired of the burdens of the Cold War, or tired of the killing in the Balkans, so too are hard-line Serb and Russian leaders.

Those who project their own sense of post–Cold War fatigue to others should ask themselves: why is it that U.S. domestic problems must constrain an assertive U.S. foreign policy, while far graver domestic problems are no obstacle to far more assertive Serb and Russian foreign policies?

Fallacies of projection underlie the stubborn U.S. expectation that the "carrot and stick" of integration with Europe will influence men like Milošević. In 1990–91, U.S. policy hoped Yugoslav prime minister Ante Marković's successful but short-lived economic reform would neutralize Milošević and ensure unity and democracy for Yugoslavia. In early 1992, U.S. policy hoped that Milošević, appeased in Croatia but threatened with pariah status should he attack Bosnia, would desist from further aggression. In late 1992, U.S. policy hoped that a Serb émigré businessman from California, Milan Panić, would wrest control of Serbia from Milošević by promising peace and capitalism. Now, U.S. policy hopes that giving Milošević much of Bosnia and then lifting economic sanctions will deter him from further aggression there and to the south.

On Russia, U.S. policy projects Clinton campaign slogans ("It's the economy, stupid") onto Russian developments, by reducing the fascist Vladimir Zhirinovsky phenomenon to an economic protest vote, and defining economics as the decisive factor for overall Russian domestic and foreign behavior over the next few years.[8]

(2) Denial, or the refusal to recognize or assimilate alarming information. Denial is as much a willful instrument as an unconscious cause of U.S. appeasement, but the borders between willful and unconscious appear to break down over time. For Serbia, instances of U.S. denial are legion. The United States was reluctant to recognize the pattern of Serb military activity in Croatia in 1990–91 and in Bosnia in late winter-spring of 1992, or the reality of Serb-run concentration camps in Bosnia in the summer of 1992. The United States remains reluctant to acknowledge Serb genocide in Bosnia in 1992–94, the personal responsibility of Serb leaders, and its human costs (the preferred State Department line is that "it is impossible to say how many have died").[9]

For Russia, there is a similar pattern of denial: U.S. reluctance to recognize the growing weakness of preferred interlocutors (Gorbachev, Yeltsin), or to draw conclusions about Russian military interventions, the ominous evolution of official Russian national security policy, the projected rise in Russian military spending, and the exhaustion of domestic Russian reform.

(3) Wishful thinking. This is a close corollary of projection and denial. For Serbia, U.S. policy has nourished chronic false hope that Milošević would be toppled by domestic opponents or UN economic sanctions, that he would moderate his objectives when appeased, or that he had reached his territorial aims. In Russia, U.S. policy hoped the parliamentary elections of December, 1993, would

consolidate both Yeltsin and reform; it now hopes against all evidence that Yeltsin's January, 1994, summit vow to Clinton to press ahead "full speed" on economic reform has predictive value not just for the economy but for Russia's overall policy course.

(4) Defeatism. This has been a strange flip side to the projection, denial, and wishful thinking of U.S. policy on Serbia and Russia. U.S. defeatism is applied to their actual or potential victims. U.S. policy has consistently underestimated the will and capacity of Croatia and Bosnia to resist a Greater Serbia, as well as the persistence of Bosnian aspirations for multiethnic democracy. The same defeatism seems now to inform official U.S. perceptions of Ukraine and the degree to which it will resist partition or reabsorption by an imperial Russia.

In the 1980s, U.S. Cold War policy was based on the conviction that history was on the side of freedom and resistance to evil, and that the United States was a key player in achieving victory. Now, U.S. appeasement is based on the rationalization that because the administration lacks the will to act, the outcome of history in the 1990s must be either unimportant or beyond the influence of the United States.

The types of policy behavior characteristic of U.S. appeasement of Serbia and Russia include the following: (a) *equivocation* (Bosnia is a case of genocidal aggression but also mostly a civil war; Russian conduct in the Caucasus is "troublesome" but also praiseworthy); (b) *amnesia* (the disappearance of the principled themes in the Clinton administration's first policy statement on Bosnia in early 1993, or the U.S. obliviousness to the fact that Russian foreign minister Andrei Kozyrev's December, 1992, warning to the CSCE of what a dangerous, reactionary Russia would look like if democracy failed has already been more than fulfilled); (c) *legitimation of nationalist Serb and Russian propaganda* (that Croatia and now Bosnia are civil wars, or that an eastward expansion of NATO can legitimately be viewed as a hostile act by Russia); (d) *redefinition* to suit domestic U.S. political convenience (Bosnia is a strategic interest or merely a humanitarian concern; Russia is a state with which we have a "mature strategic partnership" or a sometimes partner which can also be an adversary); (e) *dishonesty and Orwellian double-speak* (the refusal to call the Serb campaign in Bosnia genocide under the UN Convention, or the assertion that U.S. mediation on Bosnia aims for a "voluntary, peaceful settlement" as opposed to the capitulation of the Bosnian government to aggression and genocide); (f) efforts to establish *moral equivalency* between victims and aggressors; (g) *refusal to take sides* between victims and aggressors; (h) *empty threats and rhetorical posturing;* (i) *efforts to disarm potential and actual victims* (the arms embargoes on Croatia and Bosnia, or the pressure on Ukraine to give up nuclear weapons); (j) persistent *emphasis on the risks of U.S. action,* and deemphasis of the risks of U.S. inaction; and (k) *repeated retreats* in practice and then in principle from initial stands and commitments.

Neville Chamberlain was straightforward about his strategy toward Hitler's Germany. U.S. appeasement of Serbia and Russia amounts to a "stealth strategy" vis-à-vis the U.S. public. U.S. government denial of the realities in Serbia and Russia, and of the realities of U.S. policies, preclude and appear designed to preclude a genuine national debate on the right U.S. response to Serbia and Russia. Despite significant protest from within the American political elite, the Clinton administration appears set on slipping its appeasement policies by the American public.

Transmission Belts: The Vicious Circles

SERB FASCISM AND U.S. APPEASEMENT

The interaction between Serb Fascism and U.S. appeasement has been extensively described over the past three years by the U.S. media, senior foreign policy experts, and congressional critics of Bush and Clinton administration policies.[10] To conceive of this interaction as a vicious circle—a dynamic, escalatory process whose two elements reinforce each other—helps explain the persistence of failed U.S. policies, and their degradation from ineffective resistance to Serb aggression in 1990–91, to active complicity in Serb aggression and genocide in 1992–94. It also broadens the field of examination to how the interaction between Serb Fascism and U.S. appeasement relates to other policy areas.

Even the architects of current U.S. policies accept, intermittently, that tolerating Serb aggression and "ethnic cleansing" erodes the credibility, authority, and power of the United States, UN,

CSCE, and NATO, and encourages further threats to U.S. interests.[11] It also stands to reason, unless one posits a Dr. Jekyll/Mr. Hyde duality to U.S. foreign policymaking, that the habits and techniques developed by U.S. policymakers in appeasing Serbia — equivocation, evasion, denial, cover-ups, tolerance of the ostensibly intolerable, retreat, the abdication of leadership — spill over into U.S. policymaking in the similar but higher-risk Russian context.

U.S. APPEASEMENT AND RUSSIAN FASCISM

U.S. appeasement reinforces Russian Fascism both indirectly, via the demonstration effect and precedents set by U.S. appeasement of Serbia, and directly, via conciliatory U.S. policies framed in the specific context of Russian aggressivity. Russian aggressivity, in turn, reinforces U.S. appeasement, including toward Serb Fascism.

Such linkages are exemplified by two arguments commonly heard within the State Department and attributed to the "Talbott Approach" to Russia: (1) that the U.S. must not let a "marginal" issue like Bosnia interfere with U.S. grand strategy toward Russia; and (2) that the U.S. must not confront Serb aggression because this would inflame Russian hard-liners and thereby undermine Yeltsin. These two arguments beg the question: how is it, exactly, that capitulating to Serb Fascists and appeasing Russian proto-Fascists will strengthen Russian democrats?

SERB FASCISM AND RUSSIAN FASCISM

The direct dynamic between Serb Fascism and Russian Fascism has been little studied, despite Western awareness that Serbia has been the hottest foreign policy issue for Russian nationalist-communists, and that Russian policy has grown increasingly protective of Serbia.[12]

Serb Fascism strengthens Russian Fascism directly by (a) providing a successful ideological, strategic, and tactical model; (b) providing a "trojan horse" policy issue for Russian nationalist-communists to use against the Yeltsin regime and its initial Westernizing aspirations — an issue where pan-Slavic and pan-Orthodox rhetoric masks a pan-Fascist agenda, and where the nationalist-communists' increasing influence over Russian foreign policy strengthens their influence over Russian domestic policy as well; (c) legitimizing aggression and even genocide ostensibly on behalf of "threatened" ethnic brethren in neighboring states; (d) providing the possibility of direct organizational, financial, military, and training cooperation between Serb Fascists and Russian Fascists, whether via Russian volunteers fighting in Bosnia (or indeed, Russian UN peacekeepers in Croatia and Bosnia, notorious for their intimate relations with, for example, the death squads of Serb paramilitary leader Željko Ražnjatović (Arkan), reciprocal visits of political party leaders, or ties established between Serb Fascist leaders in Belgrade, Pale, and Vukovar and Russian parliamentary and executive branch officials.

Russian Fascism strengthens Serb Fascism through these same channels, and through the political and de facto military support extended by the Russian government to Serbia and its allies in Croatia and Bosnia: Russian opposition to lifting the UN arms embargo from Bosnia, Russian opposition to NATO air strikes against Serb forces on the ground in Bosnia, and Russian support for Serb objectives in the UN/EU and now U.S./Russian mediation process.

Conclusion

I predict that genocidal Serb aggression will destroy Bosnia (at least for the historical short term) and eventually spread to Kosovo and Macedonia, that Russia will continue to grow more aggressive to its neighbors, and more hostile to the West, and that U.S. policy will continue to appease both Serbia and Russia. The history of this century has shown that it is not in the nature of fascism to be contained by appeasement, and that it is not in the nature of appeasement to give way to will and courage until fascism becomes an absolutely clear and present danger to the national survival of the appeaser. Even then, if past is precedent, it takes leaders of the stature of Winston Churchill and FDR to begin effective resistance, and dramatic national mobilization to make that resistance prevail.

That America and Russia can destroy each other with nuclear weapons may avert the repetition of total war as the culmination of the fascism/appeasement cycle of the 1990s. However, the reinforcing dynamic between fascism and appeasement, in the 1990s as in the 1930s, suggests that some sudden and dramatic shock—and a national security team neither predisposed to nor conditioned by appeasement—will be necessary to lift the United States out of the vicious circles outlined above.

And yet—post–Cold War America is stronger and wiser than Chamberlain's World War I–shaken Britain, or FDR's isolationist society. Fascism is a discredited force. Appeasement is a discredited way of dealing with it. America is not condemned to relive past tragedies. All it needs is leaders who will honestly face up to the challenges.

Notes

1. On the Russian diaspora, see Vera Tolz, "The Burden of the Imperial Legacy," *RFE/RL Research Report* 2, no. 20 (May 14, 1993); Andrew Wilson, "Crimea's Political Cauldron," *RFE/RL Research Report* 2, no. 45 (Nov. 12, 1993); Leon Gudkov, "The Disintegration of the USSR and Russians in the Republics," *Journal of Communist Studies* 9, no. 1 (Mar., 1993); and William D. Jackson, "Russia After the Crisis: Imperial Temptations: Ethnics Abroad," *Orbis* 38, no. 1 (Winter, 1994).

2. See Zbigniew Brzezinski, "The Premature Partnership," *Foreign Affairs* 73, no. 2 (Mar./Apr., 1994): 67–82; Paul Goble, "Russia and Its Neighbors," *Foreign Policy* 90 (Spring, 1993): 79–188; Paul Goble, "Can We Help Russia Become a Good Neighbor," *Democratizatsiya* 2, no. 1 (1994); Roman Szporluk, "Statehood and Nation-Building in Post-Soviet Space," draft of an introduction to forthcoming *The Influence of National Identity,* edited by Roman Szporluk, vol. 2 of *The International Politics of Eurasia: Newly Independent States Enter the Twenty-first Century,* edited by Karen Dawisha and Bruce Parrott (New York: M. E. Sharpe, 1994); Roman Szporluk, "Conflict in Soviet Domestic and Foreign Policy: Universal Ideology and National Tradition," in *Behavior, Culture and Conflict in World Politics,* edited by William Zimmerman and Harold K. Jacobson (Ann Arbor: University of Michigan Press, 1993); and Alexei G. Arbatov, "Russia's Foreign Policy Alternatives," *International Security* 18, no. 2 (Fall, 1993): 5–43.

3. See Roman Solchanyk, "The Politics of State-Building: Centre-Periphery Relations in Post-Soviet Ukraine," *Europe-Asia Studies* 46, no. 1 (1994): 47–68.

4. See Fiona Hill and Pamela Jewett, Back in the USSR—Russia's Intervention in the Internal Affairs of the Former Soviet Republics and the Implications for United States Policy Toward Russia, *Report,* Harvard University, John F. Kennedy School of Government, Jan., 1994; Thomas Goltz, "The Hidden Russian Hand," *Foreign Policy* 92 (Fall, 1993); Pol Kolsto and Andrei Edemsky, "The Dneister Conflict: Between Irredentism and Separatism," *Europe-Asia Review* 45, no. 6 (1993): 973–1000; James H. Slagle, "New Russian Military Doctrine: Sign of the Times," *Parameters* 24, no. 1 (Spring, 1994); Frank

Umbach, "The Security of an Independent Ukraine," *Jane's Intelligence Review*, Mar., 1994; and the following analyses of evolving Russian foreign and military policies, with particular regard to the "near abroad," in *RFE/RL Research Reports:* Jan S. Adams, "Who Will Make Russia's Foreign Policy in 1994?" 3, no. 6 (Feb. 11, 1994); Suzanne Crowe, "Russian Parliament Asserts Control over Sevastopol," 2, no. 31 (July 30, 1993); Suzanne Crowe, "Processes and Policies," 2, no. 20 (May 14, 1993); John Lough, "Defining Russia's Relations with Neighboring States," 2, no. 20 (May 14, 1993); Suzanne Crowe, "Russia Seeks Leadership in Regional Peacekeeping," 2, no. 15 (Apr. 9, 1993); Suzanne Crowe, "Russia Adopts a More Active Policy," 2, no. 12 (Mar. 19, 1993); Elizabeth Fuller, "Russia's Diplomatic Offensive in the Transcauscasus," 2, no. 39 (Oct. 1, 1993); Bess Brown, "Central Asian States Seek Russian Help," 2, no. 25 (June 18, 1993); and Keith-Martin, "Tadzhikistan: Civil War Without End," 2, no. 33 (Aug. 20, 1993).

5. For texts of the remarks of Deputy Secretary Talbott, Ambassador Pickering, and President Clinton, see State Department and White House transcripts as well as *U.S. Department of State Dispatch,* Feb. 21, 1994.
6. See John J. Mearsheimer, "The Case for a Ukrainian Nuclear Deterrent," *Foreign Affairs* 72, no. 3 (Summer, 1993): 50–66.
7. Author's conversation with Paul Goble, Senior Associate, Carnegie Endowment, Washington, D.C., Feb., 1994.
8. See Deputy Secretary Talbott's Jan. 25, 1994, testimony to the House Foreign Affairs Committee.
9. See Richard Johnson's chapter in this volume, "The Pinstripe Approach to Genocide."
10. See for example the public statements of Richard Nixon, Zbigniew Brzezinski, George Shultz, Casper Weinberger, Jean Kirkpatrick, Margaret Thatcher, Senators Bob Dole, Dennis DeConcini, Joseph Biden, and Richard Lugar and Congressmen Frank McCloskey, Steny Hoyer, and David Bonior.
11. See for example President Clinton's radio address on the U.S. stakes in Bosnia on February 19, 1994, on the eve of the end of the NATO Sarajevo air strike ultimatum.
12. See, however, Frank Umbach, "The Consequences of Western Policy Toward the Yugoslav Conflict and Its Impact Upon the Former Soviet Union," *European Security* 2, no. 2 (Summer, 1993); Suzanne Crowe, "Russia's Response to the Yugoslav Crisis," *RFE/RL Research Report* 30 (July 24, 1992), and "Reading Moscow's Policies Toward the Rump Yugoslavia," *RFE/RL Research Report* 44 (Nov. 6, 1992); Jack Snyder, "Nationalism and the Crisis of the Post-Soviet State," *Survival* 35, no. 1 (Spring, 1993); and Allen Lynch and Reneo Lukic, "Russian Foreign Policy and the Wars in the Former Yugoslavia," *RFE/RL Research Report* 2, no. 41 (Oct., 1993).

CHAPTER EIGHT

Boris Yeltsin as Abraham Lincoln
ALBERT WOHLSTETTER

In the two years since this essay was written, events in Chechnya and the Balkans have provided additional evidence in support of Professor Wohlstetter's central thesis. He therefore considered this essay unfinished, and, in the weeks prior to his death on January 10, 1997, was preparing to update and revise it. Even though this chapter is unfinished, it is published here, with the permission of his wife, Roberta Wohlstetter, because it captures perceptively the central themes of the present volume: For the Clinton Administration to draw parallels between Boris Yeltsin and Abraham Lincoln is to engage in the conceit of innocence. Yeltsin is no Lincoln. Moreover, the parallels between Moscow-sponsored brutality toward the Muslims in Chechnya and Belgrade-sponsored brutality toward the Muslims in Bosnia are ominous and deserve much more attention than they have received up to now. Finally, Professor Wohlstetter exhibits in this and all his other work on U.S. foreign policy the boldness, commitment to principles, and moral stance that I have characterized as the innocence of a by-gone era. For all these reasons, it is an important piece that needs to be published even though Professor Wohlstetter, the quintessential perfectionist, would have revised it had he been able to.

—*Ed.*

Andrei Kozyrev, Russia's foreign minister, has been defending the bombing of Chechen civilians to suppress the independence that the

Chechens declared in 1991. He compares Yeltsin's war to Lincoln's Civil War against the secessionist South. And Michael McCurry, then about to debut as the new White House spokesman, offered some smooth support for Yeltsin's and Kozyrev's "new democracy . . . in the former Soviet Union," saying, "in *our* long history as a democracy . . . we dealt with a secessionist movement in an armed conflict called the Civil War." He added later that while "we don't like innocent civilians losing their lives . . . Chechnya is by international recognition part of Russia."

So was Yeltsin's Russia by international recognition part of Gorbachev's Soviet Union in 1991, when Soviet soldiers killed innocent civilians in Vilnius seeking independence for Lithuania, shot at citizens in Baku to head off independence for Azerbaijan, and fired into a peaceful demonstration in Tbilisi to stop Georgian independence. Yeltsin in 1991 was president of the Russian republic and was *for Russia seceding*. He denounced the use of the Soviet army against Soviet citizens in the Baltics as a violation of the Soviet constitution—just as now civilian leaders of the movement toward democracy in Russia and some of Russia's highest ranking generals are unconstitutional, barbarous, and a political disaster.

In a January, 1990, editorial, George Will observed that "the contrast between Lithuania's arguments now and South Carolina's then [in 1860] is striking, beginning with the fact that Carolinians wanted secession to preserve slavery, whereas Lithuanians want secession to escape it." He wrote, "The best the Soviet Union can hope for is the choice between imploding and exploding." If Gorbachev didn't choose, Will suggested, the Soviet Union "would suffer both fates—implosion and explosion—simultaneously." The same might be said for Russia and Yeltsin today. Unfortunately, Western policies, by encouraging both internal repression and external expansion, make both fates more likely.

Secretary of State Warren Christopher's immediate reaction to the bombing and shelling of Chechen civilians was to express "sympathy" for Yeltsin—the bombardier. He had only "done what he had to do to prevent [Chechnya] from breaking away." He was as "restrained as [he] could be." *In 1995, as in 1991, Western Europeans and U.S. leaders are blindly resolved to preserve the integrity of states whose subjects have to be bombed into subjection.* Western leaders expressing pious concerns about the killing of Chechen innocents resisting Russian domination cannot escape all responsibility for it if they insist on Russia's unconditional right to keep the Chechens in subjection.

So, while Bill Clinton and Warren Christopher are saying it's an "internal affair" for Russia, Russian democrats and some top Russian generals are saying that, in the days of instant global television, no slaughter of innocent civilians is an internal affair.

The situation in Chechnya, a place that Boris Yeltsin vows to cleanse of "gangsters"—using the word broadly enough to apply to any Chechen who resists—is an affair that is neither local nor confined to Russia. Its ramifications extend far beyond Chechnya, to other Russian republics and to now-independent former Soviet republics (FSRs) where Yeltsin and Kozyrev have been using the latest incarnation of the KGB, as well as Russian troops acting as "peacekeepers," to stir up ethnic conflicts that drive civilians on all sides from their homes and leave Russian troops in place, frequently on former Soviet military bases. Yeltsin's assaults on Chechnya and the FSRs, moreover, are closely related to Slobodan Milošević's cleansing of non-Serbs from former Yugoslav republics and from Kosovo, an internal part of Serbia seized in 1913, to which two U.S. administrations have inconsistently issued a guarantee against Serbian attack.

Milošević was the only European head of state who sent a letter of congratulations to the plotters of the August, 1991, coup in the Soviet Union. Yeltsin, who was at the top of the plotters' hit list, denounced Milošević's barbarism; in April, 1992, Yeltsin joined the United States in voting for UN sanctions against Serbia for its seizure of land and "forcible expulsions" designed to "change the ethnic composition of the population" of Bosnia and its "continued expulsion of non-Serb civilians" from Croatia. There was no doubt about the source of the genocidal aggression. But the steady retreat of Western mediators from even a show of enforcing the sanctions against Serbia taught Yeltsin and Kozyrev that they could answer Russian critics of their Western bias against asserting Russian interests in Eastern Europe and the FSRs by adopting the critics' own program of Great Russian expansion—and still be "Western." Until late in the assault on Chechnya, U.S. and other Western leaders have largely ignored fears of Russia expressed by the newly independent states and some Russian republics. And Western "mediation" has helped Milošević create a Greater Serbia.

Russia soon became the most overt supplier of the tools of war that Serbia was sending to its proxies in Bosnia and Croatia. By the summer of 1994 Yeltsin and Kozyrev had announced that Russia had no international borders other than those of the former Soviet Union; and they have made clear that Russia's sphere of interest extends to its "near abroad" and beyond that—even to Bosnia and Croatia, which have never been in Moscow's sphere of interest. Milošević's Greater Serbia had become the model for the Greater Russia of Yeltsin and Kozyrev.

In fact, the assault on Chechnya resembles in detail Milošević's 1991 assault on Croatia: for example, his use of fifth columns and paramilitary and military forces from Serbia (initially in disguise and then used openly to "separate" the combatants); the bombing into rubble of hospitals and other buildings in Croatian towns like Vukovar; brazenly silly claims that it was the victims who were bombing and shelling their own women and children and their own slender means of defense; the offer of cease-fires as a means of disarming the victims; and, above all, the use of terror to drive out the population of strategic towns. All to be repeated in Bosnia.

For some time now, Russia, as a member of the Contact Group, has surpassed the Europeans in openly supporting a confederation of Serbia with its proxies. The confederation would make sure that a heavily-armed Serbia will continue after the Contact Group "peace" to send soldiers and war materials to complete the creation of a contiguous Greater Serbia at the expense of Bosnia and Croatia, which the Contact Group persists in trying to deprive of arms.

Western governments supported Gorbachev against Yeltsin in the years leading up to the August coup, just as they now back Yeltsin against any alternative. But they are mistaken now, just as they were then, to support an individual rather than a path of evolution toward democracy, free markets, and conformity to international norms banning the seizure of territory by force and genocidal attacks on civilians. Western policy makes it more likely that Russia will keep moving in the wrong direction.

The expansion of Russian control and influence in its near and not-so-near abroad has dire implications for the future of democracy and free markets in Russia, as well as in the FSRs, and for the future of Russia as a trustworthy "partner" for peace and for arms-control agreements. In fact, the "new democracy . . . in the former Soviet Union" referred to by McCurry—unlike that of Lincoln—has yet to come into being. Russia has a long way to travel to reach a democratic government with the checks and balances of a parliament, presidency and judiciary under the rule of law. Yeltsin has himself said that "Russia comprehends democracy poorly. . . . In our history, it has been all or nothing. Either revolutionary anarchy or a ruthless regime."

It's most unlikely that Yeltsin's repeated bombardments interlaced with pledges to stop bombing civilians in Grozny and surrounding villages indicate that he is not in charge—that General Pavel Grachev, the defense minister, has repeatedly surprised Yeltsin by disobeying orders to stop. Yeltsin can hardly have been repeatedly surprised in Chechnya, as some pundits suggest; the attacks appeared in Russian media as well as on CNN International. In the October, 1993, confrontation between Yeltsin and the parliament, it was Yeltsin who ordered Grachev to bring tanks into Moscow to use against parliament. And it was a reluctant Grachev whom Yeltsin described as hostage to the "deeply democratic slogan" that "the army is outside politics."[1]

Yeltsin made his narrow escape in that confrontation with the Supreme Soviet by, as he says, "formally . . . violating the constitution, going the route of anti-democratic measures and dispersing the parliament, all for the sake of establishing democracy and the rule of law in the country, while the parliament was defending the constitution in order to overthrow the lawfully elected president." Yeltsin applies his doubts about parliaments much more widely than to the Supreme Soviet, the congress conceived by Gorbachev. He doesn't think much of the "bandits, fascists and criminals" who make up the Supreme Soviet. He says, with heavy sarcasm, that, bad as it is, it is no "freak in the wonderful family of parliaments of the world." His appraisal extends to the U.S. Congress: "The word *congressman, deputy* or *senator* in various languages is not surrounded by such a glowing halo. We have only to recall Mark Twain to realize that this elected body has long been associated in the minds of Western people with corruption, official sloth, and an inflated and empty self-importance ... constantly beset with scandals and exposés." Yeltsin's reference to Twain recalls Pudd'nhead Wilson's humorous statement that "probably ... there is no native American criminal class except Congress." But Yeltsin is no humorist.

His low opinion of the present Russian parliament—on which the West relies for ratifying extensions of the Anti-Ballistic Missile (ABM) Treaty, the Strategic Arms Reduction Treaty (START), and so forth—exceeds his contempt for the parliament that ratified the original treaties. *Yeltsin says that the latter—Congress's dedicated arms controllers will be interested to learn—was only "feigning advocacy for disarmament [and] peace throughout the world." The present parliament is "not even pretending to pass itself off as peaceloving, as its predecessor in the era of Communist stagnation had done."* None of this qualifies Russia as a believable North Atlantic Treaty Organization (NATO) "partner for peace," or as a trustworthy signatory of *new* treaties on strategic arms and strategic defense, or as a credibly impartial member of a group working out a "just and lasting peace" in the Balkans.

In the Balkans, the American, British, French, German, and Russian leaders of the five-nation Contact Group have been trying to compel the acceptance of their continually changing "take it or leave it" "peace" plan. After three and a half years of Serbian ethnic cleansing, Jimmy Carter has made a breakthrough, we are told, and the State Department has joined him in pressing Bosnians and Croats to accept the peace plan. Meanwhile, the Krajina Serbs in Croatia continue to punctuate Carter's "cease-fire" with cross-border attacks violating Bosnian and Croatian sovereignty, and have just stated that their next step will be to unite with the Serbs in Bosnia and, as a step after that, with Serbia itself.

That just happens to be the Contact Group's deliberately obscure "peace plan." It would create a contiguous Greater Serbia. And that, as any fine-grained analysis of the thoroughly mixed demography shows, means "cleansing" the area of non-Serbs, severing Croatia, and breaking Bosnia into a half dozen islands under Serbian siege with no defendable connection with each other or with the outside world of trade and investment they need to survive. It would mean increased forced migrations and civil disorder in a Europe whose imperial past has left its populations irrevocably impure.

The overreaching of Eurocrats, who confidently expected to "solve" the Balkan problem quickly, has already revived old antagonisms among the members of the new "united" Europe and has bitterly divided the Atlantic Alliance.

Ideas for a NATO expanded to the east by the inclusion of Russia as a "Partner for Peace," as well as the Eastern European and former Soviet republics, appear mutually incompatible rather than merely utopian. It is a resurgent, expansive Russia from whom these FSRs and former members of the Warsaw Pact need protection.

The last five years of European and American policy for southeast and east central Europe and for the FSRs have resulted in both implosion and explosion—neither peace nor containment. *It is time for a basic reassessment of policy for the world emerging from the fall of the Communist dictatorships.*

The new Congress is taking as part of its first order of business hearings for a "Peace Powers Act of 1995" to replace the War Powers Resolution. It will cast a critical eye on the wild growth of "peace-keeping" where there is no peace to keep. What most urgently needs consideration, based on Balkan recent history, is the assurance that no American forces will be used in peacekeeping operations inconsistent with the UN Charter and the Convention Against Genocide: that they will not be used to consolidate a country's hold on territory seized by violence; that they will not facilitate the cleansing from that territory of any ethnic group; and that American forces will be able to achieve a clearly defined political objective and to defend themselves without fear of veto by any country supporting the aggressor. Congress should also consider imposing constraints on the billions of dollars now used, directly or by way of international organizations such as the International Monetary Fund (IMF) or the World Bank, to support "peacekeeping" operations by other countries that do not meet the above criteria.

In hearings on a "Bosnia and Herzegovina Self-Defense Act," Congress will review the increasingly zany political arguments advanced by the Mitterrand and Major governments for continuing an arms embargo that never validly applied to Bosnia since it violates the inherent rights of Bosnia, a recognized, independent member of the UN, to receive arms for its self-defense. The Clinton administration, at its outset, strongly opposed the embargo but characteristically reversed itself under European pressure, just when European policies in the Balkans and the embargo itself had become admitted failures. The administration now is making an all-out effort to silence doubts and to muster the Pentagon and the intelligence community in support of the failed policy.

Besides rigorously examining the old bad arguments for starving the victims of means of self-defense, the new Congress should outflank the administration by going to the heart of the problem: the persistent failure of Europe and the UN bureaucracy, since May, 1992, even to try enforcing the valid ban on Serbia's reinforcement and resupply of its proxies in Bosnia and Croatia. Russia has been in the lead of Britain and France in an effort to legalize Serbia's reinforcement and resupply of its proxies, even though that puts U.S. and other NATO airmen as well as anUN peacekeepers at risk and would make even riskier a complex and dangerous operation of withdrawing them.

That operation in particular would bring out an essential connection between the changes these two pieces of legislation should make. For a dangerous operation engaging so many American foot soldiers and airmen, it would be essential for U.S. commanders to be in control of the campaign and to be able to decide (without UN second-guessing) on when, where, and how to suppress enemy capabilities to disrupt the operation and inflict serious harm on our own and allied forces.

Notes

1. As Yeltsin writes: "Grachev raised his hand and addressed me, slowly squeezing out the words: 'Boris Nikolayevich, are you giving me sanction to use tanks in Moscow?' I looked at him in silence. . . . 'I'll send you a written order,'" p. 278, in Boris Yeltsin, *The Struggle for Russia* (New York: Times Books, 1994).

CHAPTER NINE

A Tale of Two Serbias
CHANDLER ROSENBERGER

The brutality with which contemporary Serbia has pursued conquests in Bosnia and Croatia has confounded the West. In seeking the cultural sources of the savagery, commentators have turned to history, arguing that the backward Balkan peoples are simply not members in good standing of the modern world. But does this mean the Serbs are not a "modern" nation, that they are somehow trapped in the past? A closer look at the origins of Serbian national identity demonstrates that its roots are in traditions of Romanticism—German and Russian—that are entirely modern. Rejection of Western principles such as rationality and moderation are nearly as old—and just as "modern"—as those principles themselves. For nations whose intellectuals were as disappointed with the Enlightenment as were the thinkers of Serbia, the romantic tradition provided and provides as much solace—and as much recourse to violence—as it did for shapers of German and Russian national identity.

The tale of contemporary Serbia is a tale of the blossoming of these two traditions. It is first a tragic story of how Karadžićes— Vuk in the nineteenth century, Radovan in our own—have turned from the Enlightenment toward self-styled primitivism. While Vuk Karadžić (1787–1864), codifier of the modern Serbian literary language, helped to forge the Serbian national identity in a romantic, anti-Enlightenment mold, his intellectual successor, Radovan Karadžić (1945?–), the paramount political leader of the Serbian enclave within Bosnia, used this national vision to justify mass murder. But the story of the Bosnian tragedy is also a tale of how two Markovićes — Svetozar in the last century, Mihailo in ours — placed the hope of Serbian renewal in the rule of "scientific," "antibureaucratic" elites. Svetozar Marković (1846–75) first brought to Serbia an ideology of positivist socialism and revolutionary terrorism; his intellectual heir, Mihailo Marković (1923–), preached a doctrine of reformed, decentralized Marxism both at home and in the West before returning to Belgrade to make policy for the ruling Socialist Party of Serbia. The genius of the Serbian president Slobodan Milošević has not been, as is often argued, to slip from Communism to nationalism, to "control the steam" of brewing ethnic hate. Milošević's brilliance has rather been to recognize how deep both the traditions of the Karadžićes and Markovićes ran in his native land, and how easily they came together as one.

Balkan Christians before Serbian Nationalism

From the fourteenth to the seventeenth century the Ottoman sultan ruled the territory that was to become Serbia from the top down. The government, or Porte, recruited most of its military and civilian administrators through the *devshirme* system, whereby Christian boys of unusual intelligence were taken from their homes, trained in Constantinople, and converted to Islam. (Muslim boys could not be enslaved.) After their education the slaves either remained in the capital to join the Porte or were sent as *janjićari* into provinces, where they maintained local defenses by running large agricultural estates. Together, the Porte and the janjićaries provided defense and enforcement of the sultan's laws. Muslims were expected to obey the *sheriat,* a body of law based on the Koran. Christians, however, were only expected to follow secular laws, or *kanuns.* Intra-Christian disputes were mediated by elected local officials (the *knezes*) gathered in loose associations called *zadrugas,* and representatives of the Orthodox Church, who answered either to the patriarch for speakers of Greek in Constantinople or to autocephalous patriarchs in Ohrid and Peć (who used Old Church Slavonic). These Christian representatives suited the Porte's interests: the clerics could be relied upon to inculcate passivity among their flock by arguing that Muslim rule was punishment for earthly sins, while the *knezes* were scattered widely enough not to pose a unified threat.[1]

Since the terrible tragedy of Constantinople's rule was to become a theme of Serbian Romantic writers, it is important to remember that the writers who knew the Ottoman empire firsthand seemed not to mind it. One of the oldest examples of Serbian epic poetry on record was collected from the countryside in the seventeenth century and portrays the exploits of Marko Kraljević, a Serb in the service of Ottoman sultan Sulieman the Magnificent. Marko certainly has a dark side. When mocked by a woman whom he and two friends court, he gouges out her eyes and taunts, "Choose now, thou maid Rosanda, choose now which thou wilt!"[2] But he is hardly shown to be suffering under the Ottoman yoke. He fights bravely and proudly for "his" Sultan and literally (and regularly) gets away with murder.

His lesser crimes are also overlooked. When, for example, he is told by the Sultan himself that he may not drink or dance during Ramadan, he shoves his ruler against a wall and protests, "Father Sultan Sulieman / If I drink wine in Ramadan / If indeed I drink / my faith alloweth it." The Sultan's response is mild, to say the least. "The Sultan put his hand in his pocket," the poem continues, "And drew forth a hundred ducats / and gave them to Kraljević Marko. / 'Go Marko,' quoth he, 'Drink wine to thy heart's content.'"[3]

How could Marko drink knowing his nation languished under the Sultan's whip? Because no such nation yet existed. In fact, the poems that portray the torments of oppressed Serbia were penned long after Serbia had achieved a measure of autonomy under the rule of a pig farmer turned king. And they were written not by men suffering under Constantinople but by frustrated intellectuals eager to make a silk purse from sow's shepherd.

The Creation of a Prenational Serbian Identity

The delicate balance of Islamic Porte and Christian quiescence began to break down when the empire reached the limits of its expansion at the gates of Vienna in 1683. Deprived of war booty, the Porte was forced to abandon the expensive devshirme training and instead to sell its highest offices to unqualified Muslims. The new breed of janjićari were more and more likely to be loose cannons, disobedient and unscrupulous in their accumulation of personal wealth. In order to maintain the loyalty of Christian knezes, the Porte turned to a loose affiliation of Greek merchants (known as the Phanariots) close to their Patriarch to serve as a bridge to Christian villages. The Phanariots deployed their own *dragoman,* or "facilitators," to serve as an administration running parallel to the crumbling Ottoman system. The dragoman in turn built ties to Christian militia, known as *armatoles,* whose mission it was to defend villages from the most unscrupulous janjićari.

Unlike the passive clergy, the dragomani preached a message of Christian exclusionism; the Ottomans, they believed, were destined to lose control of their empire eventually, at which time the Byzantine empire would be restored. The autocephalous church based in Peć cooperated with the dragomani but responded to Phanariot ambitions with a message of its own: its subjects were heirs, not of Byzantium, but of the medieval Serbian kingdom. It henceforth referred to its ecclesiastical territory as the "Serbian lands."[4]

Loyal only to their villages and their church, the Orthodox Christians walked a tightrope throughout the eighteenth century between the Ottoman and Hapsburg empires. Since 1688, Belgrade and lands just to the north had been in Hapsburg possession, forming a "military frontier" against Constantinople; lands to the south and larger cities such as Niš remained in Ottoman hands. As practitioners of the Orthodox rite, the Serbs preferred Ottoman rule, since they feared forced conversion to Catholicism, but were willing to entertain Hapsburg offers of autonomy in exchange for their cooperation during Vienna's campaigns southward.

In 1690, Hapsburg emperor Leopold I offered religious liberty and free election of local leaders to Christians willing to fight under the Hapsburg banner; with the encouragement of Peć, families streamed across the Danube to establish autonomous settlements along the "military frontier" and a religious and cultural center in Sremski Karlovci. From 1718 to 1737, Hapsburg empress Maria Theresa was able to fulfil her predecessor's promises. Territory as far south as Niš was captured; elected knezes divided the lands into fifteen districts, which were overseen as one by an Austrian official (who took the Germanized title *oberknez.*)

When the Ottomans reclaimed the lost territory in 1739, they left the reformed knez system in place but abolished the patriarch of Peć. Religious authority among the "Serbs" could now only be found in the Hapsburg lands. Since Serbs who had fled enjoyed cultural autonomy regardless of their location, even they who settled and studied in Vienna were allowed to vote at councils of the metropolitan in Sremski Karlovci. "The regular meetings of the councils," Barbara Jelavich writes, "came to resemble national assemblies. They were held primarily to choose bishops and the heads of monasteries, but they also discussed general problems and matters of interest to the Serbian community."[5]

The move of the center of Serbian identity from Peć to Sremski Karlovci split the creators of Serbian culture — the clerics — from territory of the kingdom they had imagined for themselves. The Serbs of the Hapsburg empire prospered as merchants but remained marginal, insecure citizens, forbidden to purchase property outside the military frontier and dependent on the goodwill of the Viennese government to protect them from forced assimilation into Catholic and even Hungarian society. Denied a place at the center of Hapsburg affairs, they plowed their earnings back into their kingdom of dreams, establishing an array of educational and literary foundations in Sremski Karlovci and following events among the Serbs of the Ottoman Empire closely.

But while meetings of the Orthodox metropolitan may have *resembled* national councils, no mention of a "nation" or "people" (*narod* meaning both in most Slavic tongues) appears among the Serbs until the 1790s,[6] when two well-traveled Orthodox clerics returned home inspired to write on secular affairs. Jovan Rajić, a cleric from Sremski Karlovci, found inspiration in two trips to Russia for his "History of the Several Slavic People, Particularly the Bulgars, Croats and Serbs." Published in 1794, it focused mostly on the Serbs. About the same time Dositej Obradović, also of the Hapsburg military frontier, returned from travels in Western Europe to develop a Serbian literary language. Having seen the "enlightened nations of Europe," Obradović felt the urge "to communicate my thoughts to my fellow men and to tell them whatever good and sensible things I have heard and learned from others."[7]

The Re-Evaluation of Western Values: One Strand of Serbian Romanticism

Infused with the national idea they found circulating in Europe—especially in Russia—the Serbs of the Military Frontier had high hopes for the liberation of the largely Serbian *pashaluk*, or province, around Belgrade. Under Austrian and Russian pressure, the Porte had withdrawn the janjićari from the province in 1791, leaving its government largely to the Christian knezes. When they abruptly returned in 1801 (against Constantinople's wishes) the knezes were suddenly denied rights the Porte had guaranteed them. While plotting a strategy of self-defense in February, 1804, seventy-two Serbian elders and knezes were murdered by janjićari. The attack prompted an immediate and initially successful uprising among the remaining knezes.

To the Serbs of Sremski Karlovci, this marked the first steps to the foundation of a Serbian nation-state. Within the first few months Metropolitan Steven Stratimović had submitted an unsigned "Draft for the Establishment of a New Slavo-Serbian State" to Russian foreign minister Prince Adam Czartoryski. Sava Tekelija, also of the Military Frontier, sent a memorandum to Napoleon in June, 1804, asking him to help establish a friendly "Slavic state" to be named Illyria. When the French ruler turned him down, Tekelija asked the same of the Austrians.[8] Obradović, the first codifier of the Serbian language, moved to Belgrade shortly after the revolt began; there he attempted to establish a modern educational system.[9]

All were to be terribly disappointed, both by the Great Powers they hoped would act as saviors and by the people they hoped to save. Not only did Napoleon turn them down, he added insult to injury by founding the "Illyrian Provinces" in 1809 on coastal territory populated by Croats and Slovenes. In 1805 the Hapsburgs, concerned about the French and eager to keep a peaceful southern border, officially declared neutrality. Russia declared war on the Ottomans in 1806, but was chiefly concerned with acquiring the Danubian principalities. Serbia barely figured in the Czar's plans.

The Christian residents of the pashaluk, too, proved to be of little use; they were good soldiers but poor nationalists. After expelling the janjićari in 1806 (initially with the help of the Ottoman administration), the leader of the local population, a livestock trader named Djordje Petrović, at first sought merely to increase his powers within the empire. Petrović, immortalized in Serbian Romantic poetry as "Karageorge," only turned on the Porte when the Russians, eager that the Serbs should continue to draw Ottoman forces away from the Danubian principalities, plied him with bribes. Petrović then relaunched the war by reneging on a peace agreement and murdering the Porte's diplomats and guard without warning.[10] When this second campaign failed, Petrović fled into Austrian territory, leaving the newly born Serbian nation with little more than that with which it had begun — its language and its peripheral status in the two empires it straddled. Worse, the Serbs of Sremski Karlovci learned how indifferent, duplicitous, and savage were the cousins in whom they had placed so much hope, and how little the great powers of the day cared for their plight. It was an inauspicious beginning for a "nation" that they had hoped would learn from the "enlightened."

Fortunately for the sake of their self-esteem, the Serbs of the Hapsburg empire were quickly provided with a means by which to translate their meager cultural resources into a source of national pride. Intellectuals of the German principalities too had been bitterly disappointed by the Enlightenment doctrines of Prussia; promised higher social status after earning university degrees they were instead relegated to a life of embittering poverty. The German writers took their revenge by forging Romanticism, a vision in which the virtues praised by the Enlightenment became vices and its vices — for example, irrationality and brutality — became badges of honor.[11]

The German Romantic J. G. Herder, for example, began in radical relativism. There was no use comparing nations, Herder claimed; God had divided mankind into a variety of nations in order to fulfil a grander plan in which the characteristics of each would play a part. "The creator," Herder wrote, "is the only one who can see all nations in their diversity without losing sight of their unity."[12] Nothing was more necessary to this "unity in diversity" than the wide range of human languages, each of which was composed of particular words and logical connections necessary for particular circumstances. None could be excluded, since together all languages would fulfil the divine plan. Nor was there any use attempting to translate words forged in these unique relations, since "these connections are so intensely national, engendered according to a particular disposition and viewpoint of a people and conditioned by the time and circumstance of a country."[13]

Should one like a peek at which nations and languages God favors, however, Herder provides it. As Liah Greenfeld has pointed out, Herder's tolerance of the great diversity of life did not extend to "modern, that is, 'enlightened' society—at that time represented by France, England, and Prussia. The fact that this society put a premium on reason," Greenfeld writes, "was not interpreted as a reflection of its material conditions; the reality of the modern, rational society was not viewed as a sign of its particular perfection. Instead, modern society was considered an exception among human societies, an aberration."[14] God, acting through Nature, prefers the most "natural" nations, Herder wrote; since nature educates families, "the most natural state is, therefore, *one* nation, an extended family with one national character." Any larger states composed of "a wild mixing of various races and nationalities" are "but patched-up contraptions, fragile machines, appropriately called state-machines, for they are wholly devoid of inner life, and their component parts are connected through mechanical contrivances instead of bonds of sentiment." Only a cruel God would keep power in the hands of such "lifeless monstrosities," since they were "contrived by that kind of politics which plays with men and nations as if they were inanimate particles." But the God of Nature is not so cruel, for "history shows sufficiently that these instruments of human pride are formed of clay, and like all clay, they will dissolve or crumble to pieces."[15]

Herder's description of an ideal nation—primitive, patriarchical, dependent for its identity on its language, and persecuted by a multinational empire—should seem tailor-made for disappointed Serbs, since it was. Herder avidly collected Serbian oral epic poems and openly admired the nation that produced them. In the Serbs Herder found a people to whom he could condescend and yet in whom he could find traits which were so much more like his own beleaguered Germany than like France or England that he could celebrate backwardness without admitting to it.

The Serbs were quick to return the compliment—not the Serbs

living in the pashaluk, who were busy running a crude autonomous government, but rather those Serbs clinging to a bruised self-image as they made their precarious way through the Hapsburg empire. No one perhaps was more grateful than Vuk Karadžić, a freelance ideologue of southern Slav politics who depended on a Catholic Slovenian priest for his living in Vienna. Karadžić absorbed Herder thoroughly, setting out to collect such epic poems as he could find and writing others that cast Petrović—now "Karageorge," Turkish for "Black George"—in the Herderian image. The difference between the original poems collected and the later poems written by disaffected Romantic intellectuals is telling; while the former celebrate life under the Ottomans, the latter commemorate savagery for its own sake.

At the time of Serbian uprisings and throughout the nineteenth century, for example, the Serbian poetic tradition was taken over by academicians in Belgrade for whom the mild treatment of Marko was apparently not the stuff from which they thought nations are built. One English translator, W. A. Morrison, acknowledges that those recording Karageorge's failed uprising were composed by academics in a stiffer style. Influenced by their counterparts in Germany and disillusioned with the West that had educated them but had not come to their aid, Belgrade's intellectuals crouched over their desks and penned the "natural" epic poems that were to demonize the "Turk." Whatever these later poems lacked in grace they made up for in vehemence. Indeed, one of the most depressing aspects of looking into the Serbian mind is finding that the poems and legends that have inspired countless rapes and murders should themselves be so flat and simplistic. One would imagine that only powerful toxins could move men to commit such acts. Instead, one finds that the Serbs guerrillas of today have killed and for kitsch.

Take, for example, the tales of heroic Curta and his band of hajduks, or highwaymen. More self-consciously heroic men would be hard to sketch. "We must make our reckonings," Curta tells his men, "in accordance with the haiduk custom." A few lines down Curta congratulates his men for having "arranged our hiding-places / In accordance with ancient custom."[16] All is done, of course, not only with the best adherence to custom but with the best intentions. No more random adventures, such as those of Marko Kraljević; now, in the face of the oppressing Turk, all is done for one of two strangely anonymous masses—either the *raya* (Christians) who "could no longer pay their taxes" or the "forebears," whom every man is called to "avenge." Both, it seems, have suffered—however unconsciously—since the defeat of Prince Lazar on the field of Kosovo Polje in 1389; gone are memories of Marko's willing collaboration with the Sultan. And both are to be avenged, a religious vision at one point promises, by the beheading of Belgrade's seven Muslim *dahis*, or provincial governors. In the hands of Belgrade intellectuals, a fresh oral tradition of adventures became a stern summons to battle, stiff as a flagpole and humorless as a gun.

Karadžić had cooperated with his patron, Bartholomew Kopitar, in codifying a common south Slav language around the stokavian dialect spoken by Serbs in Herzegovina;[17] together, the two had succeeded through the 1830s in convincing skeptical Croats to accept as theirs the tongue of a people they considered somewhat primitive. But when Kopitar's group sought to use the language as a basis for a south Slav movement of "Illyrians," Karadžić and his Serbian followers turned the tables on them. Since, following Herder, a language is the hallmark of a nation, then speakers of a language must be thought to be one nation. "Under the influence of Karadžić numerous Serbs came to view stokavian as purely Serbian," Ivo Lederer writes. "This view led to the somewhat extreme view that anyone who spoke stokavian, no matter of what religion, was a Serb."[18]

One could only believe that Serbia's national destiny was to unite all Serbs if one thought of them as members of a nation and dreamed of that nation's "liberation." A "liberator" of Karadžić's model would, furthermore, have to define that nation as a linguistic collective. Djordje Petrović, who was so willing to cut deals with the Sultan, was clearly no such man. In the hands of Serbian academic poets, however, his stand-in visage—"Karageorge"—became one. "Drina water," Karageorge is portrayed as saying:

> *O, thou noble barrier*
> *Thou that partest Bosnia from Serbia!*
> *Soon the day will dawn, O Drina water*

*Soon will dawn the day when I shall cross thee
Pass through all the noble land of Bosnia.*[19]

The Illyrian movement collapsed, Hans Kohn writes, under the weight of Serbian pride. "This feeling of Serbian pride," Kohn writes, "was motivated by the fact that in their struggle for liberation from the Turks . . . the Serbs were the only Balkan people who could claim for themselves the *fara da se*. Greeks, Romanians, and Bulgarians owed their liberty to a large extent to outside intervention, to active sympathies and the military and diplomatic support of some of the great powers. The Serbs owed everything to themselves, to the heroism and ferocity of their people and the daring of their leaders."[20]

The seeds of the breakdown of Serb-Croat relations certainly lay in Serbian pride. But can one infer that it was a *confident* pride that made the Serbs aloof? Almost certainly not—as Kohn himself concedes. In desperation, the Serbian intellectuals stranded in the Hapsburg Empire had had to turn their original Enlightenment vision on its head to admire cousins so patently cruder than the Croats with whom men like Karadžić associated but whom they could not join. The legacy of Karadžić and of the writers who penned "natural" epic poems is one of common *wounded* pride, a bitterness salved only by a romantic tradition that demonized the unattainable good and worshiped the crude cruelty around them.

In an odd twist of history, the figure on the contemporary Serbian scene who has most obviously inherited Vuk Karadžić's romantic mind shares his last name. In tracing the historical origins of the mentality of Bosnian Serb president Radovan Karadžić, western journalists have often pointed uncritically to the romantic nineteenth-century poems—those that showed the Serbs locked in an eternal struggle with the Muslim world. They have unfortunately rarely asked if the poems described the actual condition of Serbia under Ottoman rule or if they were perhaps written by men frustrated more by modern society than by a distant and aloof sultan. This is too bad, since a look at the writings of the twentieth-century Karadžić reveal many of the obsessions that his nineteenth-century namesake knew.

Radovan Karadžić's poetry reveals a man who (to put it mildly) finds daily life hard going and who finds refuge in dreams of violent retribution. Like the Belgrade academicians who shaped his tradition, Radovan Karadžić daydreams of lonely landscapes shattered by guerrilla attacks. "I am finally lost," he writes in "A Morning Hand Grenade":

> *I am glowing like a cigarette*
> *On a neurotic's lip:*
> *While they look for me everywhere*
> *I wait in the ambush of the dawn.*

Trapped and alienated, the narrator longs for self-destruction, for

> *A great chance*
> *To abandon once*
> *All that my times offer to me,*
> *And to throw a morning hand grenade*
> *Loaded with the laugh*
> *Of a lonesome man*
> *With a dark character.*[21]

Nor does the Karadžić of our age have any more respect for reason than his predecessor. In *The Mad Javelin*, Karadžić implores a listener to:

> *Measure your steps, the swing of your arm*
> *The javelin that you are throwing is mad*
> *Places that wait for it are*
> *Nameless and senseless.*[22]

"For the most part," one commentator wrote, "Karadžić's poems conjure up a psychic landscape of eerie and illogical violence. His narrators often invoke the Devil as an authority on justice, and just as often they suffer from paranoia, delusions, and various manias. The overall effect is a kind of paramilitary surrealism."[23] But as Western journalists visiting Bosnian Serb soldiers have noticed, a taste for self-styled irrational (and often drunken) bravado is one Karadžić shares with many of his troops. In tracing such behavior back to Balkan primitiveness, however, those same journalists have badly misled their readers. The Bosnian Serbs are no more inherently "primitive" than was Nijinsky when he danced *The Rite of*

Spring. Their own deadly dance is a contemporary reaction against modernity and is as much a part of it as rationality itself.

For all its colorful bloodthirstiness, the tradition of the Karadžićes has merely served as a handmaiden to another radically anti-Western tradition—that of "scientific," "anti-bureaucratic" socialism. Like the worship of stern, irrational warriors, it too has its roots in anti-Western romanticism; unlike such soldiering, it is deadly serious and in control of the Serbian state itself.

Russian Romanticism and Balkan Radicalism: Svetozar Marković

By the mid-1850s the Serbian pashaluk of the Ottoman Empire had taken on many of the trappings of a nation-state. Miloš Obrenović, leader of the second uprising, had founded not only an autonomous administration but an absolutist royal dynasty, served by a foreign ministry and able to deploy ninety thousand soldiers. Monarchical succession, while colored by the competition between the heirs of "Karageorge" and Obrenović, was peaceful. The Ottoman "yoke" so lamented in romantic poetry had in fact virtually disappeared, and the Serbian monarch was afforded the luxury of declining aid from Austria and Russia for fear that the meddling of the Great Powers would prove more burdensome than rapprochement with the Porte. To the frustration of the intellectuals in the Military Frontier, leaders of the Principality showed little interest in their schemes to absorb the Bosnians and Croats. Instead, Belgrade set about wheeling and dealing its way to gaining control of the lands once held by the medieval kingdom. The *Načertanije* map drawn up by Foreign Minister Ilija Garašanin in 1844 still showed the way forward south to Peć.[24]

The Serbian principality was also acquiring cultural resources—more than enough to create embittered intellectuals of its own. Education in the Serbian language was now possible "in-country"; in 1857 there were 11,461 males and 959 females attending a range of grammar schools and the lyceé in Belgrade. Serbs who wished to get a university degree were still required to go abroad; many attended the university in Zagreb, while others went to France or Russia. With education opened, however, the principality began to create its own class of "superfluous men." Upon returning home a recent graduate had few career options; one could either serve in the bureaucracy or join a family business. Those who were poorly disposed to the former were also extremely reluctant to pursue the latter; most Serbian "industry" still required working with one's hands, something the young men saw as incompatible with status as educated.

Of this group to whom neither state service nor trade seemed appealing the overwhelming majority had been educated in Russia and had been influenced by radicalism. To serve a prince, especially ones as crude as scions of the Obrenović and Karageorgic dynasties, seemed a betrayal of their calling to apply their minds to social questions of the day. "The intellectuals among this group of unemployed members of the educated class were often, precisely because of their education at the hands of Russian revolutionaries, unable to work within society," Woodford McClellan writes. "They could not be used in society, for they were psychologically outside of it and alienated from it."[25]

Among these frustrated men of some literary talent, the influence of Russian writer Nikolai Chernyshevski loomed large. Chernyshevski's 1862–63 novel *What Is To Be Done?* seemed to offer a rank with which would come all the practical engagement of a man of state affairs without any humiliating attachments to the backward principality itself. "In the spirit of Feuerbach," Jacob Talmon writes, "Chernyshevsky appears to have envisaged his liberating mission as the task of teaching the people that their subjugation was the result of submitting to erroneous ideas, which exercised a compulsive sway over their minds, but which were the projection of social conditions."[26] Not that Chernyshevski thought, as an Enlightened Englishman might, that the goal was to free people of superstition so that they could act by the light of their own reason. The great mass of men would always merely follow their own self-interest, dressing up their actions in moral terms in hindsight, Chernyshevski wrote. He believed that in a corrupted society where everyone acted solely in his or her own interest it was up to the elite capable of seeing the truths, to create, as Talmon writes, "a social system built upon these truths and presided over by enlightened and skillful men" who would "succeed in coordinating egoistic endeavors, rewarding them [the masses] and punishing them accordingly, in making the happiness of the individual depend upon the welfare of society."[27] There would be no need to concern oneself with moral categories, since these would be exposed as frauds; one could instead rely, Chernyshevski wrote, on the "natural sciences," which "have developed sufficiently to provide a great deal of material for the exact solution of moral problems."[28]

Chernyshevski was to inspire frustrated intellectuals of communist leanings across Eastern Europe. Here finally was a code by which their alleged superior mental gifts were to be a ticket to status and power. Social problems had roots that could be discerned only by an educated elite; moral restraints that might have prevented direct action — even terrorist acts — were dismissed as so much superstition. "The people" could not possibly know their own interests; they had to be ruled by others who could think and act on their behalf.

Lenin himself was so inspired by Chernyshevski as to take *What Is To Be Done?* as the title of his first book. But the Russian Romantic also had fervent disciples in the Balkans. Chief among Chernyshevski's followers in Serbia was Svetozar Marković, an aspiring Serbian intellectual educated in Russia in the 1860s and close to Russian radicals in Switzerland. Upon returning to Belgrade in 1869, Marković launched a savage attack on Prince Michael's new constitution and the liberals who supported it. The apparent freedoms the constitution offered were merely a fraud, Marković wrote, designed to further the interests of the so-called intellectuals comprising the "bureaucratic party." Left out of the Serbian political sphere were the "ruled," the great mass of peasants who were required to perform "the most undesirable tasks" and who foolishly longed to help the Miloš dynasty by dying in wars of conquest. Before Serbia could turn its attention to the plight of cousins beyond its borders, Marković wrote, it must first abolish the tyranny within; the top priority of Serbian politics must be the "destruction of the bureaucratic system."[29]

Such criticism quickly earned Marković expulsion to the Military Frontier, where he was welcomed warmly. While disagreeing with his socialism, the émigré intellectuals delighted in Marković's Russian-trained Romanticism, adding as it did a new infusion of life to their own fading tradition. When *Matica Srpska* published

Marković's "The Realist Direction in Science and Life," the work "caused a sensation among Novi Sad intellectuals," McClellan writes; "its author was a prized addition to the groups which met regularly to discuss philosophy and politics."[30]

In addition to sharing a distaste for the government in Belgrade, Marković and the émigré intellectuals agreed that its plans for expansion south must be replaced by a campaign to absorb the stokavian speakers in Bosnia and Croatia. To seek control of historical Peć, Marković thought, demonstrated a "reactionary" disposition to the nationalities problem, while subsuming the Croats, Bulgars, and Serbs in one "south Slav" entity would be a progressive campaign, since it would both unite peoples without regard to nationality and return to them the ancient socialist institutions — the zadrugas — that Belgrade's centralized despotism had abolished.[31]

When Marshal Tito imposed Communism on Yugoslavia following World War II, Marković fell out of favor; orthodox Marxism-Leninism, then homegrown variants, instead became the order of the day. But the conviction that intellectuals could better represent the "people" than could the authorities remained in Serbian political culture and was revived, by coincidence, by one Mihailo Marković.

One might have thought that Serbian intellectuals planning to forge a nationalist campaign in the 1980s would have had very little to go on. After all, hadn't Tito reforged Yugoslavia by welding its nationalities together in a strong multinational (if not multiparty) communist state? But in fact both political and intellectual circumstances made a nationalist explosion extremely likely. What else is one to make of the fact that the political machine that launched the wars of ex-Yugoslavia is led by men who had been two of Belgrade's leading Communists? Can one really say they were mere opportunists who caught a wave of popular sentiment when they were actively shaping just that sentiment?

To understand why this is so, look at the poison pill embedded in the Leninist vision of nationhood. Lenin and Marx both thought nations were merely covers disguising how economics had divided mankind into the exploiting and exploited classes. Nations were forged by the bourgeoisie, who sought a uniform marketplace in which all consumers spoke the same language. Like the state, nations would wither away once the workers realized they had no country. "National consciousness" would then be shown to be a ruse. But unlike Marx, Lenin saw how powerful national resentment of Western wealth could be. While Marx hoped for class revolt in the rich West and dismissed poorer nations, Lenin consoled the latter with conspiracy theory. Backward countries were not poor due to their populations' ignorance or sloth, Lenin argued, but because they were entangled in the schemes of the rich and had not yet "liberated" themselves.

"Finance capital and trusts do not diminish but increase the differences in the rate of growth of various parts of the world economy," Lenin wrote in *Imperialism, the Highest Stage of Capitalism*. Rather than wait for the workers of the West to rise, Lenin called on the "proletarian nations" themselves to rebel against their exploiters.

Nowhere has Lenin's legacy proved more deadly than in the former Yugoslavia. Tensions have always run high between the more prosperous Yugoslav peoples to the north and west, the Slovenes and the Croats, and their poorer cousins in Serbia and Montenegro. But they exploded in the mid-1980s, when hard-line Serb intellectuals portrayed attempts to liberalize Yugoslav society as an anti-Serb conspiracy of Leninist scale and intricacy. Thanks to the tradition passed on to contemporary Serbia by Svetozar Marković, Mihailo Marković easily found a following.

Mihailo Marković's résumé might make him appear an unlikely nationalist. A prominent socialist theoretician since the 1960s, Marković, a member of the Serbian Academy of Sciences, has published widely in the West and was a professor at the University of Michigan in the 1970s. As a founding member of the Praxis Group, Marković was once hailed by Erich Fromm as a leading revisionist Marxist.

Just how revisionist he would become was not clear at the time. There is little, for example, in his most famous work, *From Affluence to Praxis,* to suggest at first glance that Marković is anything but a committed antifascist. But Marković's own language makes the transition from communist to fascist seem natural. "Comparing the political doctrines of liberalism, fascism and socialism," he writes: "one may immediately notice one fundamental distinction: the aim of politics and the raison d'etre of political institutions is from the point of view of the first: the isolated individual; from the point of view of the second: the nation or race; from the point of view of the third: the class, the proletariat."[32]

Whatever else the reader knows about Marković, one can see here that he already finds much in common between fascism and socialism. Both go beyond merely serving the needs of the "isolated individual" and instead provide an elite to guide the collective to a brighter destiny. Whether the collective is the "nation" or the "proletariat" is perhaps besides the point. Anticipating this objection, Marković claims that under fascism, the dictatorship is the end, while under socialism, it is merely an inconvenient middle stage made necessary by the "counterrevolutionary intervention of foreign powers: sending armies, supporting any kind of domestic resistance, organizing the military, economic and political blockade of the new revolutionary republic."[33]

This is not to say that dictatorships do not have their virtues, Marković writes. He argues that the Grand Inquisitor of Dostoyevsky's *The Brothers Karamazov* made a viable choice in denying men freedom. "One has to choose whether to grant mankind what it wants, although this alternative is degrading and demands doing horrible things. Or one can choose to accord mankind freedom with all its nobility, in which case the decision is cruel for it will torment men." The Grand Inquisitor, Marković writes, "chose to be humane, to take that terrible gift from mankind."[34] The very fact that Marković speaks of "choosing" how mankind will be disposed of speaks volumes. But his foreshadowing of Milošević's rise thirteen years before the fact suggests he, if not "one," was so empowered. "There are historical situations," Marković writes, "in which very broad masses of people suffer from collective insecurity and anxiety which can be overcome only by a far-reaching depersonalization, the identification with a great leader, and membership in strict organizations and institutions. In such a situation a leader can easily emerge, even if he is not a typical charismatic leader, even if he lacks any magic charm and any ability to immediately fascinate people."[35]

While the economic and political reforms of the 1980s slowed the amount of funds transferred from the prosperous republics to the poorer ones, Marković remained a Communist while becoming more explicitly pro-Serb. In the tradition of his nineteenth-century namesake, he struck a pose as an intellectual speaking against the state—this time on behalf of his proletarian nation. As one of three authors of the widely-published Serbian Academy of Sciences Memorandum of 1986, Marković gave Milošević the stick with which to beat his superiors—their failure to address the alleged suffering of Serbs in Kosovo. Without firm action against the restive Albanian majority, the authors wrote, Western powers would dismember Serbia and restore "bourgeois society" in the leftover pieces."[36] The crisis had been brought on, the authors later wrote, by "a restoration of the market economy, increasing reliance on Western capital loans and a growing division of political power among eight national or regional oligarchies. This was a policy that expressed particular, shortrange interests of the two developed republics, Slovenia and Croatia."[37]

In a later review of the political situation, Marković fully endorsed Milošević's campaign to strengthen the hand of the Serbian League of Communists against "federal authorities [who] did nothing serious to stop expulsion of Serbs and Montenegrins from Kosovo and the policy to make Kosovo an 'ethnically pure' province."[38] And he listed *nine* external enemies who had exacerbated the Kosovo problem to hobble his native Serbia. Among them were the Ottoman and Austro-Hungarian empires, the Vatican and, more recently, a "bureaucratic coalition within Yugoslavia itself," which had pursued a policy of "systematically weakening Serbia." Enterprises had been moved, competent managers fired, Five Year Plans skewed, and Albanian nationalists encouraged because Tito had "obviously believed" that Yugoslavia could be maintained provided that Serbia was "cut in size comparable to that of Croatia, that it would be internally unstable, and that its possible economic success would be controlled and halted."[39]

But the removal of incompetent Communists was not to be welcomed, Marković wrote in 1991, if their regime was to be replaced with "a traditional liberalist multi-party *laissez-faire* model of market economy." In a survey of anti-Communist revolutions of 1989, Marković found in the classical liberal parties only a "colossal bankruptcy of intellectuals." There was an alternative of a type Svetozar Marković would have recognized: "now after the fall of bureaucratic socialism that ground has been cleared for the emergence of democratic, humanist socialism in the East." Freedom would come, that is, with the fall of the bureaucracy. But who would then lead society? Marković answers with the article's last sentence: "Eastern European intellectuals will play a decisive role in projecting more or less rational and imaginative solutions."[40]

Shortly after publishing the above Marković was given what earlier "anti-bureaucratic" Serbian intellectuals could have only dreamed—real political power. From 1991 until his removal in 1995 Marković served as second-in-command of Milošević's Social Party of Serbia (the renamed Serbian League of Communists) with responsibility for party ideology. His mission went beyond merely designing Milošević's "anti-bureaucratic revolution" (itself no more than the transfer of Communist power from the federal to national level). In a speech to his party in the fall of 1991, Marković vowed that any independent Bosnian state would be "encircled by Serbian territory."[41] Six months later the regime he served was building concentration camps.

Marković was only removed from power after falling out with another intellectual Communist determined to protect socialism—Milošević's wife, Mira Marković. While the two differed in their emphasis—Mihailo more explicitly nationalist, Mira more obviously Communist—the two shared more than a last name. Both held a conviction that intellectuals had a duty to apply their superior brainpower to the practical political problems of the day on behalf of an anonymous and voiceless mass, be it the nation or the class. From the fact that their claim to power held any legitimacy in Serbian society, both might thank Svetozar Marković and the Russian-influenced Romantic thinkers who had laid a foundation for them.

Of course the real beneficiary of both strands of Serbian Romanticism was Milošević himself. With sinister mental agility he has slipped back and forth between them, thundering about ancient lands one month while calling for a calm return to Communist-era peace the next. That Milošević should have been able to deploy the weapons and troops of a Marxist-indoctrinated army in defense of self-styled irrational savages says more, however, about the similarity of Communism and romantic nationalism than it does about the Serbian president's management skills. One may hope that both the social-nationalists and the national-socialists in Serbia are recognized for the modern phenomena that they are, if only so that the

West is more prepared to act should their Russian counterparts fully unleash a bloody fury of their own.

Notes

1. Barbara Jelavich, *History of the Balkans, Vol. 1: Eighteenth and Nineteenth Centuries* (Cambridge: Cambridge University Press, 1983), 41–44.
2. D. H. Low, ed., *The Ballads of Marko Kraljević* (Cambridge: Cambridge University Press, 1922), 44.
3. Ibid., 152.
4. Jelavich, *History of the Balkans*, 91.
5. Ibid., 149.
6. A Croatian Franciscan monk, Andrija Kačić-Miošić, wrote a general account of the "Slav nation" (*Razgovor ugodni naroda slovinskoga*) in 1756. See Ivo J. Lederer, "Nationalism and the Yugoslavs," in *Nationalism in Eastern Europe*, edited by Peter Sugar and Ivo J. Lederer (Seattle and London: University of Washington Press, 1969), 413–14.
7. Ibid., 413.
8. Wayne S. Vucinich, "Genesis and Essence of the First Serbian Uprising," in *The First Serbian Uprising: 1804–1813* (New York: Brooklyn College Press, 1982), 5.
9. Lederer, "Nationalism," 413.
10. Stanford J. Shaw, "The Ottoman Empire and the Serbian Uprising, 1804–7," in Vucinich, *The First Serbian Uprising: 1804–1813*, 87.
11. For an excellent description of the rise of Romanticism, see "The Final Solution of Infinite Longing: Germany," in *Nationalism: Five Roads to Modernity*, by Liah Greenfeld (Cambridge, Mass.: Harvard University Press, 1992), 275–395. The concepts of national identity presented in the present chapter are entirely indebted to this work.
12. J. G. Herder, *Auch eine Philosophie der Geschichte zur Bildung der Menscheit* (Stuttgart: Reclam Universal-Bibliothek, 1990), 10. My translation.
13. J. G. Herder, "The Origin of Language," in *J. G. Herder on Social and Political Culture*, edited by F. M. Barnard (Cambridge: Cambridge University Press, 1969), 148.
14. Greenfeld, "Final Solution," 345.
15. Herder, "Ideas for a Philosophy of History," in Barnard, *Herder on Social and Political Culture*, 324.
16. W. A. Morrison, *The Revolt of the Serbs against the Turks* (Cambridge: Cambridge University Press, 1942), 5.
17. The dialects of the southern Slavs are named according to the word in each for "what." Speakers of the "stokavian" say "sto," while speakers of the "kajkavian" — Croats of the mountains around Zagreb — say "kaj."
18. Lederer, "Nationalism," 415.
19. Morrison, *Revolt*, 72.

20. Hans Kohn, *Panslavism: Its History and Ideology,* 2nd ed. (New York: Random House, 1960), 64.
21. Radovan Karadžić, "A Morning Hand Grenade," quoted in Andrew Rubin, "The Executioner's Song," *Lingua Franca,* July/Aug., 1995, p. 8.
22. Radovan Karadžić, "The Mad Javelin," quoted in Rubin, "Executioner's Song," 8.
23. Rubin, "Executioner's Song," 8.
24. Jelavich, *History of the Balkans,* 333.
25. Woodford McClellan, *Svetozar Markovic and the Origins of Balkan Socialism* (Princeton: Princeton University Press, 1964), 27.
26. Jacob Talmon, *The Myth of the Nation and the Vision of the Revolution* (Brunswick, N.J.: Transaction Publishers, 1991), 271.
27. Ibid., 273.
28. Nikolai Chernyshevski, *Selected Philosophical Essays* (Moscow, 1953), 92. Quoted in Talmon, *Myth of the Nation,* 274.
29. Quoted in McClellan, *Svetozar Markovic,* 83.
30. Ibid., 178.
31. Ibid., 186.
32. Mihailo Marković, *From Affluence to Praxis* (Ann Arbor: University of Michigan Press, 1974), 147. Some of my discussion of Marković previously appeared in the *Wall Street Journal.*
33. Ibid., 157.
34. Ibid., 162.
35. Ibid., 163.
36. Quoted in Branka Magaš, *The Destruction of Yugoslavia* (New York: Verso, 1992), 58. Mihailo Marković did his nineteenth-century namesake one better by insisting on Serbian domination of both Bosnia and Kosovo.
37. Quoted in ibid., 60.
38. Mihailo Marković, "Tragedy of National Conflicts in 'Real Socialism': The Case of the Yugoslav Autonomous Province of Kosovo," *Praxis International* 9, no. 4 (Jan., 1990): 410–11.
39. Marković, "Tragedy of National Conflicts," 420.
40. Mihailo Marković, "The Meaning of Recent Social Changes in Eastern Europe," *Praxis International* 10, no. 3/4 (Oct., 1990 and Jan., 1991): 216, 223.
41. Quoted in Noel Malcolm, *Bosnia: A Short History* (New York: New York University Press, 1994), 229.

CHAPTER TEN

Genocide:
We Are Responsible
STEPHEN W. WALKER

Since this article was written over three years ago, much has happened in the Balkans and Washington. A Washington-brokered agreement of March, 1994, did end the fighting in central Bosnia between Bosnian Croat separatists and the Bosnian army. As a result of the fragile alliance that resulted, the Bosnian army was able to smuggle a limited amount of small arms and ammunition into Bosnia and received considerable assistance from the newly armed Croatian Army in a counteroffensive against Serbian forces in western and northern Bosnia in the summer and fall of 1995.

As Serbian forces were being routed and a Bosnian-Croatian victory appeared possible, if not likely, the Clinton Administration faced its worst nightmare: the Congress was on the verge of lifting the arms embargo against Bosnia, and the UN mission was collapsing — two events that would inevitably lead to a UN withdrawal. This, in turn, would have forced President Clinton to honor his commitment to deploy U.S. forces in Bosnia to protect the retreating UN forces. Since this withdrawal might not have taken place until after the approaching Bosnian winter, the president could have been forced into committing U.S. soldiers to the war in Bosnia during an election campaign.

To prevent that political catastrophe, the administration, for the first time, aggressively pursued a political objective in Bosnia: secure a settle-

ment, any settlement, as quickly as possible so that if it did have to send troops; it would be to secure an existing "peace," and the deployment might end before November, 1996.

Using its formidable leverage on the Bosnian government, the administration essentially stopped the Bosnian-Croatian counteroffensive and "saved" half of Bosnia for Serbian strongman Slobodan Milošević and his proxies in Bosnia. A settlement, known as the Dayton Accords, was imposed on the Bosnian government and effectively partitioned the country into two roughly equal parts, one for the Serbs and the other for the Muslims, Croats, and everyone else.

Despite almost 20,000 American troops sent to Bosnia at a cost of over 3 billion U.S. tax dollars, the peace in Bosnia is increasingly threatened by Serbian and Croatian extremists who refuse to allow for the return of refugees, the freedom of movement, or free and fair elections in lands they control. Most observers believe a renewal of the war is the most likely outcome of this American "quick-fix" solution to genocide, which rewards the aggressors.

While the arms embargo on Bosnia has been lifted as part of the settlement, the Bosnian government has become largely dependent on a U.S.-led arm-and-train program to address its defense needs. Having promised an already modest program that would cost upwards of $700 million, however, the administration has delivered only half that amount, leaving the Bosnians unprepared for the terror that may lie over the horizon. The administration therefore seems destined to repeat its gravest error of the war: leaving the Bosnians defenseless in the midst of genocidal war criminals. We have a moral responsibility — and clear interests — in ensuring that we do not tie the victims hands again or fail to live up to our commitment to redress the military imbalance created by an embargo that did just that. After all, we are still responsible.

January 21, 1997

Here we are, almost fifty years after the Holocaust, approaching the twenty-first century, and we've apparently learned nothing. We call it "ethnic cleansing" because it sounds nicer, but it is genocide. Genocide is taking place again in Europe and we — yes, you and I — are letting it happen. Actually, we're not just letting it happen, we're encouraging it. We're encouraging the war criminals, the butchers, the rapists. We are responsible.

That's why I resigned my position as a specialist on Croatia at the State Department. I could no longer be a part of an administration that is aiding and abetting the Serbs as they try—successfully—to eliminate the non-Serb, primarily Muslim population in Bosnia. The trouble is, I'm still responsible. Being an American makes me responsible. It makes you responsible.

"Ancient Ethnic Hatreds," or Good Versus Evil?

Some, including the Clinton administration, would have you believe this is a confusing civil war where each group bears a fair share of the blame. They will tell you the war is the result of "ancient ethnic hatreds," that the people who live there are destined and determined to kill each other. If you believe this, we are absolved of any responsibility. But that's not how it is. The Serbs are committing genocide.

It is true that all sides—including the forces of the Bosnian government—have committed atrocities. Bosnian Croat and government forces both have killed innocent civilians and forced large numbers of civilians to abandon their homes and villages. In many cases these have been localized incidents, usually ordered by local commanders. Still, the political leaderships must be held responsible and should be expected to punish those who commit such atrocities and to use all their influence and control to prevent future atrocities.

The Serbs, however, have waged a systematic, village-by-village campaign to wipe out or force out all non-Serbs in the territories they conquer in order to create a Greater Serbia. It is on a scale that dwarfs Croat and government atrocities combined. It is a grand campaign orchestrated by Serbian leaders in Bosnia and Serbia itself. It is genocide.

The fighting in central Bosnia—which erupted between the formerly allied Bosnian Croat and government forces into a full-scale conflict this spring—is the direct result of U.S. and European Community (EC) policies. When the United States and its allies clearly opted against helping the Bosnian government this past May, the government and the Croats realized that each would be left with what they could win militarily. With only 30 or so percent of Bosnia between them and over 60 percent of the population, the pressure to grab territory from the weakest forces—each other—was unavoidable.

The U.S. Is Helping the Serbs

If you push them, senior officials in the administration will tell you that the reality is that the Serbs have won, that the war in Bosnia is hopefully in the "endgame." Well, that's partially true. The Serbs have won—so far. Bosnia, however, is not over. Nor is the broader Balkan conflict, of which Bosnia is just one critical dimension. We are certainly not in the endgame. If we allow events to continue on their present course, the Serbs will continue to slaughter and rape innocent civilians and will eventually wipe the Bosnian state completely off the map. But they won't stop there. Serb leaders will continue brutally to victimize the weak—whether they be Bosnians, Croats, Albanians, Hungarians—and to convince the Serb people that their vicious leadership is necessary to wipe out these "threats" to the Serbian nation.

The debate over Bosnia and the role of the United States has focused on whether our "national interests" are at risk and whether the United States should intervene militarily. Unfortunately, this debate has ignored a horrible fact—that the U.S. government is in fact encouraging the Serbs and their war of aggression and genocide. We are doing so in two ways.

First, the Clinton administration's public vacillations over Bosnia during the past several months have on several occasions given the Serbs a "green light." One such instance was Secretary of State Warren Christopher's July 21 press conference. The administration had been debating for several weeks what could be done to help ease the suffering in Sarajevo. Yet when asked if the United States would let Sarajevo fall, Christopher stated repeatedly that we were doing all we could consistent with our national interests. The next day the Serbs unleashed the most intense artillery attack of the sixteen-month siege on the capital. All the parties in Bosnia listen carefully to every statement made by U.S. officials. These statements have an immediate and direct impact on the ground and at the negotiating table.

Second, the Clinton administration has, since February, supported the Vance-Owen-Stoltenberg negotiations — named after the UN and EC mediators — that encourage and reward Serbian aggression. The Clinton administration initially criticized the Geneva talks for these very reasons, but decided early on that Bosnia was becoming a distraction and that a more active American role would inevitably lead to our taking on more of the responsibility for finding a just settlement. So instead, we have supported the negotiations, which are based entirely on Serb demands and the facts on the ground — which are determined by Serbian victories against defenseless Bosnians.

Clinton's Sham

While the Serbs have continued their war of aggression against the Bosnian people, we have allowed the arms embargo against the Bosnian government to continue, denying the Bosnians the right to defend themselves — a right guaranteed by the UN Charter. We have blamed the Europeans for our own inaction and assured the Bosnian government that if they agree to the present proposal to partition Bosnia into three parts that we will send troops to guarantee the Bosnians get what's coming to them. Yet, if deployed to enforce a partition agreement, U.S. troops would actually be defending Serbian military gains and allowing the Serbs to finish the genocide in the territories they now control. Lucky for us — at least for now — U.S. ground troops will probably never see Bosnian soil or Serbian war criminals. President Bill Clinton is pulling a fast one on the Bosnians. Having promised the troops to police a partition agreement, he is laying the groundwork for Congress to "block" the deployment, much as the Europeans "blocked" our feeble, halfhearted attempt to win support for lifting the arms embargo against Bosnia in May. The result will be the collapse of the negotiations and the inevitable defeat of the Bosnians, who will be left without their homes and their country. The conflict in the Balkans will return to Croatia and will likely expand to Kosovo, where the Serbs will feel free within their own borders to "ethnically cleanse" Kosovo's ethnic Albanian majority. More people will die, but Congress and the Europeans — not President Clinton — will be "responsible."

The Case for a U.S. Role

During my eight years as a foreign service officer, I considered myself a practical realist. I thought of U.S. foreign policy and national security in very practical terms and thought that our foreign policy should be guided by our national interests, not the other way around. I did, however, recognize that as the world's foremost economic, political, and military power our interests stretched across the globe and that we had more interest than any other country in protecting international peace and stability.

Bosnia has taught me that there should also be a moral content to our foreign policy. After all, a large part of the foundation for our Cold War conflict with communism was based on that system's moral corruptness. We devoted much time, energy, and resources to fight for the rights of the captives of that system. We realized that from a moral and a practical point of view, dictators and their abhorrent practices are inherently threatening, not only to their intended victims but to the health, security, and well-being of the international community as a whole. Failing to resist their aggression not only encourages their own dangerous behavior but also encourages other would-be thugs to use force and "ethnic cleansing" to address their own problems—whether they be in Eastern Europe, the former Soviet Union, or other parts of the world where our interests lie. That is why "Never again!" was one of the Cold War mottoes for the free and democratic West.

We also have other, practical interests in Bosnia and the Balkans. The threat of continued instability in Europe, greater numbers of refugees flooding into Western Europe, and spillover that could engulf the entire Balkan region—including one or more North Atlantic Treaty Organization (NATO) allies—directly impact on American interests. Western Europe is our most important trading partner, and the stability and prosperity of that region directly affect our own. If the conflict continues and expands—and, until the Serbs are stopped, it will—we will inevitably be faced with having to intervene. Better to pay the piper now.

What Can We Do to Help?

So how do we help the Bosnians without getting into the kind of bloody quagmire we find ourselves slipping into in Somalia? The answer is one the administration has held since May: It's called "Lift and Strike." The "lift" means lifting the UN arms embargo against the Bosnian government so that it can defend itself—a right it has been unjustly denied by the United States and its allies. The "strike" means using U.S. and allied air power to take out the Serbs' supply lines and the artillery sites that shell defenseless Bosnian women and children on a daily basis.

The Bosnians must be allowed to defend themselves—it is their moral and legal right. While their forces have committed atrocities, they have clearly been the primary victim and are threatened with their extinction as a state if they remain defenseless against the Serbs. The fighting in central Bosnia between the government and the Bosnian Croats should be stopped, and we should make any military assistance on our part contingent upon a cease-fire between the former allies, unless the Croats violate such an agreement. There is a wide variety of carrots and sticks at our disposal to compel and encourage Croatian compliance.

If the Bosnians continue to be denied the right to self-defense, then the UN Charter provides that the UN will defend them. This clearly is not going to happen. The United States and its allies should not send ground troops into Bosnia to take part in the conflict. In fact, it is not even necessary. The Bosnians have the troops; they lack the weapons. In order to level the playing field and prevent the Serbs from seizing one last opportunity before facing a well-armed Bosnian force, we should be prepared—with our allies—to truly enforce the no-fly zone and to use our airpower to silence the cowardly Serb artillery and cut off Serb supply lines. We owe this much to the Bosnians, and the risk would be minimal.

The results of such action would be both immediate and dramatic—on the ground and at the negotiating table. The Serbs have repeatedly backed down when faced with even the remote possibility of Western intervention. They have waged a cowardly war of aggression, preying on helpless civilians, shelling a town from afar until most everyone is dead or has fled. When the United States and its allies considered adopting the lift and strike approach in May, the Serb stopped dead in their tracks and signed on to the Vance-Owen Peace Plan. When the threat of intervention evaporated, the Serbs rejected Vance-Owen and resumed their attacks.

The Only Path to Take

Clearly, we must abandon our policy that rewards the Serbs and threatens the Bosnians with complete and total defeat. We must begin to play a more honorable and sensible role in this tragedy. The course of action I have laid out is the only honorable and sensible course to take. It has the best chance for succeeding and does not require the use of U.S. ground troops. Regardless of its results, it also is the only moral course to take, allowing the Bosnian people to defend themselves against aggression and genocide.

I, for one, am not content passively to accept the guilt of our unconscionable role in the Bosnian tragedy. I could not be a part of it, so I gave up my career as an American diplomat. For me, it was the only path to take. Some remark at the personal sacrifice I made for my principles. I marvel at the sacrifices the Bosnian people endure daily and their ability to continue to resist the Serbs and their accomplices — including you and me. After all, we are responsible.

Reprinted from TIKKUN MAGAZINE, A BI-MONTHLY JEWISH CRITIQUE OF POLITICS, CULTURE, AND SOCIETY. Subscriptions are $31.00 per year from TIKKUN, 251 West 100th Street, 5th floor, New York, NY 10025.

CHAPTER ELEVEN

Clinton's "European" Bosnia Policies
MARSHALL FREEMAN HARRIS

In December, 1995, the Clinton administration ended the fighting in Bosnia through a process of relentless diplomacy and limited military force. Proud of what was being perceived as one of his few foreign policy successes, President Bill Clinton announced that, under the U.S.-brokered Dayton Peace Accords, "refugees will be allowed to return to their homes." He continued, "People will be able to move freely throughout Bosnia, and the human rights of every Bosnian citizen will be monitored by an independent commission and an internationally trained civilian police force. Those individuals charged with war crimes will be excluded from political life."

None of these things has happened. Even worse, Bosnia is already being partitioned into three ethnicity-based mini-states. Indeed, the only success of the Accords seems to have been that they have halted the slaughter of innocent civilians. Even this, however, may be only temporary. The Accords leave hundreds of thousands of Bosnia's 2.2 million displaced persons aggrieved. In addition, three major strategic regions of the country are left indecisively addressed or unresolved: Goražde is left militarily indefensible, Sarajevo is militarily exposed, and Brčko is to be subject to a future arbitration agreement. The refusal of U.S. and other foreign troops in the North Atlantic Treaty Organization (NATO)–led Stabilization Force (SFOR) to facilitate the Accords' key civilian aspects — including the return of refugees, the apprehension of war criminals, and the conduct of free and fair elections—exponentially increases the risk that one of these potential flash points will ignite.

For now, however, the Clinton administration continues to trumpet the success of its belated intervention in Bosnia. Its most remarkable claim along these lines has been that its extraordinary leadership in marshaling intensive diplomacy and the brilliant use of military force brought peace to an embattled land and its beleaguered peoples. The Dayton peace settlement, however, represents nothing of the sort. The administration's intensive diplomacy was directed mainly toward the victimized Bosnian government, which was forced to make more and more concessions until the Bosnian Serb authorities agreed to end the war. Its military force was employed not to inflict strategic damage on the Bosnian Serb forces but merely to bring them to the negotiating table where they would be rewarded with their own state on half of Bosnia's territory. Its leadership was used not to punish aggression, redress the harm to Bosnia's victims, and drag Britain and France into support for a just and sustainable peace settlement, but rather to allow Serbia to keep most of its spoils; force the legitimately elected, multiethnic government of the UN-member state of Bosnia to surrender parts of the country's sovereignty and territory; and acquiesce to Anglo-French policies that abjured both military intervention against the Serbian forces and military as well as political support to preserve the Bosnian state.

The latter is, in many ways, the most significant characteristic of the Clinton administration–brokered settlement, which is the culmination of a lengthy process by which the United States shifted from advocacy of the use of military force and the right of self-defense to save Bosnia to full acceptance of the British and French governments' preferred policies of nonintervention and the de facto recognition of a "Greater Serbia." Rather than lead, as it has repeatedly claimed, the administration simply capitulated.

Clinton's Policies

To understand the Clinton administration's moves toward appeasement, one must examine the West's record from the beginning of the conflict. At the time of Serbia's initial attacks on Bosnia and

Croatia, the major powers and Russia accurately defined the conflict as external aggression and laid the groundwork for taking firm action to end it. The United Nations Security Council passed resolutions that respected Bosnian and Croatian sovereignty and reiterated the right of nations to come to Bosnia's defense. Most notably, Resolution 752 of May, 1992, demanded that all Serbian interference in Bosnia cease and that all forces other than those of the Bosnian Army withdraw, disarm, or surrender. Further resolutions authorized the use of "all necessary means" to ensure delivery of humanitarian assistance. To keep the pressure on Belgrade, another Security Council measure imposed economic and political sanctions against Belgrade and made their termination contingent upon Serbia's compliance with Resolution 752.

In short, UN Security Council members explicitly stated their full authority to use all means at their disposal to feed Bosnian civilians, prevent further displacements, facilitate the return of existing refugees, stop the slaughter, drive out or disband and disarm the Serbian and Bosnian Serb forces that were committing the genocide, and restore order and stability throughout Bosnian and Croatian territory. The resulting UN Protection Force (UNPROFOR) mission, however, was inadequate to its tasks in both troop strength and equipment. Indeed, the UN troop presence quickly became a substitute—or, even worse, an alibi—for effective action.

The records of the British, French, and Russian governments in the four years since these resolutions were passed call their motives and intentions into serious question. Nevertheless, their initial commitment to facilitating a just and sustainable peace was clear. The commitment of the United States was even clearer.

When Clinton took office in January, 1993, his administration seemed poised to take full advantage of the UN's reiterations of international authority to intervene. Members of the president-elect's transition team, at a very early date, demonstrated their distaste for unilateral action, which the United States, or any other nation, for that matter, was fully authorized to take. This unilateral action could have included, *inter alia*, arming Bosnian government forces, bombing Serbian targets in Bosnia, Croatia, and/or Serbia proper, and even introducing U.S. ground combat troops. Instead, the administration supported stronger action couched in the multilateralism of the UN. Candidate Clinton first displayed his ideological bent in August, 1992, when Serb-run concentration camps were discovered in Bosnia. He stated, "The United Nations demands [for Serbian aggression to be halted and the camps closed] should be backed by collective action, including the use of force, if necessary. The United States should be prepared to lend appropriate support, including military, to such an operation."[1]

After the November, 1992, election, President Clinton's transition team commissioned a complete Bosnia policy review and evaluation of available options. Unfortunately, State Department officials presented less than a full range of options to their politically appointed superiors. Career officers, who had been conditioned to temerity through two years of Bush administration inaction, inattention, and pre-election jitters, did not seem to realize that they could now speak openly and even favorably of military solutions.[2]

On February 10, 1993, the administration acted on the review by enunciating its new policy in a speech by Secretary of State Warren Christopher. The new policy represented both a step forward and a missed opportunity. The conflict was, for the first time since the early UN resolutions were drafted, defined honestly as cross-border aggression that affected U.S. interests and demanded a stronger response. Christopher stated, "Serbian ethnic cleansing has been pursued through mass murders, systematic beatings, and the rape of Muslims and others, prolonged shellings of innocents in Sarajevo and elsewhere, forced displacements of entire villages, [and] inhuman treatment of prisoners in detention camps." He also stated, "The continuing destruction of a new UN member state challenges the principle that internationally recognized borders should not be altered by force. . . . The world's response to the violence in the former Yugoslavia is an early and crucial test of how it will address the critical concerns of ethnic and religious minorities in the post–Cold War world."[3]

Christopher missed the opportunity, however, to meet the early and crucial test of the new administration's resolve by matching this strong rhetoric with a credible threat of force. In the first of many demonstrations of the administration's discomfiture with the foreign policy responsibilities and power incumbent upon the United States, Christopher pledged merely to bring "the full weight of American diplomacy to bear on finding a peaceful solution."[4] Not only were Serbian forces not presented with an ultimatum to halt the offensives and outrages that had so distressed Clinton and his team, but the administration also linked itself more directly to the European-run negotiating process. These talks had, for more than a year, not only failed to curb Serbian offensives but also enabled Belgrade, slowly but steadily, to increase its political and territorial demands.

Even the rhetoric alone, however, initiated a three-month period in which U.S. policy was at odds with those of Britain, France, and a reemerging Russian superpower. This gap grew into a chasm during Secretary Christopher's disastrous May, 1993, trip to Europe. Christopher's intent was to convince our allies to join the United States in lifting the arms embargo against the Bosnian government and, if necessary during an interim period while the Bosnians integrated the weaponry, in launching air strikes against Bosnian Serb targets.

European and Russian leaders expected Christopher to assert American leadership, as his predecessors had done many times before—by explaining Washington's firm decision to act forcefully. Instead, Christopher's interlocutors exploited his weak approach and sensed that President Clinton himself was not sufficiently committed to the new American policy. Opposition to "lift and strike" hardened rather than collapsed, and Christopher returned to Washington empty-handed. In summing up this "exchange of views" with our allies, former assistant secretary of defense Richard Perle stated, "It was an exchange all right: Warren Christopher went to Europe with an American policy, and he came back with a European one."[5]

Christopher's failed mission of May, 1993, and its continuing pernicious effects constitute the defining crisis of American policy in Bosnia. From then onward, rather than asserting its traditional leadership role and overcoming European objections to U.S. policy proposals, the Clinton administration began to capitulate to European views and redefine the conflict in terms that Europe found far more convenient.

Within only a few days of his return from Europe, Christopher signed on to the European and Russian "Joint Action Program."

What had been the Europeans' alternative proposals to "lift and strike" — specifically, designating six remaining Bosnian enclaves as "safe areas" subject to better UN protection — actually became U.S. policy. One month later, after intense lobbying by its "Joint Action" partners — Britain, France, Russia, and Spain (then in the UN Security Council presidency) — the administration agreed not to work for passage of a UN Security Council (UNSC) resolution to end the arms embargo, despite its vocal public opposition to the weapons ban. While the administration itself voted "yes," the lack of active American leadership to obtain additional support doomed the measure to failure.

In August, 1993, Serbian forces escalated the siege of Sarajevo with massive artillery and mortar fire on civilian targets. The European and Russian response was again to pressure the Bosnian government — not the Serbs — to accept the international peace plan then on offer in Geneva as the best and only deal available. Having vowed repeatedly that it would not pressure the Bosnian government to accept a particular settlement, the administration at first resisted. Then it joined in urging the victims to surrender.

By the time of the NATO summit in Brussels in January, 1994, roles had become so utterly reversed that France was able to assume the mantle of leadership in NATO by calling for air strikes to halt Serbian attacks around Sarajevo. The administration followed France's lead. As always throughout the conflict, France's motivation in seeking this threat was not to promote a just peace by reversing or even halting Serbian aggression, but rather to obtain a quick settlement. Indeed, France had, until then, been a leading opponent of air action.

In May, 1994, after more than six months of entreaties from our allies, the administration openly accepted the international mediators' formula that would leave 49 percent of Bosnia under Serbian control. Later that month, U.S. representatives joined European nations and Russia in the "Contact Group" with the goal of devising a new territorial plan to partition Bosnia. For more than a year, administration officials had vowed that the United States would not join in such "map-making." For the next two months, map-making was the top priority and principle activity of Clinton's Bosnia team.

In July, 1994, the administration argued that the Bosnian Serbs should be given an ultimatum: accept the Contact Group partition plan, or the arms embargo against the Bosnian government would be terminated. But Russia, France, and Britain persuaded the administration to back down. At the Contact Group ministerial in Geneva, Secretary Christopher, rather than continuing to advocate the U.S. position, merely echoed his European counterparts with a hollow warning that, "at the end of the day," if the Bosnian Serbs did not accept the Contact Group plan, ending the arms embargo would become "a very strong possibility."[6]

In September, 1994, the administration succumbed to British and French pressure to support and participate in an international mission to monitor Serbia's borders with Bosnia and certify whether Serbian president Slobodan Milošević was honoring his pledge to cut off all but humanitarian assistance to his Bosnian Serb proxies.[7] Throughout the spring of 1993, the Clinton administration had refused to support such a mission on two grounds: first, that such a token, largely symbolic mission could not reliably certify that the border was closed; and, second, that the isolated and poorly armed monitors would be sitting targets for Serbian troops seeking Western hostages. Yet the 1994 mission was even smaller and more poorly armed than the smallest mission to which the administration had objected in 1993.

In February, 1995, Moscow unveiled a plan to suspend UN sanctions against Serbia in exchange for a commitment by Belgrade to grant diplomatic recognition to the former Yugoslav republics. Administration officials embraced the initiative—and even claimed it as their own. The proposal revealed the Contact Group and, in particular, the Clinton administration, at their weakest. Twenty months earlier, the administration had decided to launch, albeit ineptly, a policy to halt Serbian aggression with air strikes and a full weapons program for Milošević's victims. Now, it was prepared to take no action at all against Serbia if Milošević would merely grant diplomatic recognition to his besieged neighbors. This capitulation brought Russia out of the closet and into open support of Serbia's demand for an unconditional suspension of sanctions.

Remarkably, the administration's policy free-fall was not over. Not to be out-appeased by London or out-capitulated by Paris, the administration decided in April, 1995, to restore the veneer of Contact Group unity by halting its pursuit of Bosnian recognition. Instead, it focused its efforts on securing nothing more than an extension of the winter cease-fire.

Those in Europe and the United States with desires to see the war end quickly then began to witness the unraveling of parts of Milošević's new "Greater Serbia." After tolerating more than three years of unhonored commitments from the UN to end Serbian control over regions of Croatia, Zagreb launched spring and summer counteroffensives to recapture all of its territory except eastern Slavonia. It also accepted Sarajevo's request for assistance in saving the UN-declared "safe area" of Bihać, which Britain, France, and other UNPROFOR troop-contributing nations would not protect. The Bosnian and Croatian armies then liberated vast swaths of territory in central Bosnia. In the early autumn, the Bosnian Army's Fifth Corps, together with reinforcements from other units, headed for the Bosnian Serb stronghold of Banja Luka.

The Clinton administration's response was not to pursue a just and sustainable peace settlement by, at long last, lifting the arms embargo to end the sieges of Bosnia's remaining cities or even merely by informing Zagreb of the United States' desire to see further Bosnian-Croatian cooperation in, for example, the liberation of Banja Luka; rather, for the first time, the administraton took the opportunity to try to halt the war and thereby freeze in place Serbia's remaining gains. To the Bosnian government it even made the remarkable representation that it possessed intelligence information demonstrating that further Bosnian Army counteroffensives would be thwarted by the Serbian forces. Even more remarkably, the Bosnian government accepted the reports at face value and agreed to a cease-fire.

Along with its diplomatic pressure on the Bosnian government in effect to surrender and on Milošević to bring his proxies to heel, the administration acquiesced in accepting two key British and French policy preferences regarding a peace settlement: the Bosnian Serbs would have their own para-state—that is, Bosnia would indeed be partitioned—and it would include the overrun "safe areas" of Srebrenica and Žepa in eastern Bosnia. By launching a late summer series of surgical, pinprick air strikes that momentarily interrupted the Bosnian Serb forces' ability to wage war without doing any appreciable damage to their military assets and overall strategic position, the United States and its NATO allies then convinced the Serbian and Bosnian Serb leadership to accept the new, more favorable settlement.

The Dayton Accords of December, 1995, were a triumph of American diplomacy and European policy. They halted the fighting quickly and efficiently through the introduction of massive numbers of foreign ground troops and weapons, thereby creating the satisfying illusion of an allied victory over the most brutal aggression in Europe since World War II. In fact, however, as Britain and France had advocated consistently throughout the crisis, Bosnia was being carved into two or three entities, and a "Greater Serbia" was being created. Despite the administration's pledges to the contrary, the very forces and individuals who had prosecuted the genocidal war against Bosnia and its Muslim civilian population were given absolute control over half of its territory. Refugees were not allowed to return to their homes, "ethnic cleansing" — this time, officially sanctioned — continued; freedom of movement across the new, political front lines dividing Bosnia remained a rarity, and only a handful of war criminals — including *no* Serbian political leaders — were indicted by the UN War Crimes Tribunal. It was a curious "victory" for the West, indeed.

Consequences of the Policies

Cumulatively, the results of the Clinton administration's litany of appeasement of Serbia and capitulation to Europe and Russia have been disastrous. They also make the administration guilty of two of the very charges that they have repeatedly leveled against proponents of a stronger U.S.-Bosnia policy.

First, the administration claimed throughout the conflict that more robust policies would "Americanize" the war. Instead, weak administration policies gradually escalated American involvement. They dragged the United States into multi-billion-dollar military programs that had little discernible effect on Serbian behavior on the ground; that produced extraordinarily weak results; and that have culminated in the introduction of U.S. ground troops to partition a UN-member state.

The United States' 30 percent share in paying for largely ineffective UN and NATO operations in the former Yugoslavia should give pause to this and future administrations and will give comfort to Democratic and Republican isolationists in the Congress and elsewhere. By the time the Dayton Accords were devised, the United States was paying $500 million annually for UNPROFOR, which had little or no chance of yielding a payoff in peace or regional stability. For this financial commitment, the administration enjoyed the satisfaction of supporting a mission that functioned as a peacekeeper where there was no peace to keep; subjected its troops to murder, shelling, sniping, kidnap, and detention by Serbian troops; and tolerated commanders who, for the sake of expediency, had redefined their mandate to one of neutrality and mediation rather than a concerted effort to feed the needy and support the withdrawal of Serbian forces.

In addition to UNPROFOR, the United States was the leading contributor to the billion-dollar enforcement of the no-fly-zone, which, even by the UN's own accounting, was violated more than four thousand times; resulted in the shootdown of only two planes; and did not stand in the way of Milošević's constant resupply by helicopter of his proxies in Bosnia and Croatia.

The United States was also the leading contributor to the Adriatic flotilla that enforced sanctions against Serbia and the arms embargo against all of the former Yugoslav republics. The U.S. Congress outlawed participation in the latter in 1994, so that U.S. ships could not intercept the passage of ships bearing arms for the Bosnian government. The Pentagon, however, approved rules of engagement that, in the event that a U.S. ship were to have uncovered an arms shipment bound for Bosnia, made the discovery immediately apparent to other nearby NATO ships, which could then have moved immediately to seize the cache and impound the offending vessel. Call it, "Don't ask, but tell."

In addition to its ships in the Adriatic, the United States was the leading contributor to the border-monitoring mission along Serbia's border with Bosnia. Every thirty days, the administration acquiesced as David Owen and UN negotiator Thorvald Stoltenberg, under whose auspices the mission operated, certified the uncertifiable: that Serbia's borders with Bosnia were "effectively closed." The mission was in no position to make such claims. Its monitors could neither initiate their own inspections nor detain and turn back offenders—the two principle functions of border-monitoring missions as proposed by UN Secretary General Boutros Boutros-Ghali in his 1993 recommendations.[8] Even with these restrictions, however, monitors witnessed numerous violations, which they would "raise with Serbian authorities" and then ignore. Between October, 1994, and July, 1995, they observed the following in transit from Serbia to Bosnia: 512 tanks, 506 armored vehicles, 120 heavy mortars, 130 heavy artillery pieces, 48 rocket batteries, 33 laser-guided missiles, 368 ammunition trucks, 14 artillery ammunition trucks, and 1.9 million gallons of fuel. British journalist Ed Vulliamy called this the mere "tip of the iceberg."[9] The heads of the mission, of course, made no effort to see more by eliciting satellite or similar reconnaissance. This made it easier for them to claim in each of their reports that, based on what the 180 monitors along the 375-mile border had seen, and "in the absence of any contrary information from the air," Milošević was allowing only humanitarian aid to pass.

These annual expenditures in billions of dollars, hundreds of thousands of man-hours, and incalculable amounts of American prestige and credibility were but the means to an extraordinary policy end sought by the Clinton administration: the introduction of sixty thousand U.S. and other ground troops as part of an international apartheid police force that would ensure that non-Serbs remain inside a truncated Bosnia's redrawn borders.

Second, the administration claimed that more robust policies would weaken—if not topple—Russian president Boris Yeltsin in his struggle against nationalist, antidemocratic forces. Instead, the administration's own policies allowed nationalism to dominate a Russian foreign policy that had initially grown more reformist in both the "near" and "far abroad." They gave Russia a vehicle by which it reentered the foreign policy arena as a world power and asserted a territorial claim stretching to the borders of the former Soviet Union. And they enabled Russia to claim the former Yugoslavia as part of its sphere of influence.

From the outset, Clinton's foreign policy team had too many

romantic illusions about Moscow to recognize these looming disasters. Russian reservations over Western efforts to halt Serbian aggression were given more than their due because the administration hoped that Moscow would evolve into a genuine ally and embrace our foreign policy goals. Yeltsin briefly obliged on the former, but never even feigned support for the latter. What had been open support for numerous UN condemnations and full-scale political and economic sanctions against Belgrade during the Bush administration gradually turned into grudging tolerance.

Ultimately, it became something far worse as Russia reemerged in the UN Security Council not as a cooperative partner of the Perm Five's three Western members but rather as a reconstituted, full-blown obfuscator — one that could perhaps be bought off more easily but that retained virtually all of its anti-Western predilections. One of the most disturbing of these was Yeltsin's bow to nationalists who barely disguise their desire to create a "Greater Russia." Former foreign minister Andrei Kozyrev even said publicly that Russia has no international borders short of the borders of the former Soviet Union. Such a statement would have been unutterable in 1992 or even 1993, when the Perm Five were still united in condemnations and rejections of cross-border aggression in the Balkans.

Another, more curious devolution was Russia's emergence as a foreign policy influence in the former Yugoslavia. Denied this entrée for fifty years by Marshal Tito's brand of nonaligned Communism, Moscow forged a remarkable marriage of convenience with Belgrade. At little or no cost to either party, this partnership enabled Russia to return to foreign policy prominence beyond its own — or even the former Soviet Union's — borders. At the same time, it gave President Milošević diplomatic cover for his campaign to create a "Greater Serbia." From Slovenia to Macedonia, Serbia's neighbors perceived this new marriage, quite rightly, as a destabilizing influence in the region. And they began to worry that, in international fora, Russia has been given a permanent voice on Balkan subjects even beyond the war. Some believe that the partnership will outlast the Milošević regime.

Equally curiously, while the administration claimed from the outset that its policies would protect President Boris Yeltsin against antidemocratic, old empire forces, the opposite has happened. Weak

Western policies have emboldened Russian nationalists in their expansionist policies at home and have allowed Moscow to declare an affinity with Serbian ultranationalism. It was not difficult to see this coming. It began in early 1993 when the administration allowed Russian deputy foreign minister Vitaly Churkin to serve, on behalf of the United States and European powers, as a liaison with Belgrade. Churkin and his superiors in Moscow seized the opportunity, initially, to blunt the relatively tough (by today's standards) messages that he was meant to deliver, and, eventually, to develop and exploit the special power that this gave them in determining Western policies.

In the months after Moscow first assumed this liaison role, Russia argued against air strikes to stop the major Serbian assaults on Sarajevo, Goražde, and Bihać; prevented the Organization for Security and Cooperation in Europe from making a simple statement condemning the Serbian assault on Bihać; called for UN and NATO action—including air strikes, at one point—to prevent the Bosnian government from taking back Serb-occupied territory in the Bihać region; exercised its UN Security Council veto on a political issue (a resolution that would have condemned the ongoing flow of fuel to the Bosnian Serbs) for the first time since the collapse of the Soviet Union; openly backed Milošević's demands that sanctions on Serbia be lifted unconditionally; attempted in a UN resolution to demand that Croatia give back territory that it had recaptured from Serbian occupation forces; and, most recently, refused to agree to a memorandum of understanding to regulate the assistance of the NATO-led military mission to the UN War Crimes Tribunal.

In the process, Yeltsin's supposedly democratic and pro-Western foreign policies grew steadily more nationalist, confrontational, and expansionist. Identifiable ultranationalist forces may have no more control over foreign policy than they did a year or two ago, but they do not have to: Foreign Minister Yevgeny Primakov is actively protecting their interests. Indeed, even as Secretary Christopher continued to hold hands with this Contact Group "partner," Russia prosecuted a brutal, genocidal assault against its own civilians in Chechnya. Consistent in walking away, if nothing else, President Clinton labeled this one a Russian "internal affair."

Conclusions

Throughout its tenure, the Clinton administration placed an untenably high premium on "allied unity," which is another way of saying capitulation to policies that European powers perceived to be in their national interests.

Britain and France rationalized their sway over the U.S. administration by claiming a superior knowledge and wisdom that came from hundreds of years of dealing with Balkan horrors. Stand back and stand down, their argument went: It is best to contain the fighting and allow Serbia, the largest Balkan power, to exercise its rightful hegemony over the region. It is, of course, true that British and French history and the two countries' proximity to the crisis may have initially given them some special status as arbiters. Now, however, we must judge Europe by its four-year record, which is one of failure. Ultimately, too, we would do well to remember that Anglo-French knowledge and wisdom have, too often, been as flawed historically as they are now in Bosnia. In their active form, they brought us Munich. In inaction, they brought us Hitler's unchallenged invasions of the Sudetenland and the Rheinland.

A key foreign policy failure of President Clinton's tenure is that both he and his key advisers did not learn to distinguish between sage European advice and political cant. Nor did they seem to learn a lesson that is still more urgent and important: Whether the conflict in Bosnia resumes, whether ultranationalism triumphs, whether the Bosnian state and multiethnic identity are destroyed, and whether the policies and tactics of Serbian and Croatian supremacists are imitated beyond the Balkans will be determined by whether he learns not merely to engage, but also to lead.

Notes

1. *New York Times,* Aug. 4, 1992. As subsequent U.S. forays under UN auspices in Haiti and Somalia later demonstrated, however, this profound faith in multilateralism or collectivism did not provide any insurance against the adventurism or "world police" activities that the administration forswore.
2. The opposite pattern was to emerge later in 1993, when midlevel officers regularly presented top officials with military options that were rejected out of hand. In 1992, the presentation of less than a full range of options to Clinton's transition team prompted a strong dissent by a senior official who

concluded that the department had missed its most significant opportunity to educate its political leadership.

3. *U.S. Department of State Press Release,* Secretary of State Warren Christopher's press conference and statement, "New Steps Toward Conflict Resolution in the Former Yugoslavia," Feb. 10, 1993, U.S. Department of State Bureau of Public Affairs, Washington, D. C.

4. Ibid.

5. Statement before U.S. Senate Foreign Relations and Armed Services Subcommittees, Richard Perle, June 23, 1994. The author was an eyewitness to Perle's testimony.

6. Carol Giacomo, "U.S., Major Powers Urge Serbs to Accept New Bosnia Peace Plan," *Washington Times,* July 6, 1994, p. 23.

7. The mission's weak and unintrusive mandate had been negotiated by David Owen and Milošević.

8. *Report of the Secretary-General Pursuant to Security Council Resolution 838 (1993),* United Nations Secretary General Boutros Boutros-Ghali, UN Security Council Document 2/26018, July 1, 1993.

9. Ed Vulliamy, "Serbian Lies World Chose to Believe," *Guardian* (United Kingdom), Feb. 29, 1996.

CONTRIBUTORS

AKBAR S. AHMED is Fellow of Selwyn College and Member of the Centre for South Asian Studies at the University of Cambridge. He is the author of numerous books, including *Living Islam*.

BRAD K. BLITZ received his Ph.D. in education from Stanford University. His research focuses on the processes and problems associated with the European Union, ranging from the educational system to military defense.

KEITH DOUBT is associate professor of sociology at Truman State University. He is the author of *Towards a Sociology of Schizophrenia: Humanistic Reflections* and an elected member of the American Sociological Association Theory Section Council.

GEORGIE ANNE GEYER is a writer with the Universal Press Syndicate. Her most recent book is *Americans No More: The Death of Citizenship*.

MARSHALL FREEMAN HARRIS is director of the Action Council for Peace in the Balkans and a former U.S. State Department official who resigned in 1993 to protest U.S. policy toward Bosnia.

RICHARD JOHNSON is a foreign service officer for the U.S. State Department and was the Yugoslav desk officer in 1990–92. The views he expresses in this book are his own and do not purport to have any official standing.

SLAVEN LETICA is professor of medical economics at the University of Zagreb, Croatia. He is the author of numerous books on the break-up of Yugoslavia and on Serbian aggression, including *Habits of the Balkan Heart* and *The Road from Paradise,* co-authored with Stjepan Meštrović and Miroslav Goreta.

CHANDLER ROSENBERGER was based in Central Europe from 1992 to 1994 as a John O. Crane Memorial Fellow of the Institute of Current World Affairs. He has written about Central Europe for *National Review,* the *Wall Street Journal,* and *World Policy Journal,* among other publications. He is at work on a book about post-Communist nationalism.

STEPHEN W. WALKER is director of the American Committee to Save Bosnia and a former U.S. State Department official who resigned in 1993 to protest U.S. policy toward Bosnia.

The late ALBERT WOHLSTETTER was university professor at the University of Chicago and recipient of the Department of Defense Medal for Distinguished Service. He published extensively on international relations, global communication, and Western policies regarding the recent Balkan War. His most recent publications on the war in Bosnia appeared in the *New Republic* and the *Wall Street Journal.*

Index

Ahmed, Akbar, 4
Akashi, Yakushi, 15, 17, 98, 103, 111–14
Albright, Madeleine, 23, 90
America, 6, 10–13, 17, 27, 30–33, 37, 43, 70–71, 76, 125, 158, 161, 170, 177, 231–32, 246
American civil religion, 13, 30–31, 151
American Sociological Association, 165
Anti-Ballistic Missile Treaty, 205
anti-Semitism, 16
apartheid, 43, 122–23, 129
appeasement, 5, 122, 181–99
Ash, Timothy Garton, 174
Aspin, Les, 117
Auschwitz, 39
authoritarianism, 17, 29, 76

Baker, James, 74, 75, 186, 189
Balkanization, 44, 75
Balkan War, 1–35, 81
Banja Luka, 14, 81, 132, 245
Bassiouni, Cherif, 88–90
Baudrillard, Jean, 4, 136
Belgrade regime, 4, 10, 14, 18, 20, 48, 74, 79, 118, 133, 147, 197, 211, 223, 249
Berlin Wall, 39, 74
Binder, David, 150
Bloom, Allan, 163, 165
Bok, Derek, 160–61
Bolsheviks, 28
Bosnia-Herzegovina, 4, 5, 10–13, 17, 20–23, 26–27, 37, 41–45, 49, 55, 57, 65, 68–70, 76–79, 89, 120–22, 124, 131–35, 142–47, 177, 194, 197, 233, 239
Boucher, Richard, 69
Boutros-Ghali, Boutros, 15, 17, 21, 106–109, 248, 252

Brčko, 238
Bush, George, 29, 65, 75, 117, 185, 241

Cable News Network (CNN), 97, 145, 204
Camelot, 13
capitalism, 13
Carter, Jimmy, 150, 205
Central Intelligence Agency (CIA), 20, 67, 148, 153, 173
Cerić, Mustafa, 77–78
Chamberlain, Neville, 79, 195
Chechnya, 17, 29, 166, 200–204, 250
Chetniks, 80
Christopher, Warren, 22, 68–72, 87, 90, 128–30, 181, 201–202, 233, 241–45
Churchill, Winston, 197
Churkin, Vitaly, 250
civilization, 38–39
civil religion. *See* American civil religion
Clinton, Bill, 10–18, 21, 29, 53, 65, 70, 87, 129, 168, 182, 190, 193, 194, 202, 234, 238, 242. *See also* postemotionalism, the presidency and
Cohen, Philip J., 16, 34
Cold War, 17, 37, 40, 78, 83, 111, 166, 176, 182–84, 235
collective consciousness, 30
communism, 16, 37, 39–42, 59, 92, 154, 184, 206, 225–27
compassion, of governments, 45
Conference on Security and Cooperation in Europe (CSCE), 74–75, 101, 191, 194–95, 250
Ćosić, Dobrica, 84–85
Croatia, 4, 5, 75–79, 92, 108, 142–47, 185–89, 194–97, 225–35, 245
Cushman, Thomas, 4

Dayton Peace Accords, 5, 10–13, 21–27, 120, 123–33, 170, 231, 238, 246–47
democracy, 13, 17, 47, 75, 104, 120, 192, 194
Derrida, Jacques, 162
Dinaric type, 80, 93–94
Dizdarević, Zlatko, 93
Djilas, Milovan, 75–76
Djukić, Djordje, 29, 125
Dole, Bob, 175
Donilon, Thomas, 70
Dostoyevsky, Fyodor, 117
Drašković, Vuk, 85–86
Durkheim, Émile, 17, 120, 130
Dutch United Nations peacekeepers, 19, 126. *See also* United Nations

Eagleburger, Lawrence, 67, 148
emotional empathy, 4
Enlightenment, 4, 16, 39, 158, 208, 214, 218, 221
ethnic cleansing, 4, 35–64, 68–72, 123, 129, 168–70, 181, 195, 205, 231, 234, 246
ethnicity, 41–46
ethnonationalism, 42. *See also* nationalism
European values, 38

"face work," 122–28
fascism, 6, 17, 28–30, 129, 165, 170, 182, 185–87, 194–98
fin de siècle, 4
Foucault, Michel, 162
France, 37, 40, 54, 125, 130, 215, 238–43
Fromm, Erich, 224
Fukuyama, Francis, 167

Gandhi, Indira, 49
Gandhi, Mahatma, 47–53
Gellner, Ernest, 54, 170
genocide, 5, 10–14, 29, 56, 67–72, 106, 132, 142, 158, 168, 170, 186–87, 196, 206, 237, 250; in Bosnia, 4, 10, 18–26, 29, 65–71, 111, 123, 158, 176, 193, 195; definition of, 155–56; religious, 43; in Rwanda, 4, 105, 166

Germany, 5, 20–21, 37, 40, 45, 52–54, 60, 125, 215
Geyer, Georgie Anne, 4, 10, 15
Giddens, Anthony, 40, 47, 54, 61
Glenny, Misha, 174–75
globalization, 47–53, 61
Goffman, Erving, 120–41
Goldstone, Richard, 124, 135–36
Goražde, 99, 103, 121, 126, 190, 192, 238, 250
Gorbachev, Mikhail, 187, 193, 201, 203
Grachev, Pavel, 204
Grasanin, Ilija, 220
Greater Russia, 186, 202, 249
Greater Serbia, 18, 27, 70, 76, 92–93, 122–23, 132, 147, 185–87, 194, 203–205, 232, 238, 245–46
Gulf War, 27, 41, 53, 115–17, 166

Hague, The, 25, 26, 34, 88, 89, 124, 173
hajduks, 93, 216
Hamerton-Kelly, Robert, 171–77
"happy confidence," 17
"happy face," 24
Harris, Marshall, 15, 69, 238–53
Herder, J. G., 214–16
Hindus, 36, 39–59
Hitler, Adolph, 20, 28, 52–53, 195
Hobbes, 128–34
Holbrooke, Richard, 137
Holocaust, 39, 43, 45, 56, 68, 143–45, 172–73, 231
Huntington, Samuel, 167
Hussein, Saddam, 29, 49
hyperrealilty, 126

idle curiosity, 158–59
Implementation Force (IFOR), 23, 25, 26–27, 125, 137
India, 36, 40, 42, 45, 51–56
inner-directedness, 4, 6, 10, 26, 30, 163
innocence, 5, 10, 12–17, 21–28, 30; definition of, 5; postemotional, 6
International Tribunal, 25, 26, 124, 138, 150, 173, 246, 250. *See also* United Nations War Crimes Tribunal

Islam, 36, 39, 44, 52, 55–56, 60, 77–78, 172
Izetbegović, Alija, 150, 153

janjićari, 209–13
Janvier, Bernard, 19
Johnson, Richard, 16, 29
Jović, Borislav, 18
justice, 125, 135–38

Karadžić, Radovan, 25–28, 67, 124, 136, 148, 208–209, 218–19
Karadžić, Vuk, 208, 216–18
Kennedy, John F., 13
Kinzer, Stephen, 22, 25
Kissinger, Henry, 111
Kosovo, 38, 58, 86, 93, 184–87, 197, 202, 226, 234; Battle of, 5, 16, 49, 147, 185, 217
Kozyrev, Andrei, 194, 200–203, 249
Kraljević, Marko, 210, 217
Kurds, 38, 49, 54–55

leisure class, 158–59
Lenin, Vladimir, 222–24
Letica, Slaven, 28
Lewis, Anthony, 135, 146
"lift and strike" policy, 242
Lincoln, Abraham, 17, 200–207
Lugar, Richard, 111

MacKenzie, Lewis, 115–16
Major, John, 206
Malinowski, Bronislaw, 42, 45
Mann, Thomas, 20
Maria Theresa, 211
Marković, Ante, 192
Marković, Mihailo, 209, 223–26
Marković, Mira, 227
Marković, Svetozar, 209, 222–27
Marshall Plan, 12
Marx, Karl, 222–25
Marxism, 42
McCloskey, Frank, 69–73
McCurry, Michael, 201, 204
Mearsheimer, John, 169–70, 177
media, 35–65, 114, 121, 127, 135, 158, 204
Mitterrand, Francois, 206

Mills, C. Wright, 160
Milošević, Slobodan, 18, 66–71, 76, 85, 123–24, 136–40, 150, 185–93, 202–209, 226–31, 244–49
Mladic, Ratko, 25–28, 124–26, 136, 148, 150–53
modernism, 4–5, 208. *See also* postmodernism
modernists, 42
modernity, 36, 39–49, 54, 61, 120. *See also* postmodernity
morality, 120, 235
Mostar, 93
Mother Theresa, 47
Mujahadin, 78, 153
multiculturalism, 50, 55, 162–63, 170
Muslims, 14, 16, 19, 21–26, 37–60, 65, 78–79, 136, 185, 200, 209
Mussolini, Benito, 28

Napoleon, 213
nationalism, 76, 170, 176, 182, 192, 227, 248; of Serbs, 131–38, 209. *See also* ethnonationalism
National Security Council (NSC), 66
nation-state, 54–57
Nazis, 17, 20–29, 40–43, 52, 67, 79, 135, 186–87
Nehru, Jawaharlal, 49–50
niceness, 48
North Atlantic Treaty Organization (NATO), 10, 15, 19, 22–28, 131–34, 192–95, 235, 247, 250; air strikes, 99–103, 110, 190, 197; expansion of, 194, 206; failure to arrest war criminals and, 137, 238; "partnership for peace" and, 12, 191, 205–206; policy of, toward Bosnia, 82–83
Northern Ireland, 37, 60
nostalgia, 42
nuclear weapons, 56–57, 185
Nuremburg war crimes trial, 15, 29, 90, 135

Obrenović, Milos, 220–21
Oklahoma City bombing, 7
optimism, 10, 40, 55

Orthodox Church, 93, 185, 196, 209–12
Orwell, George, 25, 93
other-directedness, 10, 17, 29, 158, 163; in academic universities, 164, 176
Ottoman Empire, 16, 209–16, 226
Owen, David, 90, 247

pacifism, 15, 104, 112
Pakistan, 36, 41, 46, 50–60
Pale, 22, 110, 147, 197
Palestinians, 38, 44, 49, 55–56
Panić, Milan, 193
Parsons, Talcott, 129–40
Perle, Richard, 242
Perry, William, 12, 171
Petrović, Djordje, 214–17
Pickering, Thomas, 190
Powell, Colin, 119
postemotionalism, 5–6, 16, 26–30; the presidency and, 11, 14; society and, 12–13, 17. *See also* innocence, postemotional
postmodern age, 38
postmodernism, 4–6. *See also* modernism
postmodernity, 37, 40, 47, 59. *See also* modernity
Potočari, 126
Praljak, Slobodan, 81
profane, the, 60
progress, 39, 42, 47, 49

racism, 14, 36, 40, 43, 54, 182
rape, 14, 23, 35, 51, 55, 122, 129, 233; as policy, in ethnic cleansing, 57–58
rationalism, 39, 42, 79, 99, 130, 134, 208
Ražnjatović, Željko (Arkan), 85–86, 151–53, 197
religion, 38–39, 42–43, 49, 52, 55, 60–61, 172
Republika Srpska, 129
Riesman, David, 5–7, 158, 160, 162, 176–78
Rojek, Chris, 61
Romanticism, 208–14
Rose, Michael, 102–104
Russia, 14–17, 53–59, 125, 181–99, 213, 240, 249–50

Rwanda, 4, 105–106, 166

sacred, 60
sacrilege, 52
safe havens, 19, 82, 121, 127, 243
Safire, William, 146
Said, Edward, 44
Sarajevo, 21–25, 79–80, 89–96, 102–103, 115, 136, 172–74, 233, 238–43, 250
Scotland, 37, 42
Serbia, 10, 22, 56, 66–68, 76, 122–23, 208–228, 234–36, 250; fascism and, 181–99
Serbian aggression, 13–17, 24, 29, 123, 128, 171, 187
Serbia's Secret War (Cohen), 16, 34
Šešelj, Vojislav, 85–86
Shakespeare, William, 56
Shattuck, John, 20
Slovenia, 18, 74, 84, 92, 108, 184, 224, 226
Smith, Leighton, 27, 137
socialism, 49, 182
social order, 128, 134
Somalia, 27
Sontag, Susan, 166, 174–77
Soros, George, 174–75
Soviet Union, 6, 11, 13–17, 29, 38, 40, 54, 75, 184–85
Srebrenica, 19–20, 121, 122–28, 245
Stalin, Joseph, 28, 38, 53
Stambuk, Vladimir, 92
State Department, 65–72, 205, 241
stokavian dialect, 217, 223

Tajikistan, 94, 190
Talbott, Strobe, 190, 196
Tarnoff, Peter, 70
television, 35, 41–52
Thatcher, Margaret, 175
Thornberry, Cedric, 78, 86
Tito, Josip Broz, 92, 184, 186, 223, 226, 249
tolerance, 45, 49–50, 59–60, 136
tradition-directedness, 162
Transcausasus, 190
Tudjman, Franjo, 18, 150, 152

Twain, Mark, 204–205

Ukraine, 87, 185, 190–91, 195
Unabomber, 7
United Nations, 37, 41, 44, 53, 55, 60, 68, 104, 122–33, 189, 195, 197, 207, 230, 234, 250; charter of, 15, 19, 206, 234, 236; genocide convention of, 65–69, 194, 206; sanctions by, 10, 123, 193, 202, 244; security council of, 121, 132, 240. *See also* Dutch United Nations peacekeepers; International Tribunal; *and specific UN organizations*
United Nations Educational Scientific and Cultural Organization (UNESCO), 81
United Nations Protection Force (UNPROFOR), 87–88, 97–98, 127, 240, 245–47
United Nations War Crimes Commission, 67
United Nations War Crimes Tribunal, 25–26, 89, 138, 173, 246, 250
Ustashe, 5, 21, 153, 185

Vance-Owen plan, 82, 88
Vasić, Miloš, 80, 84
Veblen, Thorstein, 158–78

Verne, Jules, 39
Vietnam quagmire, 145
Vietnam syndrome, 5, 14, 27
Vietnam War, 27, 97, 145
Vukovar, 79–80, 93, 123, 197, 203

war crimes, 66–70
weapons embargo, 125, 130–31, 230, 234
Weber, Max, 39
Wells, H. G., 39
Wiesel, Ellie, 70
Will, George, 201
Woerner, Manfred, 15, 82–83, 100–102
Wohlstetter, Albert, 17, 29
World Court, 132
World War II, 5, 12, 15, 21, 28, 54, 79, 83, 99, 117, 134, 185, 246

Yeltsin, Boris, 29, 53, 187, 193–96, 200–207, 248–49
Yugoslavia, 5, 16, 18, 27, 81, 92, 124, 130, 136, 168, 184–89, 224, 241
Yugoslav People's Army, 19, 128

Žepa, 120–22, 125–26, 245
Zhelev, Zhelu, 95
Zhirinovsky, Vladimir, 59, 193
Zimmermann, Warren, 92, 148–49, 174